Discourse and language across L2 instructional settings

Utrecht Studies in Language and Communication

24

Series Editors

Wolfgang Herrlitz
Paul van den Hoven

Discourse and language learning across L2 instructional settings

Edited by
Eva Alcón Soler and Maria-Pilar Safont-Jordà

Amsterdam - New York, NY 2012

Cover photo: www.morguefile.com

The paper on which this book is printed meets the requirements of "ISO
9706:1994, Information and documentation - Paper for documents -
Requirements for permanence".

ISBN: 978-90-420-3584-3
E-Book ISBN: 978-94-012-0859-8
©Editions Rodopi B.V., Amsterdam – New York, NY 2012
Printed in The Netherlands

In memoriam

WILLIS JAMES EDMONSON († 15th December 2009)

The present volume is dedicated to the memory of a great applied linguist and superb author: Willis Edmonson. He worked within the field of applied linguistics and many of his most influential publications are related to classroom discourse. Furthermore, Willis Edmonson did take an active part in the conference we organized in 2008 at Universitat Jaume I, and we feel much indebted to him.
We would like to dedicate this volume to his memory and to his family.

Eva Alcón Soler
Maria-Pilar Safont-Jordà

Acknowledgements

First and foremost, we would like to thank all contributors in the volume for accepting to take part in this project. We are also very grateful to the anonymous reviewers of preliminary versions of the chapters for their comments and thoughtful suggestions.

The figures on pages 266 and 268 were reproduced by permission of Oxford University Press from OAL: *Conversational Interaction in Second Language Acquisition,* edited by Alison Mackey © Oxford University Press 2007.

We would like to state that parts of the volume and some studies included in it have been conducted within the framework of a research project funded by *Fundació Universitat Jaume I* and *Caixa Castelló-Bancaixa* (P1.1B2011-15)

Contents

Introduction
Eva Alcón Soler and Maria-Pilar Safont-Jordà (eds.)   1

Part I. Discourse in L2 learning contexts

Primary school teachers' language practices. A four-year longitudinal study of three FL classes
Elsa Tragant and Carme Muñoz   7

Lexical scaffolding in immersion classroom discourse
Nathalie Blanc, Rita Carol, Peter Griggs and Roy Lyster   31

L1 use in primary and secondary foreign language classrooms and its contribution to learning
Rita Tognini and Rhonda Oliver   53

Repair in Japanese request sequences during student – teacher interactions
Yumiko Tateyama   79

Part II. Discourse in Content and language integrated contexts

Social perspectives on interaction and language learning in CLIL classrooms
Ana Llinares and Tom Morton   105

On the role of peer discussions in the learning of subject-specific language use in CLIL
Tarja Nikula   133

English as a Lingua Franca (ELF) and its role in integrating content and language in higher education.
A longitudinal study of question-initiated exchanges
Ute Smit   155

Part III. Discourse in new language learning contexts

Identity and face in institutional English as Lingua Franca
discourse
Juliane House 187

The voices of immigrant students in the classroom: discourse
practices and language learning in a Catalan-Spanish bilingual
environment
Josep Maria Cots and Laura Espelt 205

Email openings and closings: pragmalinguistic and gender
variation in learner-instructor cyber consultations
César Félix-Brasdefer 223

**Part IV. Issues for further research on discourse and
language learning**

Does gender influence task performance in EFL?
Interactive tasks and language related episodes
Agurtzane Azkarai and María del Pilar García Mayo 249

Exploring learners' reaction to corrective feedback from
stimulated recall interviews
Patricia Salazar 279

Code switching in classroom discourse: A multilingual
approach
Laura Portolés-Falomir and Sofía Martín-Laguna 295

Introduction

Eva Alcón Soler (Universitat Jaume I)
Maria-Pilar Safont-Jordà (Universitat Jaume I)

Studies on discourse and language learning originated in the field of general education and they focused on first language learning environments (Flanders, 1970; Mehan, 1979). However, since 1980s research on discourse and language learning has further extended its realm to include second and foreign language environments. Recently, the emergence of new language learning contexts such as computer-mediated communication, multilingual settings or content and language-integrated contexts requires further research that focuses on discourse (Allwright, 1980; Van Lier, 1988). From this perspective, on the one hand, the present volume aims to broaden the scope of investigation in foreign language contexts by exploring discourse patterns in the classroom and examining the impact of factors such as gender, explicitness of feedback, or L1 use to language learning through discourse. On the other hand, the volume deals with discourse practices and their potential for language learning in current instructional settings as mentioned above.

With that aim in mind, this volume brings together research that investigates discourse in various instructional settings: primary, secondary, and university L2 learning environments, content and language integrated contexts, and other new language learning settings. The number and variety of languages involved both as the first language (e.g. English, Finnish, Basque, Spanish, Japanese, French, Italian, and Catalan) as well as the target foreign language (e.g. English, French, Italian, Japanese, Spanish) makes the volume especially attractive. Additionally, the different approaches adopted by the researchers participating in this volume, such as information processing, socio-cognitive and ethnographic approaches, or conversation analysis, widen the realm of investigation on discourse and language learning. Finally, the strength of the volume also lies in the range of educational settings covered (primary, secondary and tertiary education) and the worldwide representation of contributors across seven different countries, including Spain, France, Austria, Finland, Germany, Canada, Australia and the United States.

The volume is subdivided into thirteen chapters. These chapters are distributed within the four parts that constitute the book. The chapters in the first part focus on analyzing language learners' discourse across L2 instructional settings, mainly foreign language and immersion settings and across educational environments: primary, secondary and tertiary education. Issues such as variation in teaching practices and strategies, use of the first language and the use of repair in student-teacher interaction are addressed. The chapter by Elsa Tragant and Carmen Muñoz focuses on early language learners and is an attempt to better understand the language practices of teachers and learners in a FL non-immersion context over a period of four years. The three case studies reported by the author show evidence that students in the three schools had quite distinct experiences ranging from quite traditional teaching practices to quite meaningful communicative ones. Also, different teaching practices often led to different patterns of classroom discourse mainly in terms of elicitation or elaboration moves, students' output and teachers' and students' use of English. In addition, the examination of the teaching style seems to point out some interesting interactions with attitudes, perceptions and linguistic development.

With an interest in describing whether effective teaching requires appropriate instructional techniques designed specifically to promote language development, the study by Nathalie Blanc, Rita Carol, Peter Griggs, and Roy Lyster analyses lexical scaffolding strategies used by teachers and their potential effect on the type of lexical processing carried out by students in immersion language learning contexts. Following a socio-cognitive perspective, the authors conducted quantitative and qualitative analyses of interactional sequences of lexical scaffolding during read-aloud activities in a French immersion primary school in Montreal, with French dominant, English dominant and bilingual eight-year-old students. The analyses revealed that while the French teacher tended to adopt a metalinguistic focus to elicit the meanings of difficult words, the English teacher sought more to recycle and explore vocabulary in contexts related to the story's content and students' prior experiences and to exploit knowledge of students' first language. The authors advocate for creating purposeful opportunities in meaningful contexts for recycling words in ways that promote lexical processing as an effective means to stimulate vocabulary development.

Including data from primary and secondary language classrooms Rita Tognini and Rhonda Oliver deal with L1 use in teacher-learner and peer interaction in ten French and Italian foreign language classes in Australian schools. The authors report that L1 use by teachers and students varied across different activities and tasks. In addition, it seems that teachers' L1 use tends to be associated with social and regulatory functions and for dealing with communication. According to the authors, although teachers' L1 use may limit opportunities for learning, L1 use in peer interaction seem to support and scaffold each other's L2 use and develop their understanding of L2 grammar.

The last chapter in Part I is written by Yumiko Tateyama. Using a conversation analytic perspective, the author examines how interactions unfold sequentially and how repair is initiated and offered when communication problems arise. Data come from student and teacher interactions as they engage in role play activity (making a request) in front of other students in a Japanese as a foreign language (JFL) class at an American university and show evidence of three repair patterns: (a) teacher inserts an exposed correction sequence within a larger request sequence; (b) teacher initiates repair and by-standing students complete repair; (c) instead of exposed correction during the interaction, teacher offers feedback on the trouble source after the role play is over. Results of the study also show that the teacher shifts back and forth between two roles – teacher and interlocutor – during the role play, assessing the student's forms and making corrections as needed, which may be relevant for the achievement of pedagogical goals. Finally, the author suggests that participants' embodied actions such as gaze and posture are issues to be further explored, since they appear to be related to their degree of engagement in offering assistance during interaction.

Part II deals with interaction and language use in content and language-integrated learning (CLIL) contexts. On the grounds that CLIL contexts seem to offer students more opportunities for interaction than traditional language classrooms, the chapters in Part II address what types of opportunities can be found and how they can be enhanced. Ana Llinares and Tom Morton examine social perspectives. They focus on a socio-interactionist approach based on conversation analysis, situated-learning theory, and systemic functional linguistics (SFL), as well as on their relevance for understanding interaction and language use in CLIL classrooms. According to these authors, a much fuller picture of the relationships between CLIL classroom discourse and learning opportunities can be gained by combining these two social perspectives of situated learning theory and SFL.

The following two chapters examine opportunities to interaction in two different CLIL settings. Using data from Finish secondary level history classrooms taught in English, Tarja Nikula explores what students' group-work interaction reveals about content and language integration. In so doing, it seeks to investigate students' joint processes of meaning making and how students co-construct understanding of a subject-specific activity, and the type of language this requires. In a similar vein, but focusing on tertiary classroom discourse, Ute Smit addresses the roles that English play in that particular context. The author carries out a longitudinal detailed analysis of question-initiated exchanges taken from critical phases throughout an English medium hotel management programme, and reports how the lecturers and students construct their interactions by relying on English as their lingua franca. Finally, it is suggested that language learning processes depend in their complexity and dynamics on English in its roles as lingua franca and as professional language.

In Part III the chapters describe discourse in new language use settings: international contexts where English is used as a lingua franca, bilingual schools and learner-instruction cyber consultations. The case study by Juliane House looks at issues of identity, face-threat and face-maintenance that emerge from ELF (i.e. English as a lingua franca) interactions between academic advisors and advisees in a German university setting. The analysis of code-switching and the discourse markers "I think" and "I mean" are chosen to illustrate that ELF face-challenging behavior in university office hours did not negatively affect a status-superior ELF speaker's face, pointing out that ELF speakers do not seek to adjust to the so called native speakers norms, but to be engaged in a specific "community of practice".
Participants' involvement in a community of practice is also addressed in the following chapter. From a linguistic ethnographic approach, Josep Maria Cots and Laura Espelt explore the connection between language learning practices and opportunities for self-expression in two contexts offered to recently-arrived immigrant to Catalonia: the reception and the ordinary classroom. In so doing, the authors analyse how students co-construct their identity in these two instructional settings and the classroom is presented as an essential environment for newly-arrived students to engage and participate in a community of practice.

The last chapter of Part III, written by César Félix-Brasdefer, is framed within the field of computer mediated discourse and it examines variation in the opening and closing sequences in email messages (L2 Spanish and L1 English) sent from undergraduate university-level students to their instructors of Spanish. Pragmalinguistic variation in the ways to open and close an email message, variation by gender, formal and informal features of email discourse and differences in politeness practices are reported. The author suggests that in order to facilitate learners' knowledge of email discourse in an L2, pedagogical intervention should be implemented by providing the learners with explicit or implicit teaching as well as exposure to the pragmatics of email discourse of the target culture.

Finally, Part IV includes studies dealing with issues on classroom discourse that require further research such as, the role of gender as an individual variable in task based interaction, the effectiveness of corrective feedback or the role of code switching in multilingual classrooms. The study by

Agurtzane Azkarai y María Pilar García Mayo aims to investigate whether gender influences conversational interaction and whether different communicative tasks have an impact on the type of interaction matched (male-male and female-female) and mixed (male-female) gender dyads engage in. The authors conclude that type of dyad did not influence the incidence of language related episodes (LREs) when pairs work on specific tasks, that the different tasks influence the learner's production of LREs and that most LREs were resolved correctly.

The effective of corrected feedback is addressed by Patricia Salazar. The author explores how foreign language learners noticed a more implicit and more explicit version of corrected feedback on learners' written production via a stimulated recall interview. The information provided during the stimulated recall interviews reveals that, regardless of obtaining a more explicit or implicit corrective feedback, it was most of the time noticed and the participants tried hard to look for grammatical reformulations. In short, Salazar's chapter challenges previous findings (Bitchener, 2008) that pointed to the lack of effectiveness of corrective feedback and, thus, calls for further research on the issue.

In the last chapter, Laura Portolés y Sofía Martín tackle the topic of cross-linguistic influence in classroom discourse by examining code-switching phenomena. The authors analyze language switches produced by Catalan-Spanish learners of English as a third language. On the basis of Williams and Hammarberg's (1998) role model for code-switching in L3 oral production, their study aims at examining the types of switches produced and the extent to which the learners resort to their L1 (i.e. Spanish) or L2 (i.e. Catalan) in their L3 (English) production. In so doing, they analyse an English as a L3 classroom including conversational interaction between 25 primary school children aged 8 and 9 years and their teacher aged 28. Findings from the study show that learners' frequently resorted to Spanish (L1) in those switches that involved meta-comments (i.e. helping or asking for help in conveying meaning). Furthermore, no role was attributed to their L2 (i.e. Catalan). Portolés and Martin attribute these results to the effect of the sociolinguistic context and the educational model followed by the school in which data were gathered. On the one hand, the students' L1 , Spanish , is the majority language in their speech community. On the other, the school followed a Spanish-medium instruction model, in which their L2, Catalan is scarcely present.

In sum, the volume provides an eclectic nature which makes it a unique contribution to the study of language learners' discourse by adopting different perspectives (i.e. FonF, CLIL, pragmatics, ELF T-ss interaction) in the study of discourse across L2 learning contexts. Furthermore, it is not reduced to one educational level (Smit, 2010), but addresses language learners of different age periods and instructional contexts. We hope the chapters included in the volume may be interesting for teachers, curriculum planners and developers, researchers in both English and non-English speaking communities, and also useful for researchers and practitioners following either European or non-European standards.

References

Allwright, D. (1980) Turns, topics and tasks: Patterns of participation in Language learning and teaching. In Larsen Freeman, D. (eds.): Discourse analysis in second language acquisition, 165-187. Rowley, Mass: Newbury House.

Bitchener, J. (2008) Evidence in support of written corrective feedback, *Journal of Second Language Writing* (17) 2: 102-118.

Flanders, N.A. (1970) Analysing teaching behavior. Reading, Mass: Addison-Wesley.

Mehan, H. (1979) *Learning lessons: social organization in the classroom.* Cambridge, Mass.: Harvard University Press.

Smit, U. (2010) *English as a Lingua franca in Higher Education: A Longitudinal Study of Classroom Discourse. Trends in Applied Linguistics: Vol. 2*, Berlin [u.a.]: De Gruyter Mouton.

Van Lier, L. (1984) Discourse analysis and classroom research: A methodological perspective. International Journal of the Sociology of Language 49:111-133.

Williams, S. and B. Hammarberg (1998) Language Switches in L3 production: Implications for a polyglot speaking mode, Applied Linguistics (19) 3: 295-333.

Primary school teachers' language practices. A four-year longitudinal study of three FL classes

Elsa Tragant (Universitat de Barcelona)
Carmen Muñoz (Universitat de Barcelona)

The present study focuses on early language learners and is an attempt to better understand the language practices of teachers and learners in a FL non-immersion context over a period of four years. Over this period of time students in three target classes underwent at least one change of teacher throughout the four grades, which allowed for the examination of any effects of the teacher factor in relation to students' attitudes, linguistic achievement and features of classroom discourse. Data were collected through non-participant observations, questionnaires and interviews and results are presented as case studies. The study concludes that students in the three schools under study had quite distinct learning experiences in their first four years of FL instruction in primary school. Also, some classroom discourse features as well as students' attitudes and linguistic gains were often sensitive to teaching style.

1 Research on primary school FL teaching

What takes place in the classroom has repeatedly proved to be vital in promoting FL learning among children. Several authors have pointed out sets of conditions for successful practice in primary foreign language learning. Hunt et al. (2005) mention active teaching methods with extensive use of songs and games as well as an emphasis on enjoyment and enthusiasm, among others. Children's participation in informal conversations in the FL as well as the provision of rich, contextualized input and contingent feedback are among a range of teaching strategies advocated by Coyle and Verdú (2000). In the evaluation report of a Bilingual Education Project in Spain, Dobson, Pérez-Murillo and Johnstone (2010) point out a number of classroom practices that seem to be associated with pupil outcomes. Some of these practices are particularly relevant at the level of classroom discourse such as pushing learners to offer more sophisticated language, asking well pitched questions or showing due concern for accuracy of language.

In spite of the above recommendations when we look at how language teachers actually teach foreign languages to young children, we often get a different picture. In an observational study conducted in Italy, experienced teachers tended to follow traditional approaches when teaching students aged 7-9 (Lopriore, 2009). In Hungary, few examples of good practice were found in novice teachers who had been advised by experienced teachers. They tended to draw heavily on grammar and memorizing vocabulary out of context when teaching children in lower primary (ages 6-10 years) (Nikolov, 2010). In an earlier study, Nikolov (2003) also found that the activities that 12 year olds were most often exposed to in class were the least popular ones and these included translation, reading aloud, grammar exercises and tests. A similar trend was found in a three-year long study involving 39 primary schools in England (Cable et al., 2010) where, even if lessons had a game-like orientation, the focus was at the word and sentence level with a predominance of interactive whole-class teaching and memorized language. In Ireland, an emphasis by teachers on traditional language practice and some reluctance to use the target language as the predominant medium of instruction were reported in the evaluation report of the National Pilot Project (Harris and Conway, 2002).

Discourse analytical studies also indicate that the interactional context and certain teaching practices may enhance or limit opportunities for learning. In the case of context, Oliver and Mackey (2003) showed that whether the classroom exchanges focused on explicit language contexts or on content and management contexts determined learners' use of teacher feedback. In the case of teaching practices, a number of studies show how poor strategies may have limit learning opportunities. In Peng and Zhang's work (2009), Chinese teachers of English gave students few opportunities to self-evaluate, guess or expand their answers and they were observed to give repetitive feedback and blanket evaluations. A predominance of the simple version of the Initiation-Response-Feedback (IRF) pattern, which is limited to 3 turns, proved to restrict learning opportunities in Western Australian schools (Tognini, 2008). Over-reliance on closed questions from teachers in the early years of a French immersion program also proved to be restrictive in Walsh and Yeoman (1999).

The pervasive use of traditional practices and a fairly controlled pattern of interaction in the primary FL classroom of some country contexts may be explained by a range of factors. One of them may be some teachers' limited linguistic FL skills (Butler, 2004). Insufficient specialized teacher training may be another factor in some countries, which may cause some teachers to resort to implementing teaching practices they experienced as language students a while ago. An additional factor is the difficulty some teachers may have in implementing what they think or learn about FL methodology. One may also consider that some teaching practices (i.e., groupwork, etc.) may just be unrealistic in the early years of foreign language learning in contexts where instructional time and out-of-school input opportunities are very limited. Also, the applicability of communicative principles may be culture-sensitive (Ghosn, 2004). In fact, little research has been conducted that .

focuses on what teachers actually do in the classroom in the early stages of FL instruction.

The present study focuses on early language learners and it is precisely an attempt to better understand teaching processes in a FL non-immersion context over a period of four years through the language practices of teachers and learners. Longitudinal studies like this are scarce both in interaction research (Philp and Tognini, 2009) as well as in early FL education (Nikolov and Mihaljević Djigunović, 2006). In this case, the longitudinal nature of the data has given us the opportunity to observe the same classes with different teachers over time and analyze predominant classroom discourse features.

2　The study

The present study took place in the context of primary education in Catalonia (Spain) where one can find great variability across different state funded schools in one same province. Frequency of EFL instruction may differ from 1 to 4 sessions a week. The duration of class sessions can also range from thirty-minute to one-hour long periods. Some primary schools are involved in CLIL projects, promoted by the Autonomous Department of Education. Even though the official age of start was 6 at the start of this study, schools had the option of starting FL instruction in infant school. The profile of English teachers can also vary greatly in terms of language proficiency as well as the amount of training in EFL methodologies. This is so partly due to a scarcity of qualified English primary school teachers and the fact that some years ago non-English specialists, who are still active nowadays, were given the opportunity to become English teachers without going through regular training. Added to these factors, schools may also differ in the availability of materials and facilities (such as Interactive White Board, from here on referred to as IWB) as well as the availability of native speaker language assistants. The location of the school is another factor to take into consideration since it greatly determines the rate of immigrant children in classes as well as the socio-educational profile of the parents and the presence of the two official languages (Spanish and Catalan) at home. Given this great variability it was clear that comparing English classes across different state funded schools was not feasible. Therefore, we opted to adopt a case study approach (Merriam, 1998) similar to that followed by Moon (2009) in her work on the teacher factor in an early foreign language program. This approach has allowed us to individually present each class/school in its context and illustrate analyses with excerpts from classroom discourse and teachers' and students' interviews.

The study aims to describe primary school classes and their English teachers over a period of four years starting in grade 1 (from here on referred to as years 1-4). The fact that over this period of time students in the target classes underwent at least one change of teacher throughout the four grades has allowed us to examine any effects of the teacher factor. More specifically the study addresses the following questions:

- How were students taught over the first four years of their primary-school English classes? In particular, what were the dominant classroom discourse features?
- To what an extent has the teacher factor had an observable effect on students' attitudes and perceptions as well as their linguistic progress?

The answers to these questions are based on classroom observations, a listening test as well as questionnaires and interviews to English teachers and their pupils as well as school principals.

2.1   The schools

This study was conducted in the framework of a larger project on Early Language Learning in Europe (ELLiE) which took place from 2006 to 2010 with the participation of 7 countries. As part of the project, a convenience sample of 6 to 8 state funded schools were selected from each country from a variety of school types allowing for both a socio-economic range and geographical spread within the sample regions. The present study focuses on 3 schools (schools 52, 53 and 54) from the Spanish ELLiE sample. Appendix 1 presents the main features of the three Spanish schools and appendix 2 shows key characteristics of their classes. Other case studies based on the ELLiE schools can be found in Tragant and Muñoz (2009) and Tragant and Lundberg (in press).

Schools 52, 53 and 54 were selected from the Spanish sample after examining the scores that students had obtained in the listening task that was administered at the end of every year but they were selected for different reasons. In school 52 comparatively low scores were obtained throughout the first four years of primary school, even if it was the school with the lowest rate of immigration and subsidized lunches. In school 53 there was a trend for students in this class to get lower scores in years 3-4 in comparison to the first two years of primary school. Finally, school 54 was selected because of sustained good scores throughout years 1-4.

2.2   Instruments and data collection

Researchers conducted one-day non-participant classroom observations at two or three points during each school year, and these constitute the primary data for this study. During these observations, which were scheduled, teachers were asked to conduct their lessons as they regularly did. A semi-open observation schedule, which had been specifically designed for the research project, was used to keep record of the different modes of classroom interaction, samples of classroom talk and teachers' and students' roles. Classes were also audiorecorded and transcribed. In addition, a number of other instruments were administered at the end of each year.

In order to gather data on the children's linguistic progress, a visually rich listening task was administered every year. A reading task was also performed in year 4 but its results will not be reported in the present study. No other proficiency measure was elicited from students. The listening task, which was collectively administered, evaluated receptive skills only and consisted of two parts. Part one had a multiple choice format consisting of three pictures per item and part two was a true/false activity based on a drawing depicting various family members at home. In designing these materials, special care was taken to use activity formats that were age-appropriate. Some items in this task were used for more than one year but most of them had to be replaced by more challenging items as students grew older. The total number of items of the listening task oscillated between 18 and 23 depending on the year. Because of this variability both in the number and content of the items, z-scores were calculated in order to be able to compare listening scores across the four years of the study. In calculating these scores only students who were not doing English as an extracurricular activity for the last two years have been taken into account. This way, we get a cleaner picture of the effect of the school teacher factor on linguistic gains. Figure 1 shows listening scores by school and year.

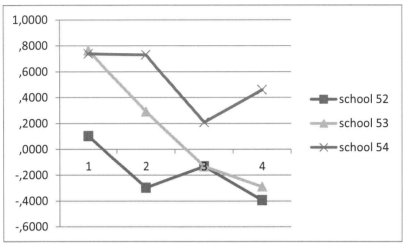

Figure 1. Listening scores by year and school

Children's attitudes were also gathered with a short structured questionnaire that was administered to the whole class. The questionnaire included items about children's general disposition towards learning English as well as towards specific learning activities and linguistic areas (i.e., listening, speaking, learning new words). In addition, six students from each class were also interviewed to get more insights about how students experienced the learning of English at school. The English teachers were also interviewed every year and were asked to describe the target class and the methodology employed in their English lessons. Finally the school principals were interviewed in years 1 and 4 to get information about the school context. For a more detailed description of these instruments see Enever (in press).

3   The case studies

3.1   School 52

School 52 is located in the suburbs a town of 65,000 inhabitants (70 km from Barcelona) and it has a good reputation. It has a very low immigration rate (1%) and the majority of parents have either secondary education studies or a university degree. Even though most students speak Catalan at home, their first language is one of the main concerns of the principal, who thinks that over the years children's level of Catalan has impoverished substantially. This is probably why this school does not schedule more teaching time to English instruction than what is required by law.

3.1.1 Learning English through controlled practice

The target class in school 52 had 27 students in year 1, 23 of whom are the same throughout the four years of the study. The number of students in this class taking English lessons outside school ranges between 6-9. This class has had three teachers since children started learning English at the age of 6: Teresa (year 1), Maite (year 2) and Roser (years 3 and 4) (not their real names). In years 1 and 2 the class was split into two smaller groups during the English sessions, which took place once a week (50'). In years 3 and 4 out of three weekly sessions, one (45') was spent on autonomous work (i.e., vocabulary book or activities in computer room). The other two weekly sessions (60') were devoted to regular English lessons.

Students in this class have used a textbook (from the same collection) every year, which the three teachers followed closely. The syllabus in the textbook series is language-based and input is heavily controlled. Teresa, Maite and Roser all have teaching experience and show to have good management skills. Nevertheless, none of them was trained as a FL instructor when they got their university degree. Following is a brief description of some of these three teachers' most salient features (see Table 1).

	Year 1 Teacher: Teresa	Year 2 Teacher: Maite	Years 3 & 4 Teacher: Roser
Teacher profile	Little experience as FL teacher to young students	Hardly any experience as FL teacher to young students	15 years as FL teacher
Materials	Exclusive use of textbook materials	Exclusive use of textbook materials	Exclusive use of textbook materials
Teacher's FL competence	Very limited	Very limited	Limited
Teacher's use of L2	Mostly L2 but minimal T talk	Hardly any L2	About 70%

Table 1. Teachers in school 52: key features

Teresa is a generalist teacher with 5 years of teaching experience but no experience teaching English in lower primary. The main focus of her lessons is on learning vocabulary with the use of different textbook resources (cards, flashcards, songs, textbook) and activities (games, T-questions, seatwork, listen and repeat). She summarizes her approach by saying 'It's mainly about repetition' and admits she gets a little bored, even though the children do not realize that 'Every unit is the same'. Teresa makes minimal use of the L2 but she hardly ever uses L1. The following excerpt is an illustration of the teacher using the L2 economically during students' seatwork to tell a student that what he is looking for (a card) is on the floor.

Excerpt 1
    S: (addressing the T) *I cannot find my* grandad.
    T: (pointing to the floor) Ah, Toni your grandad.
(fieldnotes 27.2.07, year 1)

Note that, in the above and following excerpts in this article, italics have been used as a convention to note L1 use by either the teacher or the students. Original utterances are reproduced in appendix 3. Other transcription conventions and abbreviations are stated in appendix 4.

Students in this class generally address Teresa in L1 but they are also observed to sometimes use single words in English (i.e., 'Finish', 'Yes').

Maite, the English teacher in year 2, is also a generalist teacher with over 20 years of teaching experience but hardly any teaching English. In fact, she says she is teaching English this year 'by accident'. She only uses English for a small number of routines, often inaccurately. Unlike in year 1, students in year 2 never attempt to use L2 spontaneously. Maite's linguistic limitations seem to make her very dependent on the textbook and the CD player. One day 7 pages from textbook/workbook were covered in a 45-minute session. Maite compensates her lack of expertise by drawing the students' attention in L1 to cultural aspects, spelling and handwriting, word formation and the interpretation of textbook stories. She draws heavily on practices like getting students to read aloud, repeat and translate. Excerpt 2 is a good example of these practices and Maite's extended use of L1, in this case in the context of using an illustrated story from the textbook:

Excerpt 2
    T: *Page 35, Àlex. Let's see … we will go back and look again*
             at a story we did a few days ago. Do you remember having
             done it? We will go over the story. First of all Pau will
             remind us of the characters in the story, whom we already
             know.
    P: *Rosie, Zippedy and Jack.*

> T: *Very good. In the first illustration we see that Zippedy asks a question to Rosie. Can you read it Pol?*
> P: 'Rosie, can you skip?' *which means Rosie, can you skip?, Can you skip over a rope?*
> T: *Very good.*
> (transcription 3.04.08, year 2)

Roser, a psychologist by training, used to be the school's special education teacher. However, 15 years ago she had no other option but to become the English school teacher. She feels teaching English is 'fun' but 'tiring'. She often starts the class by commenting on mistakes from students' work and then time can be spent on a combination of teacher-fronted activities like singing songs, oral word games, T-questions, textbook work and seatwork activities in which the activity book is used. T-questions require students to give short answers (i.e., 'Yes, I do'; 'No, I can't', 'on the table') or single words (i.e., 'blue', 'pasta') and are meant as focus-on-forms practice. Roser hardly ever reacts or elaborates on the content of students' answers as in the following exchange:

Excerpt 3
> T: Do you like pasta?
> S: No, I don't.
> T: Very good, very good. Questions with do, answers with do, questions with can, answers with can, yeah?
> (transcription 3.02.09, year 3)

She does not use English for spontaneous communication with students either. Neither do students use English for communicative purposes in class to address the teacher.

3.1.2 Lessons learned from school 52

When students in this class were asked about how much they liked learning English, there were more students with a positive response in years 3 and 4 (92-95% respectively) than in year 2 (41%), which could be attributable to the teacher factor. In fact, some students in year 3 said that the English class was more fun then. The fact that Maite hardly ever used the FL in class may have also had a part.

However, in spite of these positive attitudes in years 3 and 4 and an efficient use of time in class, scores in the listening tests are average to modest (see Figure 1) if compared with other schools in the sample with a similar profile. This could be due to several factors. One of them is the amount of teaching time in school 52, which was lower than in other schools. Also, both language input and output, though enjoyable, may not have been challenging enough in this class (an observation that was also made in reference to some primary school lessons in England, Cable et al. 2010). Throughout the four years a considerable amount of time was spent on vocabulary practice and activities that did not require deep processing, like singing with books open or reading aloud. This seems to be the message behind the following student's answer when he was asked about the difficulty of the English class: 'Learning things (in the English class) is easy because we only learn sentences. But if you need to learn the language, then it requires effort'.

The lack of meaning orientation on the part of the three teachers in school 52 may not have favored students' language development, either. As regards students' spontaneous L2 use, their first attempts in year 1 had no continuity in subsequent years. This could be explained by the fact that, unlike Maite and Roser, Teresa used L2 most of the time, even if her English was deficient. This is in line with what Mayfield (2005) observed in her action-research study where her students started speaking spontaneously earlier when the class was taught almost entirely in the L2.

3.2   School 54

School 54 is located in downtown Barcelona in a lower-middle class neighborhood and it has an immigration rate of around 8%. A majority of the parents are Catalan speaking and about half of them hold university degrees. The school is supportive of English instruction and more time is devoted to English than what is strictly required by law. In fact English was introduced in infant school long before other schools.

3.2.1   *Learning English as play or as work*

The target class in school 54 has got 25 children, 21 of whom are the same throughout the four years of the study. The number of students in this class taking English lessons outside school ranges between 6-9. These students started learning English at the age of 5 (three 30'-sessions a week). For the first two years of primary education (starting at the age of 6) students have had three weekly sessions of English (45'-55') with the same teacher. For the third and fourth years, a new English teacher took over and instruction time increased with longer sessions (60') and a fourth English period every fortnight for half the class. Once a week a language assistant taught this group of students in years 2 and 4.

The two teachers, Myriam and Fina (not their real names), did not originally graduate as specialist English teachers at university and got their English qualifications more than 10 years ago. Even though both of them have limited L2 skills, they use English most of the time. They do so both for planned ('Before color it finish'; 'Do you remember we have the last day beautiful song about a crocodile?'; 'Now let's sing') and unplanned classroom events ('I love math, my favorite subject'; 'Can you keep silence Kevin please?'; 'Oh, you look very nice, wow, Gisela'). With both teachers, some students also attempt to use English spontaneously with short ('Please ') or incomplete utterances ('I've got') and chunks ('What's the matter? '). With both teachers, a textbook is used part of the time and singing is a frequent activity together with other oral work. Nevertheless, groupwork and pairwork are rare throughout the four years. In spite of these similarities, the two teachers have distinct teaching styles and views about L2 learning. The following table summarizes some of these teachers' characteristics.

	Years 1-2 Teacher: Myriam	Years 3-4 Teacher: Fina
Materials	Textbook and accompanying materials (workbook, flashcards, DVD)	Textbook, workbook, online teaching materials (IWB), songs, graded readers
Feedback	Infrequent teacher correction	Frequent T correction and requests for repetition
Evaluation	T observation	Individual oral performance (i.e., song, poems) and simple written tests
Turn allocation	T hardly ever nominates students	T often nominates students

Table 2. Teachers in school 54: key features

Myriam, the English teacher in school years 1-2, has a high opinion of this group of students ('They are hardworking, participative, a nice group') and enjoys the class herself ('Sometimes sessions feel short to me'). She seems to believe students learn if they have a good experience. In this class, this is so because of the game-like nature of some of the activities (games, coloring, TPR, flashcards) as well as the atmosphere she has created. She often congratulates students and is tolerant with background noise and transitions (she had a non-directive style). She is also good at introducing new language and at elicitation. Excerpt 4, which took place after singing a song about a crocodile, is a illustrative example of Myriam's use of English in class, even if sometimes inaccurate, as well as her ability at eliciting learner talk.

Excerpt 4

T:	Tell me what's this?
SS:	The x!
T:	Do you remember the story?
SS:	Yes!
T:	Tell me what happens in the story. Tell me something, for example (DP), Oriol!
O:	(stands up)
T:	Tell me. No, no, no, no acting now. Tell me something about the story. How the story start? What does it happen here?
O:	Crocodile and frog!
S:	and delicious! (DP)
T:	and?
S:	and delicious.(DP)
S:	delicious.
T:	Ah, no the crocodile is?
SS & T:	hungry!
S:	I'm hungry.
S:	The frog delicious.
T:	Okay! The crocodile is hungry and the frog is?
SS:	delicious! Mhm!

(transcription 8.05.08, year 2)

Fina, the English teacher in years 3-4, used to be a French teacher, but even if her classroom talk is often inaccurate, she uses English most of the time. She is characterized by a controlling style and the use of materials outside the textbook. She reacts firmly to students' disruptive behavior and consequently time on task is maximized. In her opinion, learning English for students this age is no longer about playing but about making an effort. She notes that some students in this class no longer have an appropriate attitude towards English ('They think they know it all'). An important part of classtime is spent on singing (which she loves) as well as other activities that also require memorization (poems, rhymes, dialogues, question-answer sets), which students are sometimes required to perform individually in front of the class. In the following excerpt the teacher nominates several students in turn to ask each other the same question ('What do you do to help the environment?') in front of the class. Students are supposed to use words from a list but are not allowed to look at the sentences from the textbook, which the teacher expects students to remember.

Excerpt 5

L:	What, what do you do to help the environment (DP)?
T:	Can you repeat again please?
L.	What do you do, eh, to help the en, the envi (DP)
T:	the, the environment.
L:	environment.
T:	Berta? What do you do?
B:	eh.... I, I...
T:	No, don't look that, we are, remember.
B:	I go to bike, I go to bike.
T:	You use the bike, no? You go to school, you go home by bike, ok?
B:	on foot.
T:	on foot, *good.*
(...)	
S:	xx water the plants.
T:	you water plants?
S:	Ah!
T:	with?
S:	with...
T:	You water plants, with...
SS:	rain, rainy.
T:	the rain water? *Let's see.* Yes, do you remember?
S:	I xx water plants
T:	No, I ...
S:	water plants.
T:	correct, with...
S:	with, with rain water?
T:	OK. You use the rain water to water plants. OK, correct.

(transcription 7.05.10, year 4)

Students in years 3-4 are progressively challenged by Fina's use of longer or more complex texts and songs, often with the support of the IWB. Students are sometimes stretched to produce or reproduce messages that are beyond their present language abilities (i.e., 'Sunday I lazy', 'I like'), especially in year 4.

3.2.2 *Lessons learnt from school 54*

In the first two years of primary, students in school 54 were quite motivated (94% of them said they liked English in year 2) but this motivation was not sustained in years 3-4 (only 28% of students said they liked English in year 4). This may be due to Fina's directive style and/or to the difficulty of materials/activities performed, which some students commented on ('Songs are very difficult to pronounce', 'The activity book requires a lot of thinking and memorization', 'IWB activities are difficult'). Nevertheless, scores in the listening task tended to be above average, especially in year 4.This may be partly explained by a combination of factors related to teaching (i.e., the two T's extensive use of English, increasingly demanding materials/texts in years 3-4, the role of the language assistant). The fact that these students were often required to reproduce or produce rehearsed language from memory might have created opportunities for 'pushed output' (Swain, 1985), even if under controlled conditions. Other contributing factors might not be related to pedagogy such as family (i.e., fairly educated parents) and school factors (i.e., few new students and drop outs, low rates of immigration, an early introduction to the FL, more instructional time than other schools) (see Appendices 1 and 2).

3.3   School 53

School 53 is also located in Barcelona in a consolidated neighborhood where lower-middle and lower class families live. The school receives a combination of immigrant, local and international middle-class families. 39% of the students in the school had not been born in Spain at the start of year 1 even though the number of subsidized lunches is similar to that of schools with much lower rates of immigration. Most students in the target class either speak Spanish or Spanish and Catalan at home and most immigrant children's families are from South America.

A few years ago the school did not have a good reputation but this is no longer the case. Nowadays it is quite active and it has got a program to integrate immigrant children (attended by 8% of the student population), of which the principal is quite proud of ('We have done this very well'). Since 2005-06 the school has been strongly involved in a project to introduce English in infant school and implement CLIL in middle and upper primary. Like school 54, more time is devoted to English than what is strictly required by law.

3.3.1   Learning English with two proficient teachers

The target class in school 53 ranged between 20 and 25 students during years 1-4, with 4-5 new students every year and 3-4 students leaving after years 2 and 3. The number of students in this class taking English lessons outside school ranges between 1-6 depending on the year. These students started learning English at the age of 5 (four 30'-sessions a week). For the first two years of primary education (starting at the age of 6), students had the same teacher (Alícia, not a real name) and received four and three weekly sessions (30'-40') of English for years 1 and 2 respectively. For the third and fourth years, a new English teacher (Anna, not a real name) took over and taught them 4 sessions a week and English through the Natural Sciences was progressively introduced, devoting about 35% of class time to it in year 3 and 75% in year 4. All sessions in years 3 and 4 are 45' long. Throughout the four years, the class splits for one of the sessions so that one group can do oral activities and the other works with computers. The oral sessions, which students always have every two weeks, were in charge of a NS language assistant in year 1.

Both Alícia and Anna have been teaching English for three years but while Alícia has got 20 years of teaching experience as a generalist teacher, Anna has just started her teaching career (she had previously worked as a translator). As regards their EFL competence, both of them have attained level C1 according to the CEFR (Common European Framework of Reference). None of them use commercial textbooks but materials from different sources including realia and self-created worksheets and posters, among others. Table 3 presents some of these two teachers' main characteristics.

	Years 1-2 Teacher: Alícia	Years 3-4 Teacher: Anna
Teacher's use of L2	100% Some use outside class	75% Very little use outside class.
Use of time	Lessons run smoothly	Year 3 lessons move slowly with frequent disruptions Year 4 lessons run more smoothly
Teaching style	T readily helps students or provides the answer when having difficulties in speaking L2	Long T turns because of lengthy instructions and content explanations. Uses translations, examples, definitions and questions to explain unknown words.

Table 3. Teachers in school 53: key features

Alícia uses the syllabus and lesson plans of a reputed state school in Barcelona which promotes trilingualism. The approach is based on creating interesting and comprehensible contexts of learning through storytelling, songs, short dialogues, hands on activities and tasks. The following excerpt comes from a task where students had to go around the teachers in the school to ask them how they got to school. Later on the teacher elicits this information from individual students so that it can be shared in a chart:

Excerpt 6

T:	Marc, your turn. Come on ... Sh, listen to Marc.
M:	Jaume come to school on foot (reading from his notes)
T:	On foot (filling in chart on bb). A lot of teachers come to school on foot!
M:	Norma come to school by tram.
T:	first of all by train, then by?
M:	tram.
T:	and?
M:	and underground.
T:	and by underground (noting down info on bb).
S:	*but who is she, who is she?*
T:	is Norma, do you know Norma?
SS:	Yes, xxx.
S:	tram *and what else?*
T:	by train, by tram and by underground.
S:	*and* on foot on foot.
SS:	By train by tram xx.
S:	*and* on foot?
T:	No, sh. By train, by tram and by underground.
S:	xx?
T:	Train tram. Do you know the tram? Is green.

(transcription 30.04.08, year 2)

The nature of interaction that takes place in Alícia's lesson is shown in excerpt 6 where the teacher makes spontaneous contributions in L2 and students ask for clarification questions and pose confirmation checks in L1, to which the T always responds in L2.

Sometimes learning objectives include other subject areas in the curriculum (i.e., arts and crafts, math). Classroom activities often generate rich input from the part of the teacher and/or opportunities to elicit single words and structured phrases in meaningful contexts. The following are a selection of T utterances from year 1 produced while interacting with students who were drawing a shoe, trainers, etc.: 'That's very nice. What color are the trainers?'; 'What's this?' (pointing to a student drawing); 'Don't draw very small shoes (…) Look at Pablo's trainers. This size is very good' (as T shows Pablo's drawing to the rest of the class). The level of involvement of students in class is generally high ('They are very hard working' according to Alícia) and their interest often generates spontaneous task-related talk in L1 on the part of the students such as: *'Ah, we are voting now!';* 'Creu' (L1) *is cross in English?'*; S: '*How nice!*' (as T displays self-created poster)). The teacher knows how to manage misbehavior efficiently and has well-established routines, which are conducted in English.

Anna has got much less teaching experience than Alícia and, even though she has been recently trained in CLIL, she feels she still needs more training. Unlike Alícia, who is using well-tested materials and lesson plans, she is developing her own syllabus and lessons, and looking for materials from different sources. For the two years she has been observed, she seems to have done some progress as far as classroom management, but student engagement is still unequal in year 4. Unlike Alícia, she sometimes uses L1 when faced with poor behavior, and for clarification purposes. During year 4 the IWB is used more often and the teacher is very satisfied about it ('We are very much into it').

Anna's lessons usually start with some routines to be followed by a teacher-led presentation and then, if there is enough time, some oral or written T-led practice. Another feature in Anna's lessons is that they seem to be little demanding in terms of learners' production. For example, if initial routines in years 1-2 are compared with those of years 3-4, there tends to be little progress in what is expected from students to produce. The following two excerpts from years 2 and 3 about the weather at the start of the English period illustrate that:

Excerpt 7	Excerpt 8
Alícia's lesson (year 2)	Anna's lesson (year 3)
T: Well, now, Felix, what's the weather like today? (whispering so that s can repeat it)	T: Paula, what is the weather like? What is the weather like?
	P: Sun.
F: What's the weather like today? (pronounced with difficulty)	T: Sunny. Sunny.
	T: Is it cold today?
	SS: No / Yes. (loudly)
T: okay, go and look through the window!	T: Is it warm?
	SS: No / Yes. (loudly)
SS: Sunny (in a low voice)	T: It's hot?
T: Juliana?	SS: No / Yes. (loudly)
J:	T: OK OK OK Sh. Today in the class is hot. Outside?
T: It's sunny, okay great! then...	SS: Cold. (loudly)
S: Sunny delight! (making fun)	T: Cold. OK. That's OK.
T: It's sunny. Let's stick it.	

Okay? You stick.
J: (sticks plastified card on   (transcription 13.03.09, year 3)
poster)
T: Thank you. Felix, sit down.
   (transcription 8.04.08, year 2)

In excerpt 9, where the teacher is reviewing concepts related to the topic of tastes, one can see that students' productions in L2 are limited to one word utterances. For longer utterances L1 is used and accepted by the T.

Excerpt 9

T:	Now, Miguel, what is this?
M:	Vinegar.
T:	Vinegar okay. What is the taste of vinegar?
S:	*The first one tastes very good.*
T:	Is it good?
S:	(nods)
T:	Yeah, do you like it?
S:	*It tastes like the salt.*
S:	*Bitter.*
S:	*It's a bit bitter but it's better than salt.*

(it's very noisy)

T:	Okay, okay
S:	Kiwi!
T:	But it's similar to?
S:	The kiwi.
T:	To kiwi. xx. Is it salty? Is it sweet?
SS:	Yes / No.
T:	It is sour
SS:	Sour (repeat playfully with laughter)
T:	Sour
SS:	Sour sour sour (repeat playfully with some laughter)

(transcription 13.03.09, year 3)

3.3.2 Lessons learned from school 53

Anna's lack of teaching experience together with the progressive introduction of CLIL without a set of consolidated teaching materials may explain some of her students' comments about lack of understanding in years 3 and 4: 'Worksheets, I do not understand them', 'Some homework, I do not quite understand', 'Sometimes we do things that I do not understand'.

Nevertheless, when students were asked about how much they liked learning English, most students said they did (90% and 87.5% respectively in years 3 and 4). Similarly, when asked about how difficult they found learning English, only 4% of them thought it was 'difficult'.

Nevertheless, and in spite of these positive attitudes and perceptions, there is a trend in school 53 for listening scores from years 3-4 to go down when compared with those of years 1-2 (see Figure 1). Anna's more restrictive use of English in and outside class and the time she needed to spend on managing students' behavior might have resulted in less exposure to English both in quantity and quality. Also, a lack of progression in what students were expected to say in English from year to year might also have explained students' achievements in years 3-4. What seem to be low demands in terms of productive learning might have deprived learners from a more balanced set of opportunities for learning, given that productive learning typically results in more and stronger knowledge than receptive learning (Griffin and Harley, 1996). Finally, when interpreting scores we should not forget contextual variables (see Appendices 1 and 2). In comparison with schools 52 and 54, this class had a lower percentage of mothers with a university degree and the school had a higher rate of immigration. Also, there were a number of new students joining this class every year, which must have made continuity in the teaching of this group of students quite a challenging task.

4 Conclusions

It would be unrealistic to want to draw grand conclusions from these three case studies, especially if we take into account the limited number of observations per year and the fact that only one measure of proficiency was evaluated. Nevertheless, the answers to our initial research questions can lead to some reflections about FL teaching and language practices in primary education. As regards teaching, the case studies evidence that students in the three schools had quite distinct experiences ranging from quite traditional teaching practices to quite meaningful communicative ones. Also, different teaching practices often led to different patterns of classroom discourse mainly in terms of elicitation or elaboration moves, students' output and teachers' and students' use of English. Furthermore, the examination of teaching style has led us to observe some interesting interactions with attitudes, perceptions and linguistic progress. For example, even though children's attitudes towards learning English were generally positive, these were sensitive to the teacher factor. This was evident in changes in teaching style taking place in schools 52 and 54. In school 54, we also saw that less positive attitudes towards learning English did not stop students from attaining good scores in the listening task. However, what seemed to go against language progress was exposing students to tasks that were little demanding in terms of language production, something that was observed in schools 51 and 53 (years 3-4). Instead, expecting students to use English for genuine communication seemed to make a difference. It showed that students' spontaneous L2 use is not so much dependent on students' grade level, language proficiency or even the teacher's FL proficiency but on the teacher's attitude towards this issue and an unrestricted use of L2 in class. All in all, the three case studies show that even though it is not possible to evaluate FL teaching in primary schools without having into consideration family and school factors, the teaching and language practices generated by teachers and students year after year can certainly help us better understand students' attitudes, perceptions and levels of achievement.

References

Butler Y. (2004) What Level of English Proficiency Do Elementary School Teachers Need to Attain to Teach EFL? Case Studies from Korea, Taiwan, and Japan. *TESOL QUARTERLY* (38) 2: 245-278.

Cable C., P. Driscoll, R. Mitchell , S. Sing , T. Cremin, J. Earl et al. (2010) *Learning languages at key stage 2. A longitudinal study.* Final report (Research report DCSF-RR198). The Open University.

Coyle, Yvette and Verdú, Mercedes (2000) Teaching Strategies in the EYL Classroom. In Moon J. and Nikolov M. (eds.) *Research into Teaching English to Young Learners* (257-294), Pécs: University Press Pécs.

Dobson A., M.D. Pérez Murillo, and R. Johnstone   (2010) *Bilingual education project Spain: Evaluation report*, Ministerio de Educación / British Council Spain.

Enever, J. (in press) (ed) *ELLiE. Early Language Learning in Europe London*, UK: British Council.

Harris J. and M. Conway (2002) *Modern languages in Irish primary schools. An evaluation of the National pilot project*, Dublin: Institiúid Teangeolaíochta Éireann. Research report 27.

Hunt, M., A. Barnes, B. Powell, G. Lindsay and D. Muijs (2005) *Primary Modern Foreign Languages: An overview of recent research, key issues and challenges for educational policy and practice*, Warwick, UK: University of Warwick.

Ghosn, I. (2004) Story as Culturally Appropriate Content and Social Context for Young English Language Learners: A Look at Lebanese Primary School Classes. *Language, Culture and Curriculum* (17) 2: 109-126.

Griffin, G.F. and Harley, T.A. (1996) List learning of second language vocabulary. *Applied Psycholinguistics* 17, 443-460.

Lopriore, L. (2009) Developement of young learners' perception of foreign language learning and teaching. Paper presented at the AAAL, Dever, Colorado, 21-24 March.

Mayfield J. (2005) Speak it and they WILL learn. *Pacific Northwest Council for Languages* (5) (2): 3-5.

Merriam S. M. (1998) *Qualitative research and case study applications in education*, San Francisco: Jossey-Bass Publishers.

Moon, J. (2009) The teacher factor in early foreign language learning programmes: The case of Vietnam. In Nikolov M. (ed), *The age factor and early language learning* (pp. 311-336), Berlin: Mouton de Gruyter.

Nikolov, M. (2003) Angolul és németül tanuló diákok nyelvtanulási attit_dje és motivációja. [Attitudes and motivation of learners of English and German], *Iskolakultúra* (XIII) 8: 61–73.

Nikolov, N. (2010) Colloquium – Early learning of English: Learners, teachers, and discourses, *Language Teaching* (43) 1: 108–112.

Nikolov, M., and J. Mihaljević Djigunović (2006), Recent research on age, second language acquisition, and early foreign language learning, *Annual Review of Applied Linguistics* 26: 234-260.

Oliver, R. and A. Mackey (2003) Interactional contex and feedback in child ESL classrooms. *Modern Language Journal* (87) iv: 519-533.

Peng, J. and L. Zhang (2009) An eye on target language use in elementary English classrooms in China. In M. Nikolov (ed) *Early learning of modern foreign languages* (pp. 212-228), Bristol: Multilingual Matters.

Philp J. and R. Tognini (2009) Language acquisition in foreign language contexts and the differential benefits of interaction, *Annual Review of Applied Linguistics* (47) 1: 244-266.

Swain, M. (1985) Communicative competence: Some roles of comprehensible input and comprehensible output in its development. In Gass G. and C. Madded (eds) *Input and second language acquisition* (pp. 235-252), Rowley, MA: Newbury.

Tognini, R. (2008) Interaction in languages other than English classes in Western Australian primary and secondary schools: Theory, practice and perceptions. Doctoral dissertation, Edith Cowan University.

Tragant, E. and Muñoz, C. (2009, August), Young learners' oral production: contextual and teacher factors. Paper presented at EARLI. Amsterdam, the Netherlands.

Tragant, E. and Lundberg G. (in press), The Teacher's role: What is its significance in Early Language Learning? In Enever J. (ed) *ELLiE. Early Language Learning in Europe London*, UK: British Council.

Walsh, A. and E. Yeoman (1999), Making sense of the French in French Immersion: Concept Development in early F1, *Canadian Modern Language Review* (55) 3: 342-354.

Appendix 1: The school's main features

	School 52	School 53	School 54
Location	Residential area middle-size town Barcelona province	Close to waterfront in Barcelona Lower-middle and lower class families with some intl. immigrant professionals	Downtown Barcelona Lower-middle class neighborhood
Subsidized lunches*	1%	4.6%	6%
Immigration	1%	37%	8%

*The autonomous government subsidizes lunches based on the children's family income.

Appendix 2: Main features of target classes

	School 52	School 53	School 54
Parents with university degrees*	Mother 42,1% Father 21,1%	Mother 23,8% Father 33,4%	Mother 59,1% Father 45%
Languages spoken at home	Catalan 72% Spanish 0% Cat/Sp 28% Other 0%	Catalan 0% Spanish 33% Cat/Sp 53% Other 14%	Catalan 72% Spanish 4% Cat/Sp 20% Other 4%
Class size (years 1 and 4)	27/25	20/25	25/25
New students (mean)	0	4,3	1,3

FL instruction: teaching time	Years 1-2: 50' Years 3-4: 2h45'	Year 2: 1h45' Years 1 & 4: 3h Year 3: 3h15'	Years 1-2: 2h45' Years 3-4: 3h15'
Additional information about FL instruction		Years 3-4: CLIL model NS language assistant years 1-2.	NS language assistant years 2 and 4
Students taking extra FL lessons	6-9	1-5	6-9

*Based on data from the groups of students under study. Data elicited from parents in a questionnaire with a variable return rate ranging from 33-96%.
**Number of students fluctuated from year to year.

Appendix 3: original classroom excerpts

Excerpt 1
S: (addressing the T) No trobo el meu grandad. (I cannot find my granddad)
T: (pointing to the floor) Ah, Toni your grandad.
                                                            (fieldnotes 27.2.07, year 1)

Excerpt 2
T: Page 35, Àlex. A veure… ens mirarem una mica la historieta que fa dies que vam fer. Us enrecordeu que la vam fer? Recordarem una miqueta de què anava la historieta. Primer de tot el Pau ens recordarà els personatges que hi havien a la historieta, que ja els coneixem.
P: La Rosie, el Zippedy i el Jack.
T: Molt bé. A la primera vinyeta veiem que el Zippedy li fa una pregunta a la Rosie. La pots llegir Pol?
P: 'Rosie, can you skip?' Què vol dir, Rosie, pots saltar? Pots saltar a corda?
T: Molt bé.
                                                            (transcription 3.04.08, year 2)

Appendix 4: Transcription conventions

x   unintelligible word

xx	unintelligible phrase
…	pause
DP	deviant pronunciation
S, SS	student, more than one student
O, P, etc.	initials of individual students' names
T	teacher
()	non-verbal information
use of italics	originally uttered in L1
(…)	untranscribed excerpt
bb	blackboard
SS: (Yes)/(No)	Simultaneous talk.

Lexical scaffolding in immersion classroom discourse

Nathalie Blanc (Université Lyon 1 IUFM – ICAR UMR 5191)
Rita Carol (Université de Strasbourg IUFM – ICAR UMR 5191)
Peter Griggs (Université Lyon 2 – ICAR UMR 5191)
Roy Lyster (McGill University)

Research in the field of vocabulary learning has shown that child L2 learners need to meet words again and again in new contexts in order to expand and deepen their word knowledge. In an instructional setting, cognitive processing is enhanced not only by the interplay between language use and metalinguistic reflection during classroom interaction but also by the activation and articulation of different sources of knowledge. Building on this research within a socio-cognitive perspective, we conducted quantitative and qualitative analyses of interactional sequences of lexical scaffolding during read-aloud activities in a French immersion primary school in Montreal. In a class composed of a mixture of French dominant, English dominant and bilingual eight-year-olds, French and English versions of the same storybook were read aloud and discussed in alternate lessons by two different teachers. The analyses revealed differences between the two teachers' lexical scaffolding strategies. While the French teacher tended to adopt a metalinguistic focus to elicit the meanings of difficult words, the English teacher sought more to recycle and explore vocabulary in contexts related to the story's content and students' prior experiences and to exploit knowledge of students' first language. These results point to the pedagogical potential of lexical scaffolding that goes beyond word definitions and aims instead to increase learners' depth of processing through connections to cross-lingual, epistemic and experiential knowledge.

1 Introduction

One of the most widely substantiated outcomes of immersion programs is that students' first language (L1) development and academic achievement are similar to (or better than) those of non-immersion students (Genesee, 1987, 2004; Swain & Lapkin, 1982; Turnbull, Lapkin, & Hart, 2001). Another finding common across immersion programs is that students develop much higher levels of second language (L2) proficiency than do non-immersion students studying the L2 as a subject for about 40 minutes each day. At the same time, research on the L2 proficiency of French immersion students in Canada has long suggested that even higher levels of proficiency approximating native-speaker norms might be attainable through improved instructional strategies (Allen, Swain, Harley, & Cummins, 1990; Harley, 1993; Harley, Cummins, Swain, & Allen, 1990; Swain, 1988, 1996). Arguably, the instructional practices designed to foster continued L2 growth through immersion were initially formulated rather tentatively and thus underlie the attested shortcomings that characterize students' L2 proficiency.

Immersion pedagogy drew on input-based communicative language teaching theories that emphasized content goals over language goals and avoided explicit attention to language, whereas researchers working across a range of content-based contexts now argue that language learning goals should become more prominent and explicit (e.g., Dalton-Puffer, 2007; Lyster, 2007; Swain & Lapkin, 2002; Fortune, Tedick & Walker, 2008;).

In the present study, we explore the instructional discourse of both the French and the English teacher of the same group of French immersion students involved in a biliteracy project. We draw more specifically on the notion of scaffolding (Wood, Bruner, & Ross, 1976) with a view to identifying effective instructional techniques targeting vocabulary development in the context of teacher-student interaction.

2 Research background

2.1 Instructional strategies

Lyster (2007) proposed a systematic integration of form-focused and content-based instruction through *counterbalanced instruction*, which promotes continued language growth by inciting learners to shift their attentional focus in a way that balances their awareness of learning both language and content together. One way for immersion and other content-based teachers to integrate form-focused instruction is through literacy practices that fit within broader educational objectives. This is because at the core of early literacy instruction is the need to nurture learners' awareness of oral language and their ability to conceptualize language: "becoming aware of it as a separate structure, freeing it from its embeddedness in events" (Donaldson, 1978, p. 90).

Previous research into literacy instruction in immersion settings has revealed an overall lack of planned vocabulary instruction as well as an overemphasis on decoding and understanding difficult words during reading activities (e.g., Allen, Swain, Harley, & Cummins, 1990). Stemming from this research are recommendations for more explicit vocabulary instruction within communicative contexts that include cross-lingual teaching strategies and reference to cognates to alert students to differences and also similarities between their L1 and L2 (Allen et al., 1990; Clipperton, 1994; Cummins, 2007). Other studies advocate focusing students' attention on the interplay between language knowledge and epistemic knowledge in immersion settings as a way of enriching lexical processing (Carol, 2008; Serra & Steffen, 2010).

In line with these recommendations, research into vocabulary development through reading points to an important role for 'depth of processing' in vocabulary instruction (Hulstijn, 2003; Laufer, 2003, 2006). Cameron (2001) summed up the importance of depth of lexical processing even for young learners as follows:

> Vocabulary development is not just learning more words but is also importantly about expanding and deepening word knowledge. Children need to meet words again and again, in new contexts that help increase what they know about words. Teaching needs to include the recycling of words. (p. 81)

To facilitate the recycling of words in this way, teachers are encouraged to focus on frequent and useful words while adopting an explicit approach to help learners, especially at the beginning stages, to make connections between form and meaning (Schmitt, 2008). Cameron (2001) stresses that, with young learners, exposure to new words in this way needs to occur not only in isolation but also in meaningful discourse contexts.

2.2   A socio-cognitive view of learning

Content-based instructional approaches to second language learning and teaching generally draw support from a range of theoretical perspectives. As Echevarria and Graves (1998) stated in reference to sheltered content classrooms, "effective teachers typically use a balanced approach that includes choices rooted in different learning theories" (p. 36). The theoretical perspective adopted in our study attributes complementary roles to both cognition and social interaction in L2 learning, and thus draws on a socio-cognitive perspective, which brings together Anderson's work on skill acquisition (Anderson 1982) and Bruner's work on scaffolded interaction (see Bange, Carol, & Griggs, 2005; Griggs 2007). Incorporating Bruner's (1971) argument that "growth of mind is always growth assisted from the outside" (p. 52), a socio-cognitive view of learning applies aptly to school settings, where "learning is a social as well as a cognitive process, one influenced by the relationships between student and teacher and among students" (August & Hakuta, 1997, p. 85).

With respect to skill acquisition, Bange et al. (2005) argued that, in second or foreign language teaching, there has been a tendency for instruction to be considered sufficient even if it aims only to develop declarative knowledge, without proceeding to the next step of providing opportunities for students to proceduralize their declarative knowledge. They also identified an obvious challenge in this regard: the development of procedural knowledge entails "learning by doing" (see Bruner, 1971), so learners are expected, paradoxically, to participate in tasks which they are not yet able to accomplish autonomously. They argued that the solution to the paradox lies in social interaction and, more specifically, in Bruner's notion of scaffolding between expert and novice, which "enables a child or novice to solve a problem, carry out a task or achieve a goal which would be beyond his unassisted efforts" (Wood, Bruner, & Ross, 1976, p. 90). Taking on the mentoring role, teachers promote the appropriation of new knowledge as they provide the amount of assistance that students need until they are able to function independently.

3   The present study

The study we report on in this chapter was conducted in a grade 3 French immersion classroom in the province of Quebec, where Canadian French immersion programs were first launched with homogenous groups of English-speaking children in 1965 (Lambert & Tucker, 1972). Classrooms in this context are, however, increasingly heterogeneous, now consisting of a mixture of French-dominant, English-dominant, and French/English bilingual students (Lyster, Collins, & Ballinger, 2009).

In this study, we examine the ways in which the French and English teachers of the same group of French immersion students draw attention to vocabulary during a bilingual read-aloud project. Vocabulary-focused episodes were selected from 4 hours of teacher-student interaction relating to a chapter book about ancient China that was read aloud to a grade 3 class of 24 8-9-year-old children. This particular dataset comes from a transcribed corpus of 27 hours of interactional data collected by Lyster, Collins, and Ballinger (2009) in the context of their bilingual read-aloud project in which French and English teachers read aloud to their students from the same storybooks alternating between chapters in French and English. The goals of their study were (a) to raise teachers' awareness of the bilingual resources of their students, (b) to encourage students' cross-linguistic collaboration, and (c) to promote teachers' cross-curricular and cross-linguistic collaboration.

Their study involved six teachers and their 68 students, with one pair of English and French teachers teaching a grade 1/2 class, a second pair teaching a grade 2 class, and a third pair teaching grade 3. Their data consisted of video-recordings of the read-aloud sessions and discussion about the stories. The transcribed corpus is rich in interactional data because, before each read-aloud session, teachers asked their students to summarize the content of the previous chapter (read in the 'other' language), and, after each reading, they asked students to make predictions about the next chapter. Interaction ensued as well during the actual reading aloud of each chapter as teachers frequently stopped to ask questions about the narrative or specific words to ensure comprehension.

In the present study, we zero in on the two grade 3 teachers because it was this grade level that proved most suitable to the selected storybooks, all of which were written by Mary Pope Osborne, published in English in the Magic Tree House series by Random House and in French in the Cabane Magique series by Bayard Jeunesse. The theme across all three stories was "books" and how writing changes across time and space. The main characters in each story were the same two children who were given a mission in each story to travel back in time in a magic tree house to recover books in danger of being lost or destroyed. In the present study, we chose to examine interaction during the reading of the second of three books, which was *Day of the Dragon King* (Osborne, 1998) in English and *Le terrible empereur de Chine* (Osborne, 2003) in French. In this story, the duo is sent to ancient China to retrieve the Chinese legend of the silk weaver and the cowherd. Readers become aware that, in ancient China, before the invention of paper, books were made of bamboo strips displaying Chinese calligraphy.

The grade 3 class consisted of 24 students: 8 English-dominant, 8 French-dominant, and 8 French/English bilinguals. The French teacher was a francophone with minimal knowledge of English. She had taught at the school for 7 years. She had a Bachelor of Education degree from a French-speaking university, with a focus on special-needs students, but no specific teacher training in L2 teaching. The English teacher was bilingual in English and Greek and had some knowledge of French. She had completed a one-year teaching program prior to becoming an elementary school teacher and, like her counterpart, had no specific training in L2 teaching. She had taught grades 3 and 4 at the school for 22 years and had begun teaching English language arts in the French immersion stream 10 years earlier.

Both teachers focused a great deal on vocabulary during their reading of the story as well as before and after while students were retelling the previous chapter and making predictions for the next. However, the teachers appeared to use very different strategies to focus on vocabulary; hence the idea of a descriptive study of two different teachers working with the same group of students on related content (i.e., the same story) but in two different languages.

Our goal in this chapter is, first, to identify these strategies and the extent to which they engage students, and second, to speculate about their potential effectiveness in the light of the recommendations highlighted in our literature review whereby child L2 learners need to meet words again and again in new contexts, ideally in communicative contexts, in order to expand and deepen their word knowledge. We examine classroom discourse as two teachers take on a mentoring role to facilitate the appropriation of new vocabulary by scaffolding the interaction in ways that promote varying degrees of lexical processing.

4 Method of coding

Our coding categories are data driven, deriving from repeated viewings of the videos and careful readings of the transcripts. Our analysis of the two sets of classroom data led us first of all to identify what we refer to as lexical scaffolding episodes. These are characterised by the signalling and decontextualisation of lexical forms or meanings during a read-aloud or summary phase of the lesson, followed by an interactional sequence which involves the class in a lexical search giving rise to the emergence of the targeted lexical form or meaning.

The dominant underlying interactional pattern which emerged from our analysis of both teachers was the discourse sequence *Initiation–Response–Feedback* identified by Sinclair and Coulthard (1975). This determined the way in which we apprehended the structure of each lexical episode, the lexical search generally presenting itself in the form of a sequence initiated by the teacher. In most cases, the initiation takes the form of a question which triggers the lexical search. In example 1, the teacher's question focuses on a difficult word in the text and asks for a definition :

Example 1
> FT   je vais te demander des mots difficiles, je veux savoir si tu comprends bien « Il dévale les escaliers » Mmm… dévaler, le verbe... » (FT-3).

In example 2, the lexical search is set off during a student turn in which the appropriate word in English is missing :

Example 2

S   they went... they went in their [cabane].

ET: they went in their [cabane]. What's another word for [cabane]? (ET-1).

We identified four types of orientation underlying the instructional interaction during these episodes, determined either by the teacher's scaffolding strategies or by the students' output (responses or autonomous turns).

A *(meta)linguistic orientation* involves a search for a lexical form or a word definition, calling on language knowledge which may also include reflection on language. This orientation naturally underlies all the lexical scaffolding episodes and systematically constitutes the opening orientation in so far as the episodes are initiated by the decontextualisation of language knowledge (see example 1).

A *cross-lingual* orientation entails reference to the knowledge of the "other" language and can either be triggered by the teacher or emerge in the students' production (see example 2).

An *epistemic orientation* relates either to general world knowledge or to the content of the story being read, as in the following example:

Example 3

ET   [Ancien.] Did you hear that word [ancien] or ancient country in the previous book that we read? (ET-1).

An *experiential orientation* draws on knowledge based on students' personal experience. In the following example, the teacher has recourse to objects and activities linked to the personal lives of the students in order to clarify the meaning of the lexical item "thread":

Example 4

ET   Cotton threads, so it's cord any kind of cord that we weave into cloth. How many of you have tents at home? Tents? How many of you go camping or have a little tent in your backyard? (ET-17-10).

As language necessarily articulates form and meaning, the boundaries between linguistic and non-linguistic orientations are often difficult to define. Our coding decisions are therefore not always unequivocal but based on our judgment of the degree to which a word is, on the one hand, the object of metalinguistic focus and, on the other hand, embedded in a communicative activity.

Finally, a distinction was made between student responses and autonomous student turns according to whether the student output is linked or not to a previous teacher initiating turn in the elicitation sequence.

5   Quantitative analysis

The aims of this quantitative analysis are (a) to classify and quantify different orientation patterns, (b) to measure their effect on the amount of student output, and (c) to explore the effects of orientation changes on lexical processing.

5.1   Classification   and   quantification   of   orientation patterns

The first elements which appear in our quantitative analysis are that 32% of the French teacher's (FT) episodes display a single orientation which is exclusively linguistic or metalinguistic, whereas in the English teacher's (ET) class the percentage of single-oriented episodes is less than half as much (12%) (Table 1). Furthermore, 61% of FT's episodes have a double orientation and only two episodes out of 28 (7%) show a triple orientation. On the other hand, ET's episodes present a much richer configuration of patterns, with a significantly higher rate of episodes combining three orientations (24%) and 5% of episodes combining all four.

	FT	ET
Single orientation ((meta)linguistic)	9	5
	(32%)	(12%)
Double orientation	17	24
	(61%)	(59%)
Triple orientation	2	10
	(7%)	(24%)
Quadruple orientation	0	2
		(5%)
total	28	41

Table 1: Number (and percentage) of sequences per teacher with single, double, triple or quadruple orientations

The sequences in the multiple-oriented episodes show, for both teachers, a preference for scaffolding patterns combining a (meta)linguistic and an epistemic orientation. In the double orientation category, this is the case for 46% of FT's episodes and for 34% of ET's episodes (Table 2) and this combination is also the most recurrent in triple-oriented episodes with 7% for FT and 22% for ET (Table 3). The predominance of this scaffolding pattern can be explained by the fact that the lexical processing takes place in the context of a content-oriented pedagogical activity. The most substantial distinguishing feature between the two teachers is that, in comparison to FT's lexical scaffolding episodes, those of ET incorporated a higher proportion of experiential references (19% vs. 10%) and an even greater proportion of cross-lingual references (42% vs. 11%) as a means to explore and consolidate the meaning of words (Tables 2, 3, & 4).

	FT	ET
(meta)linguistic + cross-lingual	3 (11%)	8 (20%)
(meta)linguistic + epistemic	13 (46%)	14 (34%)
(meta)linguistic + experiential	1 (3%)	2 (5%)
total	17 (60)	24 (59%)

Table 2: Number (and percentage) of sequences per teacher with different double-orientation combinations

	FT	ET
(meta)linguistic + cross-lingual + epistemic	0	6 (15%)
(meta)linguistic- + cross-lingual + experiential	0	1 (2%)
(meta)linguistic + epistemic + experiential	2 (7%)	3 (7%)
total	2 (7%)	10 (24%)

Table 3: Number (and percentage) of sequences per teacher with different triple-orientation combinations

	FT	ET
(meta)linguistic + cross-lingual + epistemic + experiential	0	2 (5%)

Table 4: Number (and percentage) of sequences per teacher with a quadruple orientation

5.2   Effects of orientation patterns on the amount of student output

Our first hypothesis deriving from the notion of depth of processing presented in the literature review and from the results of the preceding quantitative study was that lexical scaffolding engaging students communicatively should benefit lexical processing in that it fosters the recycling of words in a meaningful discourse context. Working on this hypothesis, we sought to relate the categories of scaffolding orientation to the amount of student output generated during the interactional sequence. The effect of lexical scaffolding on the quantity of student output was measured in terms of the number and the length of student turns. For both teachers, we counted the average amount per episode of student turns and the average amount per episode of student turns containing one sentence or more.

Table 5 shows that the average amount of student turns per episode increases in proportion to the number of orientations within the episode: an average of 2.7 turns for single-oriented episodes, 4 turns for double-oriented episodes, 10.2 turns for triple- and quadruple-oriented episodes. A similar rate of increase can be observed for the number of student turns containing one sentence or more: an average of 0.9 for single-oriented episodes, 1.7 for double-oriented episodes, 4.5 for triple- and quadruple-oriented episodes. Table 5 also shows that these rates are similar for both FT and ET and do not appear therefore to be affected by the teacher variable.

orientations		number of episodes	average student turns	average student turns of one sentence or more
single	FT	9	2.8	1.2
((meta)linguistic)	ET	5	2.5	0.2
	FT + ET	14	2.7	0.9
double	FT	17	4.4	2.4
	ET	24	3.7	1.1
	FT + ET	41	4.0	1.7
triple & quadruple	FT	2	8.0	5.0
	ET	12	10.3	4.4
	FT + ET	14	10.2	4.5

Table 5: Volume of output related to orientation patterns

Table 6 relates student output to combinations of lexical orientations within multiple-oriented episodes. A distinction is made between episodes involving combinations where the linguistic orientation (i.e., (meta)-linguistic and/or cross-lingual) is dominant and those where the non-linguistic orientation (i.e., epistemic and/or experiential) is dominant. Average student output is shown to be higher in episodes where non-linguistic orientations exceed linguistic ones. In double-oriented episodes, combinations of linguistic and non-linguistic orientations generate an average of 4.2 student turns compared to 3.5 in exclusively linguistic ((meta)linguistic/cross-lingual) combinations and an average of 1.9 student turns of one sentence or more in the former compared to an average of 1 in the latter. In triple- and quadruple-oriented episodes, the gap between non-linguistically and linguistically dominant orientations is even greater: an average of 12.5 compared to an average of 3.5 for the rate of student turns and an average of 6 compared to an average of 1.2 for the rate of student turns of one sentence or more.

number of orientations	combination of orientations	number of episodes	average student turns	average student turns of one sentence or more
double	(meta)linguistic/crosslingual	11	3.5	1.0
	linguistic/non-linguistic	31	4.2	1.9
triple & quadruple	linguistic dominant	12	3.5	1.2
	non-linguistic dominant	5	12.5	6.0

Table 6: Volume of output in linguistically dominant and non-linguistically dominant orientation episodes

The results of this quantitative analysis show therefore that student output increases in proportion to the diversity of orientations underlying the teachers' lexical scaffolding strategies and to the degree to which these orientations are non-linguistic. According to our first hypothesis, such instructional strategies should be beneficial to lexical processing in that they engage students communicatively and thereby allow words to be recycled.

5.3   Effects of orientation changes on lexical processing

Our second hypothesis was that lexical processing is enhanced in this instructional setting by the interplay during classroom interaction between different sources of knowledge. In the light of this hypothesis, we decided to count the number of changes, whatever type of orientation they involve, which take place during the multiple-oriented episodes. This led us also to examine more precisely who initiates these changes, the teacher or the students.

We counted as changes switches in orientation initiated both by the teacher after feedback and by students in their responses or autonomous turns. Thirty-seven orientation changes were found in the 28 episodes scaffolded by FT, giving an average rate of 1.3 changes per episode, whereas for ET the rate is much higher, amounting to 97 changes of orientation in 41 episodes, with an average of 2.4 per episode. On the other hand, the relative proportions are inverted in the two teaching contexts regarding the number of changes initiated by the students or by the teacher: 43% of these changes are initiated by the students in FT's case, whereas for ET, the rate is lower at 29%. These figures show, therefore, that in FT's class, the pupils take more responsibility for changes in orientation than in ET's class.

As for the number of autonomous turns taken by the students, an opposite tendency can be observed. Indeed, 11 student autonomous turns were counted in FT's episodes, giving an average of 0.4 per episode, while in ET's class, this figure is more than doubled: 35 autonomous turns were found with an average of 0.8 per episode. The relative proportion of different types of orientation within the autonomous student turns also varies according to the teacher. In the case of FT, 63.6% of these student turns are (meta)linguistically oriented, 27.3% have an epistemic orientation and 9.1% an experiential orientation. In ET's case, the relative proportion is different and more balanced and also includes cross-lingual oriented turns. The highest rate (40%) is that of epistemic orientation, with (meta)linguistic orientation at 31.4%, experiential at 22.8% and cross-lingual at 5.8%.

These results imply that in ET's class the students' output is both more content-based and more spontaneous, seeming in the second case to contradict the previous results showing that it is in FT's class that the students take more responsibility for orientation changes. The lower rate of student-initiated orientation changes in ET's class could be explained by the fact that she herself switches orientation a lot more than FT. The rate of switches is lower in FT's case, but the percentage of changes initiated by the students is higher. We speculate therefore that the students themselves feel the need to switch orientation in order to process vocabulary and that this need is not addressed sufficiently by FT's scaffolding strategies based primarily on a (meta)linguistic orientation.
In the light of the research presented in the literature review, the results of the quantitative analysis lead us to formulate two further hypotheses regarding the effect on lexical processing of these changes in orientation :
-    Hypothesis 1: A switch from a linguistic to a non-linguistic orientation during a scaffolding episode may both facilitate lexical

access by clarifying meaning through a process of contextualisation and increase the depth of lexical processing by recycling vocabulary in communicative discourse.

- Hypothesis 2: A switch from a non-linguistic to a (meta)linguistic or cross-lingual orientation may allow the learners to consolidate meaning and deepen lexical processing by articulating different types of language knowledge.

6 Qualitative analysis

In order to explore these two hypotheses we carried out a qualitative analysis of two lexical scaffolding episodes representative of the strategies displayed by the two teachers and both involving multiple orientations: the episode « paisible » taken from FT's class and the episode « pasture » taken from ET's class. This qualitative analysis draws on socio-cognitive theory by relating the scaffolding strategies used by the two teachers to the type of pedagogical relationship that emerges during the interaction.

The "paisible" episode is triggered when FT draws the students' attention to a difficult word (*paisible = peaceful*) in order to check comprehension during the read-aloud activity.

"Paisible" Episode: Extract 1

1FT	Alors, je commence? « Un pays si paisible » **Qu'est-ce que ça veut dire le mot paisible?** un pays paisible, mmm… quelqu'un là qui parle beaucoup anglais à la maison, serait capable de me dire ça? xxx, tu parles anglais beaucoup à la maison - comment?
2S	**Comme c'est l'eau…**
3FT	**Un pays pais--.** xxx! pense au mot *paisible*, tu lèves la main. C'est beau? xxx baisse la main tout de suite, assis-toi sur tes fesses, xxx! **Alors, un pays… pense à la Chine…** un pays paisible, j'aimerais ça là, quelqu'un qui par--… xxx, tu parles beaucoup anglais à la maison dis-le donc
4Sd	**euh… c'est un pays… beau…**
5FT	**Beau? Non Pense à un autre petit mot dans le grand mot.** Vas-y donc ..ah…xxx! dernier avertissement. Paisible ? xxx;
6 Sd	euh.. encore un exemple ….eh…**quelqu'un qui pèse beaucoup ?** *(laughter)*
7FT	**Qui pèse beaucoup ? Non..**

8Sd	Je sais, je sais!
9FT	Pour moi c'est un mot facile, mais je crois que c'est difficile. Oh la la! xxx?

In Extract 1, three attempts by FT to elicit the meaning of "paisible" lead to student responses which all receive negative feedback from the teacher. An initial linguistically oriented elicitation "qu'est-ce que ça veut dire le mot paisible?" gives rise to the student response "comme c'est l'eau" which attempts to define the word by associating it to an analogous context, that of water. In so doing the student departs from a purely linguistic orientation to evoke a context more embedded in personal experience. In contrast, the third elicitation, strongly focusing on lexical form – "pense à un autre petit mot dans le grand mot" – imposes a strict metalinguistic framework which induces a student to produce a wrong answer: "quelqu'un qui pèse beaucoup", which nevertheless shows evidence of a clever metalinguistic deduction. Between these two (meta-)linguistically oriented elicitations, FT changes to an epistemic orientation in order to facilitate the lexical search through the evocation of China, the country in which the story is set : "alors un pays... pense à la Chine... un pays paisible." However, this change in orientation also leads to an inadequate reply ("c'est un pays... beau"), as the feature targeted by the teacher in the very general context she evokes is not sufficiently evident to be mutually recognized by the group.

We consider that the failure of FT's elicitations to achieve the expected outcomes in this extract can be linked to the type of pedagogical relationship she establishes with the class. By choosing to explore language in a predominantly metalinguistic framework, which she herself and the French-dominant students master better than the English-dominant students, she induces a more asymmetrical relationship in which knowledge is exchanged on an unequal basis and constructed according to the expectations of the teacher. The task of lexical processing is thus made all the more difficult especially for English-dominant students. This asymmetry is reinforced by her insistence on specifically designating English-dominant students to respond to her elicitations (turns 1 and 3) and by her deliberate choice, repeated in other sequences, of drawing students' attention to difficult words. When her scaffolding strategy does take on a non-linguistic epistemic orientation, the features she tries to bring to the students' minds through the context she evokes are not sufficiently manifest to support lexical processing.

In contrast, FT achieves her objective at the end of the same sequence, in Extract 2, by presenting the word in a shared framework constructed on the basis of the students' personal experience – "quand tu as la paix, disons à la maison? Tu es comment? Tu te retrouves, c'est...? " – thus allowing students to rapidly find appropriate synonyms "tranquille" and "calme".

"Paisible" Episode: Extract 2

17FT	Ok! sh...quand tu as la paix, disons à la maison? Tu es comment? Tu te retrouves, c'est...?
18Ss	Tranquille
19FT	Tranquille! Alors, qu'est-ce que ça veut dire un pays paisible. Sh....non, je vais aller voir (?) qui a la main levée
20Sd	euh... calme?
21FT	Bon! un pays calme. Ça va? On y va!

The "pasture" episode, taken from the corpus of the English class, takes place during a summary phase in which the teacher isolates the word "pasture" as part of a comprehension check of the chapter which has just been read aloud. The analysis of the extracts shows how the scaffolding sequence triggered by this word leads the students to explore the word's semantic field by switching to and fro between linguistic and non-linguistic orientations.

After ET's linguistically oriented initiating turn fails to elicit an adequate response in Extract 3, she switches immediately to an epistemic orientation in which she reconstitutes contextual features taken from the story so as to help the students infer the targeted meaning. By recycling the students' previous output she reinforces the mutually recognized context: "on a farm where **someone said** like a garden where you have a field, animals go to the to pasture (...) you have in the countryside **most of you said it**." When this strategy also fails to lead the students to an adequate response, ET carries on in the same orientation by showing a picture from the book. This picture serves as a semiotic tool enabling knowledge to be shared.

"Pasture" Episode: Extract 3

1ET	Did everyone understand the word pasture? Raise your hand if you know what pasture is. There was the word pasture. What's a pasture? *(points to one student)*
2S	It's- ok, I don't remember
3ET	**On a farm where someone said like a garden where you have a field, animals go to the to pasture.** What does that mean? Animals go animals go to pasture. **You have in the countryside most of you said it**. There were gardens next to the garden is usually a pasture. xxx what's a pasture?
4S	I think it's like in a barn or something

5ET	No it isn't, it's not a building.
6Sd	On a farm.
7ET	It's on look... look behind and you can see the pasture *(shows picture in book)*.

Later on in the sequence in Extract 4, ET switches, with the same objective of building shared knowledge, to an experiential orientation. This generates a large amount of student output based upon personal experience, leading them to recycle words of the same semantic field (farm, acres, field, yard) in a meaningful context. Furthermore, the teacher's authentic questioning ("how many of you have ever gone on a farm?", "ok so when you look out the window from your papa's house what do you see outside?") induces a symmetrical relationship by inverting the typical pedagogical interaction with regard to the source of knowledge.

"Pasture" Episode: Extract 4

15ET	If we, **how many of you have ever gone on a farm?** *(Some hands go up)* Ok xxx you've gone on a **farm**?
16Sd	So it's kind of a farm it's where my papa lives he lives in this big big area.
17ET	**Ok so when you look out the window from your papa's house what do you see outside?**
18Sm	Well usually I see like **yards** with **acres** and **acres** of **yard** and stuff like that.
19ET	Acres and acres of what?
20Sm	Yard.
21ET	Yard? Do you mean what, a **field**?
22Sm	Yeah.
23ET	A field.

At the end of this sequence in Extract 5 the class first returns to a linguistic orientation and then finally switches to a cross-lingual one. Within the experiential context collectively constructed by the class, the teacher's question – "What are they standing on?" – takes on a lexical orientation by directly pointing to words that are linked to the targeted meaning. This question enables the class to constitute through their interaction a network of associated words ("grass", "field", "land", "trees"). By evoking a shared experience – "so you've all walked across a pasture" - the teacher then goes on to establish these words as belonging to the same lexical field as "pasture".

Finally, in order to consolidate further the meaning of the word, the teacher asks French-dominant students to provide a translation in French. A more symmetrical relationship is thus once more induced by an inversion in the normal flow of knowledge: French-dominant students are designated in their capacity as "experts" in their native language while the teacher herself masters only partially what for her is a foreign language.

"Pasture" Episode: Extract 5

29ET	You just saw animals. Where were they standing? **What were they standing on?**
30Sm	They were standing on the …
31Sd	**Grass?**
32S	Yeah
33ET	Grass. So another word for grass in the countryside is pasture. How many?
34S	**Fields?**
35ET	Fields yes fields of grass is a pasture.
36Sd	**Land.**
37ET	Land, **trees.** F1 How many of you like to run in the fields in the countryside? *(most students raise their hands)* So you've all walked across a pasture.
38S	Ah, Miss xxx?
39ET	So, how would we say pasture in French? Who would like to take a chance? xxx?

(…)

47ET	So what does that mean, [pasture]? xxx I'm concerned now that you're talking because you're not listening.
48S	[Pasture] means-
49ET	So [pasture], xxx do you know what [pasture] means in English or in French?
50S	[Un champs]
51ET	[C'est un champs] a field exactly.

In summary, therefore, the main difference between the instructional strategies of FT and ET is that the latter are characterized by a more communicative and symmetrical mode of pedagogical interaction in which information is exchanged more horizontally and knowledge constructed more collectively in shared contexts. We hypothesise that this mode of pedagogical interaction, involving the exploration of vocabulary in different discourse contexts, is more likely to develop procedural lexical skills by encouraging the recycling of words in meaningful contexts and to foster depth of processing through the interplay between different sources of lexical knowledge.

7 Conclusion

Starting from the premise that effective teaching in immersion contexts requires appropriate instructional techniques designed specifically to promote language development, this study has analysed lexical scaffolding strategies used by teachers and their potential effect on the type of lexical processing carried out by students. In view of the descriptive nature of its research design, the aim of the study was not to measure the effects on vocabulary learning of different types of lexical scaffolding strategy, but rather to explore the correlations between teachers' scaffolding strategies, students' cognitive focusing and the pedagogical relationships established during instructional interaction. Our quantitative analysis of the lexical scaffolding episodes managed by the two teachers participating in this study revealed differences in the strategies they use. While the French teacher favoured a metalinguistic focus to elicit definitions of difficult words from students, the English teacher tended to recycle and explore vocabulary in different contexts, thus allowing words to be processed in relation to epistemic content, students' prior experiences, and students' first language. In the light of the research literature, the quantitative analysis suggested that the scaffolding patterns in the English class provide particularly favorable interactional conditions for the recycling of words and for depth of processing. The qualitative analysis, drawing on a socio-cognitive perspective, then allowed us to explore more deeply these interactional conditions and to show how they correlate positively with the type of pedagogical relationship the teacher establishes with her students.

Creating purposeful opportunities in meaningful contexts for recycling words in ways that promote depth of lexical processing is advocated as an effective means to stimulate vocabulary development. Yet, how teachers can effectively employ such strategies during online interaction with students is less well documented and requires concrete examples that might serve as models for professional development. Noteworthy in this regard in our analysis is how one teacher in particular was able to recycle words within a single lesson by shifting students' attention from metalinguistic and crosslinguistic orientations to epistemic and experiential orientations. She maintained a recursive interplay between these orientations, thereby counterbalancing a focus on language and content in ways that required shifts in students' attention and thus deeper levels of lexical processing. We expect to continue this line of research by investigating in more detail the discourse features that enable teachers to orchestrate their lexical scaffolding in this way.

References

Allen, P., Swain, M., Harley, B., & Cummins J. (1990) Aspects of classroom treatment: Toward a more comprehensive view of second language education. In B. Harley, P. Allen, J. Cummins, & M. Swain (Eds), *The development of second language proficiency,* Cambridge, UK: Cambridge University Press: 57-81.

Anderson, J. (1982) Acquisition of Cognitive Skill. *Psychological Review, 89* (4), 396-406.

August, D., & Hakuta, K. (Eds) (1997) *Improving schooling for language-minority children: A research agenda.* Washington, DC: National Academy Press.

Bange, P., Carol, R. & Griggs, P. (2005) *L'apprentissage d'une langue étrangère : cognition et interaction,* Paris: L'Harmattan.

Bruner, J. (1971) *The relevance of education,* New York: Norton.

Cameron, L. (2001) *Teaching languages to young learners,* Cambridge, UK: Cambridge University Press.

Carol, R. (2008) Langue et cognition : apprendre les concepts de couleur et de taille en classe d'immersion à l'école primaire. *Etudes de Linguistique Appliquée 151*: 319-331.

Clipperton, R. (1994) Explicit vocabulary instruction in French immersion, *The Canadian Modern Language Review, 50*: 737-749.

Cummins, J. (2007) Rethinking monolingual instructional strategies in multilingual classrooms. *Canadian Journal of Applied Linguistics, 10*, 221-241.

Dalton-Puffer, C. (2007) *Discourse in content and language learning (CLIL) classrooms,* Amsterdam: John Benjamins.

Donaldson, M. (1978) *Children's minds,* New York: Norton.

Echevarria, J., & Graves, A. (1998) *Sheltered content instruction,* Boston: Allyn & Bacon.

Fortune, T., Tedick, D., & Walker, C. (2008) Integrated language and content teaching: Insights from the immersion classroom. In T. Fortune and D. Tedick (Eds), *Pathways to multilingualism: Evolving perspectives on immersion education,* Clevedon, UK: Multilingual Matters.

Genesee, F. (1987) *Learning through two languages: Studies of immersion and bilingual children*, Cambridge, MA: Newbury House.

Genesee, F. (2004) What do we know about bilingual education for majority language students? In T. K. Bhatia & W. Ritchie (Eds), *Handbook of bilingualism and multiculturalism,* Malden, MA: Blackwell: 547-576.

Griggs, P. (2007) *Perspective sociocognitive sur l'apprentissage des langues étrangères*, Paris: L'Harmattan.

Harley, B. (1993) Instructional strategies and SLA in early French immersion, *Studies in Second Language Acquisition, 15*: 245-259.

Harley, B., Cummins, J., Swain, M., & Allen, P. (1990) The nature of language proficiency. In B. Harley, P. Allen, J. Cummins & M. Swain (Eds), *The development of second language proficiency*, Cambridge, UK: Cambridge University Press: 7-25.

Hulstijn, J. (2003) Incidental and intentional learning. In C. Doughty & M. Long (Eds), *Handbook of second language acquisition*, Oxford: Blackwell: 349-381.

Lambert, W., & Tucker, R. (1972) *Bilingual education of children: The St. Lambert experiment,* Rowley, MA: Newbury House.

Laufer, B. (2003) Vocabulary acquisition in a second language: Do learners really acquire most vocabulary by reading? Some empirical evidence, *The Canadian Modern Language Review, 59:* 567-588.

Laufer, B. (2006) Comparing focus on form and focus on forms in second language vocabulary learning,*The Canadian Modern Language Review, 63:* 149-166.

Lyster, R. (2007) *Learning and teaching languages through content*, Amsterdam: John Benjamins.

Lyster, R., Collins, L., & Ballinger, S. (2009) Linking languages through a bilingual read-aloud project, *Language Awareness, 18*: 366-383.

Osborne, M. (1998) *Day of the Dragon King*, New York: Random House.

Osborne, M. (2003) *Le terrible empereur de Chine*, Paris: Bayard Jeunesse.

Schmitt, N. (2008) Review article: Instructed second language vocabulary learning, *Language Teaching Research, 12*: 329-363.

Serra, C. & Steffen, G. (2010) Acquisition des concepts et intégration des langues et disciplines dans l'enseignement bilingue. In Carol, R. (Eds) *Apprendre en classe d'immersion. Quels concepts? Quelle théorie?,* Paris: L'Harmattan: 129-186.

Sinclair, J., & Coulthard, R. M. (1975) *Towards an analysis of discourse: The English used by teachers and pupils*, Oxford: Oxford University Press.

Swain, M. (1988) Manipulating and complementing content teaching to maximize second language learning. *TESL Canada Journal, 6*: 68-83.

Swain, M. (1996) Integrating language and content in immersion classrooms: Research perspectives, *The Canadian Modern Language Review, 52*: 529-548.

Swain, M., & Lapkin, S. (1982) *Evaluating bilingual education in Ontario: A Canadian case study*, Clevedon, UK: Multilingual Matters.

Swain, M., & Lapkin, S. (2002) Talking it through: two French immersion learners' response to reformulation, *International Journal of Educational Research, 37*: 285-304.

Turnbull, M., Lapkin, S., & Hart, D. (2001) Grade 3 immersion students' performance in literacy and mathematics: Province-wide results from Ontario (1989-99), *The Canadian Modern Language Review, 58:* 9-26.

Wood, D., Bruner, J., & Ross, G. (1976) The role of tutoring in problem solving. *Journal of Child Psychology and Psychiatry: 17,* 89-100.

L1 use in primary and secondary foreign language classrooms and its contribution to learning

Rita Tognini (Western Australian Department of Education)
Rhonda Oliver (Curtin University)

The bilingual nature of foreign language classrooms is often ignored in SLA research. However, L1 use in teacher-learner and peer interaction is a reality in these classrooms. Studies of teacher-learner and peer interaction have found varying levels of L1 use in different contexts. They have tended to highlight its limitations to learning but have also identified cognitive and social functions for L1 use that could contribute to learning. Research in both contexts draws attention to the lack of a principled basis for optimum L1 use for SLA. This chapter explores L1 use in 10 foreign language classes in Australian schools. The chapter is based on findings of a four month study in ten French and Italian classes and focuses on the context and purpose of L1 use in teacher-learner and peer interaction. L1 use by teachers and students varied across different activities and tasks. Teachers' L1 use tends to be associated with particular classroom contexts. Although it serves important social and regulatory functions, its consistent use, especially for dealing with communication difficulties, may limit opportunities for learning. In contrast, L1 use in peer interaction helps learners support and scaffold each other's L2 use and develop their understanding of L2 grammar.

1 Background

Research studies have demonstrated that interaction facilitates language learning in a number of ways (Mackey, 2007). At the same time there is growing evidence of the impact of context on the nature and purpose of interaction (Alcón, &. García Mayo, 2009; García Mayo & Alcón,, 2002; Mackey & Gass, 2006). A learning context that has received limited attention in interactionist research is that of the primary and secondary foreign language (FL) or, as they are called in Australia, Language Other than English (LOTE) classrooms, where both teacher-learner and peer interaction often includes use of L1 as well of L2. This chapter draws on a study of the nature and purpose of interaction in primary and secondary LOTE classrooms in Australia (Tognini, 2008) to examine the use of L1 in teacher-learner and peer interaction in this context and explore its contribution to learning.

Interaction occurs when learners are under pressure to communicate (Gass, 2003). It provides them with opportunities to receive valuable input and to try out language that they are in the process of acquiring. As they push their output they can receive feedback about the effectiveness of their communicative efforts. In turn, the feedback learners give each other as part of the interaction stimulates them to notice difference between their interlanguage and the target language. For example, Swain (1995; 2005) demonstrated that this feedback pushed learners to make their output more precise, coherent and appropriate. This finding is particularly relevant to the current study.

The contribution of output to second language learning has been established by a number of studies. As well as giving learners an opportunity to apply the insights they have gained about aspects of the target language from feedback, successful output helps them to consolidate prior knowledge and increase fluency through automatic retrieval of form (Nobuyoshi & Ellis, 1993; McDonough, 2005; Swain, 1995, 2005).   Output thus provides evidence of what is occurring in terms of learner acquisition. It is also the way that teachers assess learners and judge their development. This dynamic process of learner output, as part of the interaction, and teacher assessment (and possible invention as a consequence) was the focus of analysis in the current FL/LOTE study. The nature of learner output in teacher-learner, and within peer interaction, is examined particularly with respect to L1 and L2 production.

2   Foreign language/LOTE classroom learning

For the majority of primary, secondary and tertiary students across the world, second language learning often occurs in FL/LOTE classes. These classes are characterized by limited time allocation, a feature that is marked in most primary and some secondary school LOTE classes in Australia. The pedagogy of Australian LOTE primary and secondary classes can be described as broadly communicative, with learning outcomes that focus on developing students' ability to communicate effectively and appropriately in the target language orally and in writing. Teachers are expected to provide students with opportunities for interaction with themselves and importantly with peers through a range of activities and tasks and to encourage reflection on L2 form.   However, despite the large number of FL/LOTE classroom learners, there is a dearth of research in this interactional context, especially with regard to the amount and purpose of L1 used.

What is known is that there appears to be a high level of L1 use by FL/LOTE teachers in teacher-learner interaction: This has been documented by research carried out in Australia (Crawford, 2002), Canada (Calman & Daniel, 1998; Duff & Polio, 1990; Turnbull, 2001; Turnbull & Arnett, 2002),

New Zealand (Kim & Elder, 2005) and the United Kingdom (Mitchell, 1989; Macaro, 1997). One exception to this general pattern was found in a study by Macaro (2001) of six FL student teachers who only used L1 between 5%-7% of the time. Further, a high level of teacher linguistic proficiency in the L2 does not necessarily appear to guarantee correspondingly high levels of use. Duff and Polio (1990) and Kim and Elder (2005), whose studies were of university and secondary school FL classes respectively, both found that teachers who were native speakers also recorded low levels of L2 use. However, considerable individual variation in levels of L1/L2 use between teachers has featured in number of these studies (Duff & Polio, 1990; Turnbull, 2001; Kim & Elder, 2005).

A number of factors have been identified as influencing levels of L1/L2 use. Teaching experience is one factor, although the results across studies are not consistent. In their study of five French teachers in the UK, Mitchell and Martin (1997) found that the three experienced teachers used L2 between 91%-100% of the time, while the two inexperienced teachers only used L2 between 37%-60% of the time. Another factor found to influence L1/L2 use is activity type. For example, Rolin-Ianziti and Brownlie (2002) found that the university teachers of French they studied generally demonstrated high levels of L2 use (82%-100%), however, during grammar lessons there was more L1 use. Polio and Duff (1994), in a follow-up study that examined data of six of the thirteen teachers from the earlier Duff and Polio (1990) study, identified some of the common purposes for L1 use. They were: grammar instruction; classroom management especially that related to student language and comprehension difficulties; expressions of empathy and/or solidarity with students; L1 language practice for the teachers; and, promotion of student interaction. In the school context students' age, corresponding to the students' school year levels, may have an influence on L1/L2 use. For instance, Crawford (2002) found higher levels of L1 use in primary school classes than in secondary school classes, and the highest level of L2 use was in the final two years of secondary school. For this reason, data from both primary and secondary classroom were included in the current research.

3   Peer interaction

In addition to interaction with teachers, peer interaction also occurs frequently in communicative classrooms. When students share an L1 it is not surprisingly that some of the interaction occurs in that language. Previous studies show that the use of L1 is part of formal and informal interaction between child and adult peers in immersion (Blanco-Iglesias, Broner &

Tarone, 1995; Tarone & Swain, 1995; Swain & Lapkin, 2000) and in conventional classroom second language learning contexts (Platt & Brooks, 1994; Brooks, Donato & McGlone, 1997; Antón & DiCamilla, 1998).

The use of L1 in second language classrooms has both social and cognitive functions. Antón and DiCamilla (1998), investigating adult learners, found that on a social level, learners in their study used L1 to collaboratively define the nature of the task in which they were engaged, in other words, to develop a shared perspective or *intersubjectivity*. On a cognitive level, learners utilized L1 to provide each other with strategies to manage and expedite the completion of the task. These included: enlisting and maintaining each other's interest in the task throughout its performance; developing strategies for making the task manageable; maintaining focus on the goal of the task; and, foregrounding important elements of the task. Anton and DiCamilla (1998, p.321) also suggest that L1 was used by their learners "to explicate and build on each other's partial solutions to specific problems throughout the task". The learners do this by using L1 to access L2 forms; by engaging in metalinguistic analysis of the language they are producing in L1; and, by evaluating and understanding the meaning of text in L2 through L1. Finally, they used L1 to direct their own thinking about linguistic and other issues through private speech that is externalized forms of one's inner reflections or speech (Antón & DiCamilla, 1998, p.317).

Swain and Lapkin (2000) identified three main purposes for L1 use by learners in the immersion classes they investigated: 1) moving the task along, i.e., getting themselves started and managing linguistic and organisational aspects of task completion; 2) focusing attention, in other words, concentrating on aspects of vocabulary and grammar; and, 3) interpersonal interaction, including disagreements and off task exchanges. Most L1 use (54%-60%, depending on the task) had to do with various aspects of task management. Focusing on the linguistic aspect of a task, usually more vocabulary than grammar, accounted for between 22%-35% of L1 use. L1 use for interpersonal purposes was mainly for 'off task' reasons and occurred between 12%-17% of the time. On the basis of these findings, Swain and Lapkin also conclude that L1 use has important cognitive and social functions and could contribute to learning and, therefore, should not be prohibited. However, they qualified this cautious endorsement by advising against actively encouraging L1 use, arguing that this could diminish rather than support L2 learning.

A further function of L1 use is suggested by Blanco-Iglesias, Broner and Tarone (1995) and Tarone and Swain (1995), who argue that it enables the signaling of group identity. Blanco-Iglesias et al., (1995) discovered an interesting shift in language use between grades 3 and grades 4 and 5 in five of the six immersion classes they studied. The pattern in classes from kindergarten to grade 3 showed a trend towards exclusive use of Spanish both in students' interactions with the teacher and with each other. In grades 4 and 5, however, use of English by the learners reasserted itself and a mixture of both codes was the norm. The authors suggest several reasons for this trend towards L1 use. The L1 used by learners was characterized by "highly vernacular language forms to mark the speakers as in-group members of a pre-adolescent speech community" (Blanco-Iglesias et al., 1995, p. 251). As learners did not usually possess this form of L2, they reverted to L1 to signal the desired group identity. It may also be that these learners regarded English as the language of relaxation, as their interactions during transitions from one class to another were usually in L1.

Tarone and Swain (1995) examined the social and linguistic factors that influenced L1 use by older secondary learners in non teacher-directed peer interaction in immersion classes. They highlighted the functional distinction the students made between L1 and L2, paradoxically reserving L2 for academic topics (which require more complex syntax and vocabulary) and L1 for social interaction (which generally makes less complex demands on speakers). Like Blanco-Iglesias et al., (1995), they conclude that a key influence on L1 use appears to be learners' lack of the L2 vernacular required for informal peer interaction which is essential, in adolescence, for establishing and maintaining group identity.

There is ongoing debate about the role of L1 in L2 learning in relation to both teacher-learner and peer interaction (Wells, 1999; Cook, 2001; Turnbull & Arnett, 2002).   There are practical classroom management, cognitive and social reasons for L1 use in teacher-learner interaction. There is evidence that L1 use has positive cognitive and social functions in peer interaction. However, the use of L1 by teachers and learners reduces already limited L2 input and output opportunities in FL/LOTE classes. Furthermore, there appears to be a differential impact in teacher and peer interaction.

The key issue appears not whether L1 use should be encouraged, but the steps taken to ensure an appropriate balance between the use of L1 and L2, so as to maximize the benefits for learners. The observations on this made by Wells (1999) in his response to Antón and DiCamilla (1998) are very pertinent:

> The data…appear to have been collected in a quasi-experimental situation in which the use of L1 was positively encouraged. If this approach were taken to its logical conclusion, however, there would be a danger of the oral use of L2 being completely neglected – a

situation that would no doubt be unacceptable to the students as to the teacher. I assume …an attempt was made to encourage oral interaction in L2 as well as L1. However, the principles on which the balance between L1 and L2 is struck also need to be enunciated and justified.

(Wells, 1999, p.253)

These principles and a rationale for their use are crucial for maximizing opportunities for L2 development in conventional language learning contexts, and especially in FL/LOTE classrooms. However, they are yet to be developed. In order for this to happen there is first a need to examine the context, nature and purpose of L1 use in these classes and to explore the implications for L2 learning. This is the aim of the current study.

3   Methodology

3.1   Participants

The participants in this study were learners and teachers of French and Italian from ten schools in Western Australia, seven of which were government and three non government schools. Data were collected from four primary school and six secondary LOTE classes. Two Year 6/7 classes of French and two of Italian made up the primary school data set. There were between 22-30 students in each primary school class. They received between 50-80 minutes of instruction per week/cycle and had studied the language an average of 3.8-4.7 years   Three Year 10 classes of French and three of Italian comprised the secondary school data set. The secondary school classes averaged between 17-24 students, who received between 105-200 minutes of instruction per week/cycle and had studied the language an average of 3.2-6 years.

All ten teachers were female. Two teachers of Italian (one primary and one secondary school) and one secondary teacher of French were native speakers or near native speakers. The other teachers of Italian were background speakers. The primary school teachers had all taught as generalists for between 20-35 years and had retrained to teach foreign languages. Thus, their LOTE teaching experience was less than their experience as generalists, ranging from 7-28 years. The secondary school teachers were all foreign language specialists and their teaching experience spanned an even greater number of years, ranging from 7-34. All but one of these teachers had also taught other foreign languages apart from French or Italian.

3.2   Data collection

Five complete lessons in each class were audio and video recorded over a four month period. The lessons recorded were those normally prepared by the teacher for the unit of work being covered. A detailed summary of each teacher's set of lessons was produced and 23 of the 50 lessons were transcribed and coded, eight from primary classes and 15 from secondary classes.   Segments of other lessons involving peer interaction were also transcribed and coded.

3.3   Data analysis

The teacher-learner data were analyzed by determining the proportion of L1 versus L2 use in lessons overall, identifying the instructional contexts each language was used for within lessons and determining the nature and purpose of L1 use within these contexts.   The instructional contexts were adapted from Oliver and Mackey (2003) and covered four areas: Management; Form; Meaning; and, Content, which are defined in Table 1:

Context	Teacher-learner interaction	Peer interaction
Management	Exchanges related to the management of learners, tasks, the learning environment and resources and equipment.	Exchanges related to learners' management of their roles, the task, the environment and personal/interpersonal issues.
Form	Exchanges and tasks whose main focus is instruction about, modelling and practice of elements of the L2 grammatical system.	Exchanges and tasks that focus on rehearsal, practice or performance of L2 form.
Meaning	Exchanges and tasks that focus on communication. Learners rely on well-rehearsed as well as spontaneous language to communicate their message.	
Content	Exchanges that impart knowledge and/or elicit information on a content or skills area.	

Table 1: Definition of instructional contexts for teacher learner and peer interaction

The peer interaction data were analyzed in the following ways: First, as with

teacher-learner interaction, the four instructional contexts for L1 and L2 use as per Oliver and Mackey (2003) were identified and the nature and purpose of L1 use within these contexts were established. Next, the activities and tasks were classified according to two categories taken from Ellis (2001):
• functional language practice activities; and,
• focused communicative tasks.
Functional language practice activities are defined as "instructional materials that provide learners with the opportunity to practice producing the target structure in some kind of situational context" (Ellis, 2001, p. 20). In contrast, Ellis describes focused communicative tasks as "designed to elicit production of a specific target feature in the context of performing a communicative task" (Ellis, 2001, p. 21). They differ from communicative tasks in general in that learners are required to use some feature of language that has been specifically targeted.   What distinguishes communicative tasks from functional language practice activities is their primary focus on meaning rather than on form.

4 Results

4.1 Teacher-learner interaction

Teacher-learner (T-L) interaction was the most prevalent and most readily quantifiable interaction for L1 and L2 use. The analysis estimated the time where interaction was mainly in L1, mainly in L2 and in a mixture of L2 and L1. 'Mainly L1' was defined as use of L1 80% or more of the time, 'mainly L2' as use of L2 80% or more of the time and a 'mixture of L2 and L1' involved roughly equivalent time using each code.

School/ Class	Mainly L1		Mainly L2		L1 & L2	
	Range (%)	Mean (%)	Range (%)	Mean (%)	Range (%)	M ea n (%)
Correa Yr 6/7 French	39-92	62	0-51	20	4-48	22
Hibbertia Yr 7	N/A	5*	N/A	80*	N/A	15 *

French*						
Pittosporum Yr 6 Italian	0-23	11	12-68	46	9-79	43
Wilga Yr 6 Italian	0-84	36	16-75	41	0-100	23
Eremophila Yr 10 French	0-55	28	0-65	30	7-100	42
Orania Yr 10 French	4-81	28	4-31	14	15-89	58
Sassafras Yr 10 French	0-39	18	28-74	49	4-67	33
Acanthus Yr 10 Italian	14-56	38	14-34	25	8-63	37
Danthonia Yr 10 Italian	9-43	22	3-18	4	39-91	74
Nardoo Yr 10 Italian	5-61	35	2-27	14	27-69	51

Table 2: Proportion of L1/L2 use in teacher-learner interaction

Note that in Table 2 in the Hibbertia class the students were working on self-access tasks, and therefore most teacher-learner interaction was interaction between the teacher and individual or small groups of students, and the figures refer to this participation structure. T-L interactions involving the whole class occurred mainly as part of classroom management at the beginning and end of lessons and tended to include higher amounts of L1 than interaction between the teacher and individuals and small groups. Because of this and the limitations of the recording equipment, it was not possible to estimate range of use for each category within the five lessons from the data collected in this class.

The data in Table 2 shows the considerable level of L1 as well as L2 use within the lessons in each class. It also shows the variation for all three categories of language choice, within lessons and between classes. The most characteristic language choice in teacher-learner interaction was a mixture of L1 and L2, especially in the secondary classes where this occurred, on average, between 33%-74% of the time. The teachers interacted with students mainly in L1 an average of between 5%-62% of the time, with the lowest and highest percentage being in primary school classes. The range was less marked in the secondary classes: 18%-38%. Teacher-learner interaction that occurred mainly in L2 showed notable variation in both the primary and secondary classes. However, L2 use by teachers was higher in the primary than secondary classes, averaging from 20%-80% across the four classes when Hibbertia Primary was included and 20%-46% when it was not. In the six secondary classes interaction mainly in L2 averaged from 4%-49%, with only three of the six classes in the 25%-49% range.

Teachers' language choices for each of the instructional contexts, management, form, meaning, and content (as described in Table 1) are now examined. First, Table 3 presents these choices for the management context where teachers are talking about the organization of the class or lesson. It was evident that these exchanges occupied a considerable proportion of teacher-learner interaction. Further, it should be noted that the response required from the learner being 'managed' was frequently in terms of action rather than speech. When the interactional exchanges were of a limited nature, they were often carried out in L2; however, those that needed more extended use of language were generally conducted in L1.

Instructional context	Exchanges and tasks	Language choices
Management	1. Greetings, leave-takings, positive reinforcement of appropriate behaviours	L2
	2. Classroom discipline	L1 & L2
	3. Acknowledgement, praise, encouragement for L2 use	L2
	4. Turn taking	L1 & L2
	5. Explanation/organisation/monitoring of tasks	L1
	6. Distribution/collection of materials or equipment	L1
	7. Other e.g., explaining excursions.	L1

Table 3: Language choices in T-L interaction in the management context

This can be seen in the following excerpt where the teacher explains a worksheet that has to be completed by the class. The teacher begins in French, but after several utterances reverts to English, seemingly to ensure comprehension by all class members:

T: Très bien. Ok. Maintenant vous allez parler. D'accord? Do you understand that. Ok. *(The teacher distributes sentence building sheet.)* Ok, I'm sure you've done this before. This is like a sentence building exercise. The first column, 'pendant les vacances', then you choose from the second column, then from the third column. *(Gives a number of examples using the sheet.)* And on the dotted line you can add anything else you like, another sentence.
Very good. Ok. Now you're going to talk. Agreed?... The first column, 'during the holidays'...

> *(Sassafras Secondary)*

In T-L interaction, exchanges and tasks that had form as their focus involved either the practice of particular linguistic items (e.g., numbers 1 and 4 from Table 4 below) or explanations about linguistic items (e.g., numbers 2 and 3) and one type of exchange often grew out of the other.

Table 4 shows teachers' language choices in exchanges and tasks in this context.

Instructional context	Exchanges and tasks	Language choices
Form	1. Q/A drills, pattern practice	L2
	2. Incidental review/instruction on L2 form, including metalinguistic commentary, in context	L1 & L2 L1
	3. Formal instruction on an aspect of the L2 grammar	L1 & L2
	4. Games focusing on practice of vocabulary/grammar.	

Table 4: Language choices in T-L interaction in the form context

Question and answer drills and pattern practice were more evident in the primary than secondary classes, as is illustrated in the following excerpt where the teacher revises the items to be used in asking for directions:

> *T:* ...Now *(names a student)* I'd like you to ask someone how

to get to the bank. Now it's very easy. Pour aller, pour aller *(student repeats)* à la banque *(student repeats)* s'il vous plaît? *(student repeats)* Excusez-moi Monsieur or Madame, pour aller à la banque, s'il vous plaît? Pour aller à la banque, s'il vous plaît? To get to the bank please? And they will have to tell you, la banque c'est à gauche. La pharmacie c'est à droite. Au café -continuer tout droit. Do you think you can ask somebody?
Please, what's the way to the bank?   Excuse me Sir or Madame, how do I get to the bank, please...The bank is on the left. The chemist is on the right. To get to the café go straight ahead.

Std 1: (doesn't say anything)

T: (prompting) Excusez-moi, pour aller - come on. Pour aller-
Excuse me, to get to ... to get to –

Std 1: Pour aller –

T: Pour aller à la banque, s'il vous plaît? - *(to other student)* you have to answer. La banque.
To get to the bank, please? ...The bank.

Std 2: La banque *(tries to say à droite)*

T: I think you say à gauche.
...on the left.

Std 2: à gauche
...on the left.

T: La banque c'est à gauche. Ok, you get to ask someone else.
The bank is on the left.

(Correa Primary)

Incidental, contextualized 'focus-on-form' occurred in both primary and secondary classes, while traditional pre-emptive instruction on aspects of grammar featured only in all the secondary classes and in all but one of them occupied the whole or a significant part of a lesson. The following excerpt of incidental instruction on form is from a secondary class:

T: What was the key word that would have told you about hotels, about having problems when staying in hotels?

Std 6: la problema.
...problem.

T: Is it 'la problema? It looks as though it should be 'la', but it's actually 'il problema', 'il problema'. Ok. If it's more than one problem, it's 'i' problemi'. OK *(writes word on board.)* It's an irregular word, an irregular noun, problema, problemi.
...the problem ...the problems ...problem, problems.
(Danthonia Secondary)

Exchanges and tasks in the meaning focus area are those that concentrate on exchanging information in L2 rather than on aspects of L2 grammar or form. However, in LOTE classes included in this study, meaning-focused exchanges in T-L interaction often involved the exchange of information in a rather restricted sense. There are two reasons for this: The first is the low proficiency level of learners, which means that they have very limited capacity to respond spontaneously in L2; The second is the language rather than content orientation of the teaching program. Thus the meaning-focused exchanges that occurred during T-L interaction in the exchanges and tasks listed in Table 5 are partially communicative in nature, but may also require learners to focus on a particular grammatical feature.

Instructional context	Exchanges and tasks	Language choices
Meaning	1. Q/A 'conversations' – exchanging personal information or opinions on a topic	L2 L1 & L2
	2. Brainstorms, pooling of ideas	L2
	3. Informal exchanges in the L2 between teacher and learner	L1 & L2
	4. Review/discussion of learner generated texts	L1 (secondary)
	1. Reviewing/discussing responses to L2 text (aural or written).	L1 & L2 (primary)

Table 5: Language choices in T-L interaction in the meaning context

In the data, T-L interaction tended to feature different kinds of meaning-focused exchanges and tasks in different classes. Warm-up question and answer 'conversations' at the beginning of lessons were a feature of three secondary classes in particular, but were not in evidence in any of the remaining secondary or in the primary classes.

> *T: (Writes initial question on board.)* Qu'est-ce que tu aimes faire pendant les vacances? Par exemple, moi, moi j'aime aller en Europe et visiter les musées, les galleries d'art. Oui, j'aime aussi aller aux concerts. Tu aimes aller aux concerts?
> *What do you like doing during the holidays? For example, I, I like going to Europe and visiting the museums, the art galleries. I also like going to concerts. Do you like going to concerts?*

> *Std 7 M:* Oui.
> *Yes.*

> *T:* Oui. Quel genre de concert? Les concerts de rock?
> *Yes. What kind of concert? Rock concerts?*

> *Std 7:* Je ne sais pas.
> *I don't know.*
>
> (Sassafras Secondary)

In these three secondary classes such exchanges were given a communicative emphasis, while at the same time providing an opportunity for learners to practice a targeted language feature. The 'conversations' were often quite extended, lasting ten minutes or more. An extract from one of them, where the teacher discusses the kind of dishes eaten in each course at dinner with students, is provided in the following excerpt:

> *T:* Di solito, a che ora mangi la cena?
> *When do you usually have dinner?*

> *Std 2:* Le 9.30.
> *9.30.*

> *T:* La cena, la sera. La cena. Non la prima colazione, non il pranzo. La cena la sera.
> *Dinner. Evening. Not breakfast, not lunch. Dinner in the evening.*

Std 2: Alle sei.
At six.

T: E di solito cosa mangi come antipasto? -
And what do you usually have for entrée.

Std 2: Uumm. -

T: Come antipasto, mangi la bruschetta? -
Do you have 'bruschetta' as entrée.

Std 2: Uumm, mangio la bruschetta .
... I eat bruschetta.

(Acanthus Secondary)

While this 'conversation' targets meal time vocabulary, its main purpose is the exchange of information.

The LOTE classes studied provide few opportunities for exchanges and tasks that focused on content in the conventional sense. As illustrated in Table 6, Teacher-Learner interaction with a content focus in these classes usually occurred as part of tasks concerned with the presentation and discussion of L2 culture.

Instructional context	Exchanges and tasks	Language choices
Content	1. Presentation and discussion of aspects of L2 culture.	L1 & L2

Table 6: Language choices in T-L interaction in the content context

Exchanges focusing on aspects of the L2 culture often emerged from other tasks, as teachers dealt with queries or illustrated points they considered significant. This is demonstrated in the following extract, which occurred when the teacher was assigning parts for a restaurant role play and involved discussion of the word 'apéritif'. As was often the case in other classes, during the exchange the teacher reverted to English to explore this issue.

T: What kind of an appetiser?

Std O: Umm?

T: What kind of an appetiser? Like chips or -?

Std O: Yeh, like nibblies.

> *T:* I see. It's actually a drink. Apéritif   Un apéritif *(writes word on board)* - is a very European habit.   Before a meal you might have an apéritif.   It basically opens the appetite. You'll find the stem (underlines apér) refers to open. Apéritif, it opens the appetite. These days in Australia you more often have appetisers. Un apéritif, it doesn't have to be alcohol, but very often it is a sort of alcoholic drink.   The appetisers you're talking about, the French call them 'les amuse-gueules'. 'Gueules' the best English equivalent would be 'gob'. Little things that are for putting in your mouth, 'les amuse-gueules'
>
> *(Sassafras Secondary)*

The findings shown in Tables 3-6 suggest that L2 use by teachers tended to be confined to those exchanges and tasks that did not require extended, unpredictable or more complex use of language. Exchanges and tasks in which a mixture of L2 and L1 were used sometimes began in L2 and a problem with learner comprehension or the complexity of the explanation or the task triggered the change to L1. This was usually the case with classroom discipline where brief and routine requests were carried out in L2, while anything perceived as a more serious breach of discipline was addressed in L1. There was also individual variation between teachers. For example, the teacher from Sassafras Secondary used mainly L2 to introduce and explain aspect of grammar, such as the use of the future tense, whereas three other secondary teachers who also presented this grammar item used mainly L1. That teacher and the teacher from Nardoo Secondary often explained points of grammar and cultural items that that emerged incidentally during lessons in L2, while the others almost always used L1. The teacher from Sassafras Secondary also presented a lesson that focused on aspects of the L2 culture mainly in L2.

4.2   Peer interaction

Again the main contexts of L1 (and L2) use between peers within lessons were categorized using the instructional contexts adapted from Oliver and Mackey (2003) outlined in Table 1 above.   A picture of the learners' language choices for exchanges and tasks in each of these contexts is provided in Tables 7-10.

Instructional context	Exchanges and tasks	Language choices
Management	1. Clarification of task 2. Assigning roles 3. Turn taking 4. Seeking/giving help 5. Personal and interpersonal exchanges	L1 L1 L1 L1 L1

Table 7: Language choices in L-L interaction in the management context

Table 7 shows that exchanges and tasks occurring in a management context were carried out mostly in L1.   Form-focused exchanges and tasks, on the other hand, were conducted mainly in L2, as demonstrated in Table 8.

Instructional context	Exchanges and tasks	Language choices
Form	1. Drills, pattern practice, Q/A rehearsing L2 form 2. Presentations and performances including role plays based on a model dialogue 3. Surveys 4. Completing written exercises on L2 form	L2 L2 L2 L1 & L2

Table 8: Language choices in L-L interaction in the form context

Those exchanges and tasks where instructional context was form-focused often made very limited and predictable linguistic demands on learners (even though appearing to concentrate on meaning).   This made it easy for them to use L2, as is evident in the following excerpt from a role play based on a model dialogue:

Std B: Je voudrais une chambre à un lit et – um – sans bain – s'il vous plaît.   Er, je voudrais payer quarante francs.
I'd like a single room ... without a bath – please.   ...I'd like to pay forty francs [a night].

Std A: Er, vous avez réservé?
Have you booked?

Std B: Non, je n'ai pas réservé.
No, I haven't booked.

Std A: Je regrette mademoiselle - er mais j'ai seulement une chambre – à une_lit – et, avec une bain.   Elle coûte soixante - francs.
I'm sorry miss – but I've only a single room – and with bath. It costs sixty francs.

Std B: Bon, d'accord, je prends cette chambre.   That's it. Umm.
Good, that's fine, I'll take that room. ...
                                                    (Eremophila Secondary)

In contrast meaning-focused exchanges and tasks were carried out in a mixture of L2 and L1, as shown in Table 9.

Instructional context	Exchanges and tasks	Language choices
Meaning	1. Information gap tasks	L1 & L2
	2. Jigsaw activities	L1 & L2
	3. Joint construction of texts for role plays, debates etc.	L1 & L2
	4. Games requiring some skill or interpretation	L1 & L2

Table 9: Language choices in L-L interaction in the meaning context

This would appear to be related to the relatively low level of learner proficiency and the less predictable linguistic demands of these tasks. Whether students used a mixture of L1 and L2 or were able to sustain more extended L2 use also depended on the task itself and the students' own capacities.   For example, the one-way information gap task undertaken by a pair at Hibbertia Primary was both extremely simple and linguistically very predictable and, after some initial assistance from the teacher, the pair was able to carry out the task mainly in L2. However, when the demands of a two-way information gap task in which the emphasis is more on exchange of information results this results in a different balance between L2 and L1, as the next excerpt shows:

> *Std A:* Est-ce que il y a une - cuisine?
> *Is there a kitchen here?*
>
> *Std B:* Umm - la cuisine - est –chez le - premier étage.
> *...the kitchen - is – on - the first floor.*
>
> *Std A:* Umm, umm - une peut – on peut
> *... (ungrammatical) – can one*
>
> *Std B:* What did you say?
>
> *Std A:* on peut?
> *can one?*
>
> *Std B:* I don't know what you're actually doing.
>
> *Std A:* I don't know. Umm *(Laughs)* - Is this all right?
>
> *Std B:* You have to say, what time is it open till.
>
> *Std A:* Yeh, I say, au premier étage.
> *... on the first floor.*

> *(Eremophila Secondary)*

As with exchanges and tasks occurring in a management context, in peer interaction those related to the content context were carried out mostly in L1.

Instructional context	Exchanges and tasks	Language choices
Content	1. Answering questions about aspects of L2 culture from information provided in an L2 text	L1

Table 10: Language choices in L-L interaction in the content context

Overall, learners relied on L1 in their interactions and were most likely to use L2 exclusively for activities and exchanges that focused on form and that required them to use or recycle well rehearsed chunks of language. Further examination of the types of interactions that occur between peers using the categories of 'functional language practice activities' and 'focused communicative tasks' taken from Ellis (2001) reveals a predominance of L1 use in the latter category. The nature of the activities associated with each of these categories in the data is summarized in Table 11:

Type	Activity
Functional Language Practice	
FLP1.	Pair work where students ask each other questions on a predetermined topic such as daily routines - in other words, question and answer practice using targeted vocabulary and structures, including survey type activities.
FLP2.	Pair or group work where students describe an item, person or a picture to each other using targeted vocabulary and/or structures.
FLP3.	Pair or group work where students engage in role play either based on a model dialogue or involving a situation which requires them to use familiar and well-rehearsed language.
Focused Communicative Tasks	
CTI.	Pair work where students engage in one or two-way information gap tasks.
CT2.	Pair or group work where students work collaboratively to construct text e.g., list questions to ask exchange students who will visit the class in the future; develop an argument for their side for a debate; create a role play; prepare part of a procedural text such as a recipe; list the ingredients of an imaginary dish.

Table 11: Description of functional language practice activities and focused communicative tasks identified in the data

An analysis of the data shows that FLP1-3 and CT1 were carried out predominantly in L2, while CT2 occurred mainly in L1. However, use of L1 was also a feature of some role plays (FLP3) and two-way information gap tasks (CT1) for task management and interpersonal exchanges, as well as for negotiation. This is illustrated in the following excerpt from a two-way information gap task where students are quizzing each other about the facilities of a Youth Hostel:

> *Std R:* Um, I'll ask you another one anyway. Um, on peut - on peut acheter des provisions ici?
> *Um, can one – can one shop here?*
>
> *Std Q:* Provisions?
>
> *Std R:* That's shopping. –
>
> *Std Q:* Les provisions est rez de saussée - rez de chaussée
> *Shopping is the ground floor – ground floor*
>
> *Std R:* What was reception on? - *(indecipherable)*
>
> *Std Q:* Elle est entrée à huit heures et *(indecipherable because of talk from others)* - [vingt–deux heures].
> *It's entered [open] between 8.00am and…10.00pm.*
>
> *Std R:* Merci beaucoup. Au revoir.
> *Thank you. Goodbye.*
>
> *Std Q:* Au revoir.
> *Goodbye.*
>
> *Eremophila Secondary)*

In the context of CT2, L1 is often used to help solve problems with L2 form. This is demonstrated in the following excerpt from a jigsaw task where students are collaborating in the outlining the content of a recipe:

> *Std I:* Why is it, why is it 'il or la'? I don't understand it.
>
> *Std K:* Because if it ends in 'a' it's 'la' and 'o' its 'il'.
>
> *Std I:* Oh, I get it. - Grattugiano – grattugiano il cioccolato. *(gets the stress right the second time)* – No, how do you say 'smash' le uove?
>
> *Std K:* Break
>
> *Std I:* Break, break - *(trying to find the word in dictionary.)*
>
> *Std K:* We'll have no break. Mix the cream and eggs.
>
> *Std I:* Mescoli

You mix

Std K: No

Std I: Mescolano. *(stress in wrong place)*
They mix.

Std K: Mescolano.

Std I: Mescolano - il crema -.
They mix the cream.

Std K: La -

Std I: Crema is – o - if I have 'o' it's il crema –

Std K: No

Std I: e le uova - e la – uova -

Std K: It's le. Ask her.

(Acanthus Secondary)

The collaborative work carried out in L1 in this CT2 activity provides students with the opportunity to engage in language form as they work out how to communicate in L2.

5   Conclusion

This study of FL/LOTE classes in Western Australia has shown that there may be notable levels of L1 use in both teacher-learner and peer interaction, thus restricting the L2 input available to learners.   This is of particular concern given the essential nature of input for L2 acquisition. When L2 was used, especially in teacher-learner interaction, it tended to be restricted to simpler and more predictable exchanges for all instructional contexts. In peer interaction there appeared to be little need for learners to rely on and to produce L2 output for real communicative purposes.   For example, opportunities that might arise for negotiation of meaning and interpersonal exchanges were often carried out in L1. It seems that this occurred because of the limited proficiency of learners. Further, the lack of pressure to resolve difficulties in L2 meant that the type of exchanges that have been demonstrated to facilitate learning were more likely to take place during teacher-learner interaction than in peer interaction. However, while the use of L1 may impede some learning opportunities, it did provide others. In peer interaction students were often able to use L1 effectively to scaffold each other's production and to manage and expedite the completions of tasks. L1 was also used as a tool for reflecting on and resolving language difficulties and, importantly, in order to solve problems with L2 form. Clearly this has implications for pedagogy. At the same time, given the dearth of research, much greater exploration of interaction in FL/LOTE classes is needed.

References

Alcón, E. &. García Mayo, M. P. Guest eds) (2009) Interaction and language learning in foreign language contexts, *International Review of Applied Linguistics* (47) 3 (special issue).

Antón, M., & DiCamilla, F. (1998) Socio-cognitive functions of L1 collaborative interaction in the L2 classroom. *The Canadian Modern Language Review, 54*(3), 314-342.

Blanco-Iglesias, S., Broner, J., & Tarone, E. (1995) Observations of language use in Spanish immersion classroom interactions. In L. Eubank, L. Selinker & M. Sharwood-Smith (Eds.), *The current state of interlanguage: Studies in honor of William E. Rutherford* (pp. 241-254). Philadelphia PA: John Benjamins North America.

Brooks, F. B., Donato, R., & McGlone, J. V. (1997) When are they going to say "it" right? Understanding learner talk during pair-work activity. *Foreign Language Annals, 30*(4), 524-541.

Calman, R., & Daniel, I. (1998) A Board's-eye view of core French: the North York Board of Education. In S. Lapkin (Ed.), *French second language education in Canada: empirical studies* (pp. 281-323). Toronto: University of Toronto Press.

Cook, V. (2001) Using the first language in the classroom. *The Canadian Modern Language Review, 57*(3), 402-423.

Crawford, J. (2002). Do languages have a place in the curriculum? A Queensland view. *Babel, 36*, 12-16.

Duff, P., A, & Polio, C., P. (1990) How much foreign language is there in the foreign language classroom? *The Modern Language Journal, 74*(2), 154-166.

Ellis, R. (2001) Investigating form-focused instruction. In R. Ellis (Ed.), *Form-focused instruction and second language learning* (pp. 1-46). Malden, MA: Blackwell Publishers.

Gass, S. (2003) Input and interaction. In C. Doughty; M. Long. (Eds.), The handbook of second language acquisition (pp.224-255). Malden, MA: Blackwell Publishing.

García Mayo, M.P. & Alcón, E. (Guest eds) (2002) The role of interaction in instructed language learning, *International Journal of Educational Research* (37) Special issue: 3-4.

Kim, S. H. O., & Elder, C. (2005) Language choices and pedagogic functions in the foreign language classroom: A cross-linguistic functional analysis of teacher talk. *Language Teaching Research, 9*, 355-380.

Macaro, E. (2001) Analysing student teachers' code switching in foreign language classrooms: theories and decision making. *The Modern Language Journal, 85*(4), 531-548.

Macaro, E. (1997) *Target language, collaborative learning and autonomy.* Clevedon, UK: Multilingual Matters Ltd.

Mackey, A. (2007) Introduction. The role of conversational interaction in second language acquisition. In A. Mackey (ed), *Conversational Interaction in Second Language Acquisition: A Collection of Empirical Studies,* Oxford: Oxford University Press.

Mackey, A., & Gass, S. M. (2006) Pushing the methodological boundaries in interaction research: An introduction to the special issue. *Studies in Second Language Acquisition, 28*(2), 169-178.

McDonough, K. (2005) Identifying the impact of negative feedback and learners' responses on ESL question development. *Studies in Second Language Acquisition,* 27, 79-103.

Mitchell, R. (1989) Second language learning: Investigating the classroom context. *System, 17*(2), 195-210.

Mitchell, R., & Martin, C. (1997) Rote learning, creativity and "understanding" in classroom foreign language teaching. *Language Teaching Research, 1*, 1-27.

Nobuyoshi, J., & Ellis, R. (1993) Focused communication tasks and second language acquisition. *ELT Journal* 47, 203-210.

Oliver, R., & Mackey, A. (2003) Interactional context and feedback in child ESL classrooms. *The Modern Language Journal, 87*, 519-533.

Platt, E., & Brooks, F. B. (1994) The "acquisition-rich environment" revisited. *The Modern Language Journal, 78*, 497-511.

Polio, C., P, & Duff, P., A. (1994) Teachers' language use in university foreign language classrooms: A qualitative analysis of English and target language alternation. *The Modern Language Journal, 78*(3), 313-326.

Rolin-Ianziti, J., & Brownlie, S. (2002) Teacher use of learners' native language in the foreign language classroom. *The Canadian Modern Language Review, 58*(3), 402-426.

Swain, M. (1995) Three functions of output in second language learning. In G. Cook & B. Seidlhofer (Eds.), *Principles and practice in applied* linguistics: studies in honour of H. G. Widdowson. (pp. 125-144). Oxford: Oxford University Press.

Swain, M. (2005) The output hypothesis: theory and research. In E.Hinkel (ed.), *Handbook of research in second language teaching and learning*. Mahwah, NJ: Lawrence Erlbaum. 471–84.

Swain, M., & Lapkin, S. (2000) Task-based second language learning: The uses of first language. *Language Teaching Research, 4*, 251-273.

Tarone, E., & Swain, M. (1995) A sociolinguistic perspective on second language use in immersion classrooms. *The Modern Language Journal, 79*, 166-178.

Tognini, R. (2008) *Interaction in languages other than English classes in Western Australian primary and secondary schools: Theory, practice and perceptions.* Unpublished doctoral dissertation, Edith Cowan University, Western Australia.

Turnbull, M. (2001) There is a role for the L1 in second and foreign language teaching, but... *The Canadian Modern Language Review, 57*(4), 531-540.

Turnbull, M., & Arnett, K. (2002) Teachers' uses of the target and first languages in second and foreign language classrooms. *Annual Review of Applied Linguistics, 22*, 204-218.

Wells, G. (1999) Using L1 to master L2: A response to Anton and DiCamilla's "Socio-cognitive functions of L1 collaborative interaction in the L2 classroom". *The Modern Language Journal, 83*(2), 248-254.

Repair in Japanese request sequences during student – teacher interactions

Yumiko Tateyama (University of Hawaii at Manoa)

This study examines student and teacher interactions as they engage in role play activity (making a request) in front of other students in a Japanese as a foreign language (JFL) class at an American university. Using a conversation analytic perspective, the study examines how interactions unfold sequentially and how repair is initiated and offered when the student encounters trouble. The analysis shows three repair patterns: (a) teacher inserts an exposed correction sequence within a larger request sequence; (b) teacher initiates repair and by-standing students complete repair; (c) instead of exposed correction during the interaction, teacher offers feedback on the trouble source after the role play is over. It is argued that context, pedagogical focus, and spatial practices between the interlocutors might have led to specific repair trajectories. The analysis also shows that the teacher shifts back and forth between two roles – teacher and interlocutor – during the role play. This allows the teacher to assess the student's forms and make corrections as needed, important in the achievement of pedagogical goals. Further, it is suggested that by-standing students' embodied actions such as gaze and posture appear to be related to their degree of engagement in offering assistance to the focal student.

1 Introduction

With a growing interest in using conversation analysis (CA) as a methodological resource for understanding second language (L2) learning and teaching, studies that examine L2 classroom interactions from a conversation analytic perspective have increased (e.g., Markee, 2000; Seedhouse, 2004; Wong and Waring, 2010; Kasper and Wagner, 2011). As Markee (2000) notes, CA uncovers "the details of how learners actually deploy talk to learn on a moment-by-moment basis (p. 3)," which has been largely ignored in the mainstream second language acquisition research. With its emic, participant-based perspective and focus on talk-in-interaction as an orderly accomplishment, CA provides us with insight into how participants make their orientations, understandings and relevancies available to each other through coordinated actions as they engage in socially situated activities (Kasper, 2004).

One of the areas where CA researchers have examined is repair. Repair in the CA sense refers to the mechanisms through which certain 'troubles' or problems in interaction are dealt with (Schegloff, Jefferson, and Sacks 1977). Repair organization describes how parties engaged in a talk deal with problems in speaking, listening, and understanding, which includes but is not limited to correction of errors or mistakes, clarification requests, checks of candidate understanding, restatements, and the like. Additionally, repair is sometimes found where there is no apparent error or mistake. Thus, repair in the CA sense encompasses the mechanisms of dealing with a much wider range of actions than what is typically referred to as error correction or negative feedback in L2 learning and teaching.

Recognition of a trouble source or repairable and its subsequent repair may be undertaken by either the speaker (self) or other participants in the talk (other). As a course of action, repair shows a sequential organization or trajectory. Hutchby and Wooffitt (2008) summarize four varieties of repair trajectories depending on who initiates repair and who resolves the problem:

> • Self-initiated self-repair: Repair is both initiated and carried out by the speaker of the trouble source.
> • Other-initiated self-repair: Repair is carried out by the speaker of the trouble source but initiated by the recipient.
> • Self-initiated other-repair: The speaker of a trouble source may try and get the recipient to repair the trouble – for instance if a name is proving troublesome to remember.
> • Other-initiated other-repair: The recipient of a trouble-source turn both initiates and carries out the repair. This is closest to what is conventionally understood as 'correction'. (p. 60)

Schegloff et al. (1977) found a preference for self-initiation and self-repair over other-initiation and other repair in ordinary conversations between first language (L1) speakers of American English. Dispreference for other-initiation and other-repair was also found in ordinary conversations between L1 and L2 speakers in non-educational discourse. For example, Brouwer, Rasmussen and Wagner (2004) found numerous instances of non-native-like constructions that were not corrected. Kasper (1985) notes that native speakers refrain from formal other-corrections of learner utterances unless the learner requests such corrections. Hosoda (2006), who examined casual conversations between L1 and L2 speakers of Japanese, also states that participants usually do not initiate or provide corrections or repair grammatical mistakes or lexical errors, except when one party invites the other party's repair as in the case of vocabulary searches, as well as when the participants encounter trouble in achieving mutual understanding. Kasper (1985) provides mutual face-support as a primary reason for abstaining from other corrections in non-educational discourse, both native and non-native. Unlike ordinary conversations, other-repair occurs frequently in classroom interactions where face risk due to other-repair can be suspended in the interest of language learning (van Lier, 1988). Because the present study examines repair in student-teacher interactions in L2, I will review studies on repair in the L2 classroom next.

2 Studies on repair in L2 classroom

Kasper (1985) and van Lier (1988) are among the first researchers who examined organization of repair sequences in the L2 classroom. Kasper (1985) found that other-initiated and other-completed repairs of learner responses were commonly observed both in language-centered (form-focused) and content-centered phases of teacher-fronted L2 class, with the teacher usually being the initiator of the repair. The delegated repair (Kasper, 1985 p. 30) in which the teacher initiates the repair and passes its completion to other learners to ensure their active participation in the learning and teaching process was frequently observed in the language-centered phase. In the content-centered phase, the teacher completed the repair instead of delegating it to other learners.

Van Lier (1988) also points out the prevalence of other-repair in the L2 classroom, noting that repair makes L2 use in the classroom significantly different from other discourse such as ordinary conversations between L1 speakers and informal talks between L1 and L2 speakers. Van Lier classifies repairs that are pedagogic in nature as *didactic repair* and repairs that are common to all face-to-face interaction as *conversational repair.* He states that we need to look at the way the trouble is addressed rather than the type of trouble per se in order to understand whether it is a didactic repair or conversational repair. After sequentially examining different repair trajectories depending on who initiates repair and who offers repair, van Lier concludes that there is a heavy emphasis on other-repair in classroom discourse unlike ordinary conversation outside the classroom. He contends that some delay of other repair maybe useful in order to promote the development of learner self-monitoring and pragmatic adjustment.

In a similar manner to van Lier's distinction between didactic repair and conversational repair, Hall (2007) distinguishes instructional correction and CA repair. According to Hall, instructional correction is part of the instructional component of the initiation – response – feedback or IRF (Mehan, 1979; Sinclair & Coulthard, 1975; see Lee, 2007 and Waring, 2008 for more recent studies), whereas CA repair and correction are interactional resources available to the interlocutors. In CA, repair is initiated and offered when speaker and hearer have problems or trouble in achieving or restoring shared understanding or intersubjectivity. As Sidnell (2011) states, "in conversation understandings emerge in the course of interaction and are revisable in light of what subsequently happens (p.13)." According to Hall (2007, p. 511), correction is one type of repair in which errors are replaced with what is correct. Hall argues that although studies using the CA perspective to examine classroom interactions employ the term *repair,* in many cases the analysis focuses on the instructional components of repair and correction where achieving intersubjectivity is not a primary goal.[1] Macbeth (2004) also states that conversational repair and classroom correction are better understood as distinctive and that the latter is "an identifying task and achievement of classroom teaching (p. 705)." In his data from an English class at a Japanese university, Hauser (2010) aptly shows an instance of teacher performing other correction of language form immediately following a repair sequence.

With regard to van Lier's call for some delay of other repair in order to promote the development of learner self-repair, Koshiki (2002) should be mentioned. Koshiki examined error correction in one-on-one student-teacher L2 writing conferences using a CA framework. One type of turn discussed in Koshiki's study is an institutional practice she calls "designedly incomplete utterance" or DIU. In the DIU, teachers intentionally leave utterances incomplete in order to elicit self-correction of focal written language errors from the student. It is shown that such practice is an adaptation of similar practices found in ordinary conversations such as word search in order to accomplish a specialized institutional task. The performance of teacher initiations with withheld corrections for the purpose of student self-correction in the subsequent slot is also reported in McHoul (1990).

Kasper (1985) and van Lier (1988) suggest that the organization of repair varies with goal orientations or pedagogical focus. Seedhouse (2004) developed this further and examined repair trajectories in three different contexts in the L2 classroom: form-and-accuracy, meaning-and-fluency, and task-oriented. In a form-and-accuracy context, exposed or overt type repair (Jefferson, 1987) was overwhelmingly found rather than embedded corrections (Brouwer et al., 2004; Jefferson, 1987). In this context, the focus of the repair was on the production of specific linguistic forms, and the teacher generally initiated repair. Repair trajectory peculiar to this context was teacher-initiated peer-completed repair. In a meaning-and-fluency context, a mixture of repair types and a mixture of repair trajectories were observed, but the focus of the repair was on enabling learners to sustain communication. In a task-oriented context, the focus of the repair was on accomplishing the task. Learners generally conduct repair while working on tasks in pairs or groups. Based on these observations, Seedhouse (2004) proposed that there is "a reflexive relationship between the pedagogical focus and the organization of repair (p. 179)."

Occurrence of self-initiated repair is reported in Jung (1999) who examined the organization of repair sequences in learner role-playing activities and teacher-fronted activities in an ESL class. Jung shows that while other-initiated other-repair in the form of IRF sequence was prevalent in teacher-fronted activities, self-initiated repair was commonly found in learner role-playing activities, suggesting that participation frameworks play an important role in the construction of repair sequences. Hellerman (2011) examined other-initiated, other-repair in learner – learner interactions using a CA framework. The data were collected longitudinally from participants in L2 classroom. Hellerman's study is innovative because it shows evidence of change over time regarding what the learners orient to as repairable and how they accomplish repair initiation and completion. Although Hellerman cautions that context might have influenced the changes observed in the learners' language use, the study demonstrates the potential of CA for examining opportunities for L2 learning.

While the studies reviewed above, in particular van Lier (1988) and Seedhouse (2004), provide useful frameworks for understanding classroom repair trajectories, Rylander (2009) is cautious about classifying classroom contexts into general categories. He demonstrates that exposed correction of linguistic forms by the teacher was observed on several occasions in his meaning-and-fluency activity data (doing presentations) in Chinese as a foreign language class. Rylander points out the need for describing a variety of L2 activities and characteristics of repair organizations within each activity.

The present study is partly motivated by Rylander's call for more studies describing repair trajectories in a variety of L2 activities. This study examines repair trajectories in interactions between student and teacher as they engage in role play activity (making a request) in front of other learners of Japanese as a foreign language (JFL) at a college-level JFL class. Seedhouse (2004) argues that repair organization in the L2 classroom varies with pedagogical focus. The present study examines how repair segments in student-teacher role plays are organized and what pedagogical focus might have motivated a particular repair sequence. Jung (1999) examined role play activities performed by students. The present study examines role plays performed by student and teacher following student role play practice in pairs. The teacher asking students to demonstrate what they have practiced is a commonly observed scenario in the L2 classroom. Examining repair trajectories in such a scenario will provide us with an insight into orientations that teachers and students display through their interactions, as well as insight into the student's interactional competence. As Kasper and Wagner (2011) notes, "interactional competence can only be studied by observing interaction locally and in great detail (p.118)."

In this chapter, I will show how a variety of repair sequences unfold during student-teacher role play activities. In Role play 1, an exposed repair completed by the teacher will be shown. In Role play 2, a teacher-initiated, peer-completed repair will be shown. Role play 3, which has very few teacher or peer-completed repairs, will be discussed in terms of spatial practices. I will also discuss the teacher's shift between the two roles – interlocutor and teacher – during the role play and its pedagogical implications. Further, I will examine how non-focal students' embodied actions such as gaze and posture might have contributed to the role play activity unfolding in front of them. I will conclude the chapter with pedagogical implications and suggestions for future research.

3   The study

3.1   Data

The data for the present study come from low-intermediate (4th-semester) JFL class video recorded as part of a larger study in progress. There were 11 students (6 women and 5 men) in class and 3 students (Brian, Kent, and Mary – all personal names are pseudonyms) who appear in the Excerpts were all native speakers of English. The class was taught by the author of this chapter, a female L1 speaker of Japanese who had been teaching Japanese in the United States for nine years.[2]

As part of a larger study, class sessions were video and audio recorded at regular intervals. A total of 12 class sessions were recorded. For the present study, analysis of three request role plays from two class sessions (fifty minutes each) will be presented: Excerpts 1, 2.1 and 2.2 come from the same class session, while Excerpt 3 comes from the session recorded approximately one week later. In the class sessions prior to the request role plays, requesting in Japanese had been a topic of instruction. Students in the class learned about the factors that people take into account when making requests, watched a video clip and live performances of Japanese request events,[3] and engaged in consciousness raising activities.

Data were transcribed following conversation-analytic conventions (see Appendix). The analysis of Role plays 1, 2, and 3 follows their chronological order. In order to examine the repair organization of the request role plays in detail, the analysis is conducted from a conversation-analytic perspective. Goffman's (1981) notion of participation framework will also be referred to.

3.2   Analysis

3.2.1   *Role play 1 (Asking for kanji dictionary)*

The interaction shown in Excerpt 1 below took place immediately after the students practiced making a request of different interlocutors such as the teacher, an upperclassman, and a friend in pairs, following prompts written on the role play card. The instructor calls Brian to demonstrate one of the role plays he practiced with her. The situation was as follows: "You are looking for a *kanji* dictionary. Ask your teacher if she could tell you about a good dictionary." In this role play demonstration, the teacher was standing in front of the class while Brian remained seated at his desk with the other students.

Excerpt 1 (B: Brian, T: Teacher, S1: unidentified student)

```
1          B: ano sensee,  chotto yoroshii <desho:: ka.>
              uhm teacher a little good  CP[polite] Q
              "Uhm Professor, may I interrupt you for a second?"
2          T: hai, nan desu ka?
              yes  what CP  Q
              "Yes, what is it?"
3          B: jitsu wa=
              fact  TP
              "The fact is"
4          T: e:.
              yes
              "Yes"
5          B:= ii    jisho   o
              good dictionary O
              "good dictionary"
6          T: un.
              uh-huh
              "Uh-huh."
7→         B: mitsu:ke-
              find-
              "(I) find-"
8          (0.5)
9→         T: un  sagashite iru.
              uhm  looking AUX
              "Uhm (I'm) looking for"
10→        B: sagashite iru.
              looking   AUX (plain)
              "(I'm) looking for"
11→        T: un (.) imasu.
              uhm     AUX (polite)
              "Uhm (.) I am."
12→        B: imasu.
              AUX (polite)
              "I am."
13         (1)
```

14   T: ah jisho   o sagashite iru n desu ne.
         oh dictionary O looking for   N CP IP
         "Oh you're looking for a dictionary, right?"
15   B: hai.
         yes
         "Yes."
16   T: ah, soo desu ka.
         oh so CP   Q
         "Oh, I see."
17   B: hai (.4) ii   jisho   o
         yes   good dictionary O
         "Yes, (I'm looking for) a good dictionary."
18   T: ee
         yes
         "Yes."
19   (3)
20→   T: ah, oshiete hoshii n desu ka.
         oh   teach   want N CP   Q
         "Oh, you want me to tell you a good dictionary?"
21→   B: oshiete.
         tell
         "Tell me."

22→   T: aa: soo desu ne. un jisho   dattara ano hawai
         uhm so CP IP FL dictionary CP if   uhm Hawaii
         "Uhm let's see. Uhm if you are looking for a
         dictionary,"
23   daigaku no sensee ga(.) kakareta jisho ga arimasu
         kara=
         university LK professor S written dictionary S have so
         "I have a dictionary (.) written by a professor from
the
         University of Hawaii so"
24   B: hai.
         yes.
         "Yes."
25   T: =jaa soo desu ne, ashita kurasu ni motte kimashoo ka.
         well so CP   IP tomorrow class P have   come   Q
         "Well, let's see, shall I bring it to class tomorrow?"
26   B: hai. doomo sumimasen.
         Yes very   sorry.
         "Yes. Thank you very much."
27   (.8)
28→ S1: tasukarimasu.
         be helpful
         "Thank you for your help."
29→   B: tasuka-
         hel-
         "your hel-"
30   (1)
31   T: haha (1) jaa ashita motte kimasu ne.
         haha   well tomorrow have come IP
         "haha (1) I'll bring it tomorrow."

```
32        B: hai.
             Yes.
             "Yes."
```

Brian begins the conversation by asking the teacher's availability with the polite expression *"chotto yoroshii <desho::ka.>* [may I interrupt you for a second?]" (line 1). This is a commonly used opening expression when asking a favor of a higher status person. With the use of *"jitsu wa* [the fact is]" in line 3, Brian prefaces the upcoming action. In line 5, he correctly produces the syntactic object, *"ii jisho o* [good dictionary]," which is pragmatically hearable as the object of a question or request in progress. This enables the teacher's understanding, as the teacher shows with the acknowledgement *"un* [*uh-huh*]" in line 6. In line 7, Brian utters *"mitsu:ke-"*, an incomplete form of the verb *mitsukeru* [to find]. A half a second gap in line 8 suggests that Brian was not able to recall the word completely or he was not sure about its usage in this context. Since Brian's action is entirely interpretable as is, the teacher could have opted for answering the question and ignoring the grammar error. Instead, the teacher orients to grammatical correctness with her action, as she engages in exposed other corrections in lines 9 – 12. In line 9, the teacher corrects Brian's utterance by replacing *"mitsu:ke-"* with *"sagashite iru* [(I'm) looking for]." Brian repeats the word as is in line 10, showing that he registered receipt of what was just said (Schegloff, 1997; Svennevig, 2004). The teacher further corrects Brian's utterance in line 11 by supplying *imasu,* the polite equivalent of the auxiliary verb *iru.* Brian accepts this correction as well by repeating the polite form of the verb in line 12, which shows his orientation to the teacher's professional authority and his performing with the teacher in front of the class (cf. Cook, 1996). It should be noted that this sequence on correcting forms is inserted in a larger sequence on requesting. That is, this is a side sequence (Jefferson, 1972), which puts the interactional business of requesting on hold. It is an exposed correction (Jefferson, 1987) and makes correcting forms an interactional business in its own right. The interaction could have proceeded directly from line 8 to line 14 without inserting the correction sequence. However, through the exposed correction sequence, the teacher shows her orientation to formal correctness as a pedagogical goal.

During the 1 second gap in line 13, the teacher was probably expecting Brian to resume the main business of requesting. However, with no such indication from Brian, the teacher initiates a repair in line 14. It should be noted that the teacher's corrections in lines 9 and 11 addressed Brian's production. In line 14, the teacher offers her understanding of Brian's previous turns for confirmation. That is, the teacher is requesting confirmation of her understanding from Brian. With the change of state token *"ah* [oh]" (Heritage, 1984) as preface, along with the extended predicate *"n desu* [it is that]" used for confirmation and the interactional particle *ne* which indexes agreement, the teacher claims a change of her understanding so far, upgrading her epistemic rights (Heritage & Raymond, 2005).

The teacher's orientation to formal correctness as a pedagogical goal is also shown in lines 14 through 21. After the teacher confirms that Brian is looking for a dictionary in line 14, she acknowledges it one more time with *"ah, soo desu ka* [Oh, I see.]" in line 16. Brian tries to formulate a sentence in line 17 but he ends up uttering an incomplete sentence, *"hai, ii jisho o* [Yes, a good dictionary]." Here again, the teacher could have opted for answering the question and ignoring the incompleteness of Brian's utterance since his action is entirely interpretable as is. Instead, the teacher offers a continuer *"ee* [yes]" in line 18 and waits for Brain to repair his utterance. However, after a 3 second gap and no self-repair from Brian, the teacher offers a repair in line 20, saying *"ah, oshiete hoshii n desu ne* [Oh, you want me to tell you a good dictionary, right?]. The goal of the task that the students had practiced prior to this role play demonstration was explaining the situation and making a request using conventionally polite request forms such as *oshiete itadakemasen ka* [Could you please tell me?] and *oshiete hoshii n desu kedo* [I would like you to tell me]. The teacher's utterance *oshiete hoshii n desu ne* in line 20 is recipient-designed to facilitate Brian's use of conventionally polite request form in the next turn, although he picked it up only partially as shown in his utterance *oshiete* [tell me] in line 21.

It is interesting to note that the teacher did not engage in lengthy exposed correction as she did in lines 9-13 after Brian said *oshiete* [Tell me] in line 21, despite the fact that *oshiete* is not a pragmatically appropriate form. It might be the case that the teacher opted for not correcting Brian's utterance in line 21 since she had already repaired Brian's utterance earlier with *oshiete hoshii n desu ne* [Oh, you want me to tell you a good dictionary, right?] in line 20 and that what he wanted her to do was clear. Opting out for not correcting the student's linguistic forms also shows the teacher's orientation to having the student focus on the task at hand, as in the case of a real life situation.

In Excerpt 1, the only instance where a by-standing student offers a repair appears in line 28 after Brian has thanked the teacher with an apologetic thanking expression, *"doomo sumimasen* [Thank you very much]" in line 26.[4] An unidentified student S1 whispers *tasukarimasu* [Thank you for your help], a thanking expression used when a request is accommodated that was introduced to class earlier. Brian tries to repeat the expression in line 29, but he does not finish it. It is followed by a 1 second gap in line 30. The teacher does not repair his utterance; instead, she simply indicates that she will bring the dictionary the next day (line 31). Schegloff et al. (1977) state that repair is not always offered or the trouble source is not necessarily repaired. Brouwer (2004) notes that when a repairable is not found troublesome, its recipient may confirm that the item is understandable through the receipt token. It appears that both of these observations apply to the present case. As Kasper and Kim (2007) note, passing up repair serves "to sustain the current line of talk and keep the L2 participants actively engaged (p. 39)."

In sum, except for one incidence of repair offered by a by-standing student, the repair trajectory in Excerpt 1 was predominantly teacher-initiated and teacher-completed, including exposed corrections inserted into a larger request sequence. At the same time, there were instances where the teacher passed up repairs. This shows the teacher's orientation to both improving the student's formal accuracy through exposed corrections and having the student actively engage in the current line of talk to complete the task at hand through passing up repairs. Both are pedagogically important aspects that L2 teachers attend to in a foreign language classroom.

3.2.2 *Role play 2 (Asking how to make websites)*

In Role play 2 (Asking a *senpai* or upperclassman about how to make websites), more instances of repair offered by by-standing students were found. The excerpt includes a pre-task talk where the teacher explains about the subsequent role play to class and nominates a student who would role play with her. I will examine this portion (Excerpt 2.1) first, followed by the analysis of the actual role play portion (Excerpt 2.2).

Excerpt 2.1 (K: Kent, T: Teacher, S1, S2, S3: unidentified students, SS: students)
```
1      T: ja, niban doo desu ka. hai. kondo      senpai desu
kedo.
           well NO.2 how  CP  P okay this time  senpai CP   but
           "Well, how about NO. 2? Okay. This time it's senpai."
2          jaa   kondo   wa watashi senpai ni narimasu node.
            well this time TP  I    senpai P    become   so
           "well this time I'll be a senpai."
3          hai. °jaa    dareka yaritai    hito.°
            okay  well someone want-to-do person
           "Okay. Well, anyone who wants to do it?"
4          (2.2)
5          Kent san doo desu ka.
           Kent Mr. how  CP  P
          "How about you, Kent?"
6          (4.2)         ← Figure 1
           ((Kent continues looking down and then tilts his head))
7      T: hai, ja   doozo watashi ni, hai.
            okay well please  me     P  go ahead
           "Okay, well please talk to me, go ahead."
8      K: Uh (3.0) uhm ((raises his head))   ← Figure 2
```

```
9              (11.0) ((looks down again))      ← Figure 3
10      K:  ((raising his head)) I didn't study hard.
11      T:  okay. can anyone help him? how he can start?
12→     S1: chotto [ii desu ka.      ← Figure 4
              a bit   okay CP   P
              "Do you have a minute?"
13→     SS:         [chotto ii °desu ka°
                     a bit okay CP    P
              "Do you have a minute?"
14      T:  un yea:h, senpai  chotto  ii  desu ka:?
            yeah yeah, senpai, a bit  okay CP   P
            "Yeah, senpai, do you have a minute?"
```

Figure 1 Kent continues looking down.

Figure 2 Kent raises his head.

Figure 3 Kent continues looking down.

Figure 4 Students raise their heads.

After announcing that she will play the role of a *senpai* 'upperclassman' this time (line 2), the teacher asks for a volunteer who will do the role play with her (line 3). With a 2.2 second gap and still no volunteer, the teacher nominates Kent (line 5). During the 4.2 second gap following the nomination, Kent who is seated second from left is mostly looking down (Figure 1) but soon after he tilts his head,[5] the teacher urges Kent to talk to her, saying "*hai ja doozo watashi ni, hai* [Okay, well please talk to me, go ahead]" (line 7). Kent minimally responds to the teacher in line 8 with "uh (3.0) uhm" and raises his head momentarily (Figure 2). By-standing students captured in the video are all looking down during this time, as shown in Figures 1 and 2. The student on the far left is writing something and the rest of the students appear to be looking at the handout distributed earlier or the textbook. During a 11 second gap that follows, Kent is again looking down; so are the rest of the students captured in the video, as shown in Figure 3. No interactions among the students were observed during the gap. When Kent raises his head again, he says "I didn't study hard" (line 10) which shows his orientation to the state of not being ready to do the role play. Following this, the teacher asks class to offer assistance, saying "can anyone help him? how he can start?" (line 11). S1 responds to the teacher's call for help with the expression, "*chotto ii desu ka* [do you have a minute?]" (line 12). Several other students also say "*chotto ii desu ka*" (line 13) before S1 finishes her sentence. In line 14, the teacher confirms that it is the correct expression, saying "*un yea:h, senpai chotto ii desu ka.* [Yeah, senpai, do you have a minute?]" This is a typical IRF sequence: the teacher initiates a question (line 11), the students reply (lines 12, 13) and the teacher offers feedback (line 14). It is interesting to note that the teacher is not playing the role of *senpai* here, despite the fact that she announced she will be a *senpai* in line 2 and urged the students to talk to her in line 7, saying "*hai, ja doozo watashi ni, hai* [*Okay, well please talk to me, go ahead.*]" The teacher shifting back and forth between the two roles (i.e., teacher and interlocutor in the role play) was observed on several occasions during the role plays. In terms of embodied actions, immediately after the teacher calls for assistance (line 11), most of the students captured in the video raise their head and look towards the teacher (Figure 4) as they respond (lines 12-13), showing that they are paying attention to what is unfolding in class.

Excerpt 2.2 shows the subsequent role play between Kent and the teacher who plays the role of a *senpai* or upperclassman. Kent asks her if she could teach him how to make websites. In this role play demonstration, the teacher was standing in front of the class while Kent remained seated at his desk with the other students.

Excerpt 2.2 (K: Kent, T: Teacher, S1, S2, S3: unidentified students)

```
15→    K: senpai, chotto ii desu ka.
          senpai  a bit  okay CP P
          "Senpai, do you have a minute?"
16     T: hai↓ nan desu ka.
          yes  what CP  P
          "Yes, what is it?"
17     K: ano: websaito=
          uhm  website
          "Uhm websites"
18     T: uhm.
19→    K: =wa: °ano° (1.0) tsukari-(.) tsukari-[tsuka-
          TP   uhm         mak-       mak-    mak-
          "As for (websites), uhm mak-  mak- mak-"
20     T:                                      [uhm tsukurikata
                                                uhm how to make
                                               "Uhm how to make"
21→    K: oh, tsukuri(.)kata=
          oh  how to make
          "Oh, how to make"
22     T: °un.°
          uh-huh
          "Uh-huh."
23→    K: =ga  wakaranai     n desu kedo.
          S  understand-NEG  N CP  but
          "I don't know (how to make websites)."
24     T: ah  soo desu ka.
          oh  so  CP  P
          "Oh, I see."
25     (1.0)

26     K: ano: (2.8) suimasen.
          uhm         excuse me
          "Uhm excuse me."
27 ,   T: un.
          yeah
          "Yeah."
28     K: uhm
29     (3.5)
30→    S2: °xxx oshiete° (.) °oshiete°
               teach          teach
           "Tell me (.) tell me."
```

```
31      T: un   soo desu ne. oshiete-
            yeah so  CP  IP    teach
            "Yeah that's right. Tell me."
32      K: oshiete
            teach
            "Tell me."
33         (3.0)
34→     S1: °kudaisaimasen ka. °
            please NEG    P
            "Won't you please?"
35      T: ((holding the handout)) uhm so you can refer to this
            sheet (1.0) and request, you know, you can (.) select
            one of these (.) oshiete-
36→     S3: °moraemasu          ka.°
            can receive (a favor) P
            "Can you?"
37→     K: oshiete   moraemasen       ka.
            teach    receive (a favor) NEG  P
            "Won't you please tell me?"
38      T: aa   ii   desu yo.
            yes  fine CP   IP
            "Yes, sure."
```

Kent starts with *"senpai, chotto ii desu ka.* [senpai, do you have a minute?]"
(line 15), the expression provided by his peers and the teacher in Excerpt 2.1.
By repeating the same expression, Kent shows his acceptance of the repair
provided. After bringing up a topic *"ano: websaito* [Uhm websites]" in line
17, Kent encounters trouble when he searches for the correct form of the verb
tsukuru 'to make'. He self-repairs his utterance saying *"=wa: ano (1.5)
tsukari-(.) tsukari- [tsuka-* [As for (website), mak- mak- mak-]" (line 19).
His third try, *"tsuka-,"* overlaps with the teacher's correction in line 20, *"uhm
tsukurikata* [uhm how to make]." With the change-of-state token 'oh'
(Heritage, 1984) in line 21, Kent indicates that he now knows the correct
form through the teacher's correction. He accepts it by repeating the form
(line 21), and successfully explains that he does not know how to make
websites (line 23). Following the teacher's acknowledgement token *"ah soo
desu ka* [oh, I see]" (line 24), Kent utters *"ano:* [uhm]" and the subsequent
2.8 second gap indicates another trouble source. Kent resolves this trouble on
his own by uttering *"sumimasen* [excuse me]" (line 26). This is an instance of
a successful self-repair. However, Kent encounters trouble again. This time
he has difficulty formulating "please tell me" in an appropriate manner.
There is a 3.5 second gap after he utters "uhm" in line 28. This time Kent
does not self-repair after the gap. A by-standing student, S2, offers assistance
by whispering "xxx oshiete° (.) °oshiete° [tell me (.) tell me]" (line 30). The
first part of his utterance is unintelligible but the word *oshiete* [tell me] is the
part that Kent can use. The teacher ratifies it in line 31, saying *"un soo desu
ne. oshiete-* [yeah, that's right. Tell me]." Kent accepts it by repeating
"oshiete [tell me]" in line 32. However, Kent encounters trouble again after

this. A 3 second gap in line 33 suggests that he is not sure what form he should use after *oshiete*. S1 offers repair, saying "*kudasaimasen ka* [won't you please?]" in line 34. After the teacher indicates that students can select one of the forms listed in the handout, S3 also offers repair, saying "*moraemasu ka* [can you?]" (line 36). With S1's and S3's assistance, Kent is now ready and says "*oshiete moraemasen ka* [won't you please tell me?]." Notice that Kent uses the negative form *masen ka* [won't you], which is perfectly fine here, instead of repeating *masu ka* [will you?] provided by S3. That is, Kent repairs the form provided by his peer and adapts it in his own way. After this, Kent handles the interaction with the teacher fairly smoothly. Excerpt 2-2 shows instances of self-repair as well as other-repair completed by both teacher and peers. These repairs contributed to the focal student's successful completion of the role play activity. In Excerpt 1, we saw an exposed correction, where the correcting of forms became an interactional business in its own right. In Excerpt 2-2, lines 30-36 can be also regarded as an exposed repair: the focal student, by-standing students and the teacher engage in collaboratively identifying the appropriate form to be used. Notice that the teacher's assessment "*un soo desu ne* [Yeah that's right]" (line 31) is uttered towards S2, instead of Kent, regarding S2's utterance in line 30. Additionally, the teacher's explanation on the task, "uhm so you can refer to this sheet (1.0) and request, you know, you can (.) select one of these (.) oshiete-" (line 35), indicates that the role play with Kent is on hold for the moment. This is what van Lier (1988) calls *activity-oriented* repair, which focuses on the organization and structure of the classroom activity. The excerpt shows that the teacher shifts back and forth between her role as Kent's interlocutor '*senpai*' and her role as the teacher who corrects the student's forms and organizes classroom activities. By doing so, the teacher displays her orientation to the achievement of pedagogical goals.

3.2.3   *Role play 3 (Asking how to use word processor)*

In Role plays 1 and 2, both teacher and by-standing students offered repair to the focal students. In Role play 3 (asking the teacher how to use a word processor), the number of repairs offered by the teacher was very limited and no instances of repair by other students were found. This role play was performed in front of the class where both teacher and student were standing facing each other.

Excerpt 3 (M: Mary, T: Teacher)
```
1      M: ano: sensee wa=
          um   teacher TP
          "Uhm teacher"
2      T: >hai<
          Yes
```

```
            "Yes"
 3   M: =ima ojikan      ga arimasu ka?
        now  time(polite) S  have   P
        "Do you have time now?"
 4   T: e: ii desu  yo. hai, nan deshoo.
        yes fine CP IP  yes, what CP
        "Yes, I have. Yes, what is it?"
 5   M:=eeto jitsu wa:
        uhm  fact  TP
        "uhm the fact is"
 6      (3.5)
 7   M: ee: ↑bunka↓     ga: (1.0) kai- (2.8) bunka  o=
        yes culture  S          wri-        culture O
        "yes culture wri- culture"
 8   T: un.
        uh huh
        "uh huh"
 9   M:=taipu<shite> taipushinakereba (.) nara↑nai↓ kara
        type and     type   have to       have to  so
        "I type and I have to type so"
10→  T: ah, pe:pa: desu ka?
        oh  paper   CP  P
        "Oh, you mean a paper?"
11   M: ha:i
        yes
        "Yes."
12   T: a: so:.
        oh so
        "Oh, I see."
13   M: um: demo sono nihon no waapuro       wa=
        uhm  but that Japan LN word processor TP
        "Uhm but as for that Japanese word processor"

14   T: ee.
        uh-huh
        "Uh-huh."
15      (0.5)
16→  M:=tsukau kata  ga wakara↑nai↓ n desu (.) kara=
        use    method S know-NEG    N CP         so
        "I don't know how to use so"
        ((errors in the form "tsukau" and the connective
        "kara" after the extended predicate "n desu"))
17→  T: [°ee°
        uh-huh
        "Uh-huh."
18→  M: [eetto sense: (0.5) nihon no wa:ppuro ga: (0.7)tsuku-
        uhm  teacher       Japan  LN word prosessor S    use-
19→     °I mean° tsukaika- tsukai- tsuka-
                how use-   use-    us-
        "Uhm Professor Japanese word processor use-
        I mean how use- use- us-"
20   SS:°haha [haha°
21→  T:       [haha
22→  M: tsukatta koto arimasu ka?
```

```
       used      N      have     P
       "Have you used it?"
23     T: ee, wa:puro       wa  hai   nando   mo  arimasu    yo.
          yes word processor TP yes many times P   have       IP
          "Yes, I have used a word processor many times."
```

The student (Mary) organizes the opening sequence with a pre-request. She asks the teacher's availability (line 3) incorporating the polite form '*ojikan* [time]' into her utterance, showing her orientation to the teacher's professional authority. After finding out that the teacher is available for talk (line 2), Mary prefaces what comes next with "*eeto jitsu wa:* [uhm the fact is]" (line 5). This is followed by a 3.5 second gap when Mary tries to explain that she has to type something (lines 7, 9), saying "*ee:* ↑*bunka*↓ *ga: (1.0) kai- (2.8) bunka o taipu<shite> taipushinakereba (.) nara*↑*nai*↓ *kara* [yes culture wri- culture I type I have to type so]." Due to grammatical and lexical problems, Mary's explanation is not clearly presented. In line 10, the teacher offers a repair to confirm her candidate understanding, saying "*ah, pe:pa: desu ka*? [Oh, you mean a paper?]." Notice that here the teacher does not engage in extensive repair of Mary's utterances that pertain to grammatical and lexical problems. She simply checks her candidate understanding so that they can reach intersubjectivity or shared understanding. Further, when Mary indicates that she does not know how to use the word processor in line 16, her utterances contain a conjugation error of the verb *tsukau* [to use] and an incorrect use of the connective particle *kara* [because] which should not be used after the extended predicate *n desu* [it is that]. Here again, the teacher does not engage in correcting Mary's grammatical and lexical problems. She simply offers a continuer "*ee* [uh-huh]" in line 17. In lines 18 and 19, Mary continues having problem conjugating the verb *tsukau* [to use] into the appropriate form. She says "*eetto sense: nihon no waappuro ga: (.) tsuku-* [uhm Professor Japanese word processor use-]" (line 18), and she offers self-repair, saying "°*I mean*° *tsukaika- tsukai- tsuka-* [I mean how use- use- us-]" (line 19), although it is still incomplete. Hearing this, by-standing students laugh quietly in line 20; so does the teacher in line 21. Here again the teacher does not correct the form that Mary uses. Mary successfully completes self-repair in line 22, saying "*tsukatta koto arimasu ka* [Have you used it?]" which is grammatically and pragmatically appropriate.

As shown in Excerpt 3, the teacher hardly offers any corrections on Mary's incorrect forms while the interaction is in progress. The video clip shows that the teacher did offer feedback about the forms that Mary had difficulty with once the role play was over. The fact that there were very few corrections by the teacher during the interaction might have something to do with the context where the role play was performed. Role plays 1 and 2 were performed immediately after students practiced role plays in pairs. Also, prior to the pair practice, the teacher went over various forms that the students could use for making conventionally polite requests. Thus, it is possible to speculate that the teacher wanted to make sure that students were using the correct forms, resulting in an exposed correction sequence on forms inside the larger request sequence. In contrast, Role play 3 was performed approximately one week later after the students had more opportunities for practicing making requests. Therefore, the teacher was able to focus more on meaning and fluency rather than on forms. These findings suggest that repair trajectories within the same activity – role play – vary depending on context and pedagogical focus.

Spatial practices between the interlocutors might have been also related to the repair trajectories observed. During the interactions in Role plays 1 and 2, the teacher was standing in front of the classroom while the nominated students remained seated with the other students. Excerpt 2.1 included a teacher monologue where she explained the upcoming role play activity and selected a student who would role play with her. When the nominated student (Kent) had difficulty with the opening part of the role play, the teacher solicited responses from other students and offered feedback in the IRF format. Thus, Excerpt 2.1 shows a typical teacher-fronted class interaction. Excerpt 1 and Excerpt 2.2 dealt with only the role play segment, but here again we saw repairs offered by both teacher and by-standing students. In these excerpts, the role plays were carried out while the teacher was standing and the focal student remained seated with the other students. This might have triggered other repairs from the by-standing students. In contrast, in Excerpt 3, the nominated student, Mary, and the teacher who performed the role play, were both standing in front of the class. Since the focal student remained seated in Excerpts 1 and 2, that might have made it easier for the by-standing students to offer assistance, as opposed to Excerpt 3 in which the focal student was away from her peers and standing right next to the teacher facing her. Thus, in addition to context and pedagogical focus, spatial practices between the teacher and the focal student might have also led to the repair trajectories observed in the present study.

One last note with regard to repairs offered by by-standing students is the fact that their embodied actions such as gaze and posture seem to be related to their degree of engagement in offering assistance to a focal student. Although video recording did not capture the entire students in class, those students who did appear were not all equally engaged in the role play interaction that was unfolding in front of them. Some were simply looking down at the handout or the textbook rather than at the focal student. Those who did look at the teacher or the focal student seem to be paying more attention and were more likely to offer repair more frequently than those who did not. These more attentive by-standing students were not merely bystanders (Goffman, 1981) who simply observed what was going on in class. Rather, they actively contributed to the interaction as official participants when the focal student had problems, as we saw in the excerpts. Providing by-standing students with opportunities to offer assistance to the focal student might increase affordances (van Lier, 2000) for learning L2 because being able to offer assistance at the right moment requires accurate assessment of the situation, as well as grammatical and pragmatic knowledge of the form to be used. Okada (2010) discusses active participation of by-standing students in classroom interactions. He claims that a talk between primary participants such as the assigned student and the teacher can become a resource for by-standing students. Tateyama and Kasper (2008) also discuss the peripheral yet active participation of by-standing students in the on-going talk unfolding in front of them in terms of affordances for learning; The by-standing students' embodied actions and vocal conduct showed that they were paying close attention to the talk performed in front of them.

4 Summary and implications

The present study examined interactions between student and teacher when they engaged in role plays where the student made a request of the teacher in front of other students. The analysis showed an exposed other correction inserted in a larger request sequence, as well as teacher-initiated, peer-completed repair that followed the IRF format when the role play was performed between the teacher who was standing and the student who remained seated. In contrast, when the role play was performed by the teacher and a student who were both standing in front of the classroom, very few other repairs were observed. Instead of exposed correction during the interaction, the teacher offered feedback on the trouble source after the interaction was over.

The excerpts (Role plays 1 and 2) show that the teacher shifts back and forth between her role as the interlocutor in the role paly and her role as the teacher. When the teacher returns to the teacher mode during role play, putting the interlocutor mode on hold, the teacher does form-focused instruction, making corrections as needed. The teacher also organizes the activity calling for active participation from other students. Shifting back and forth between two roles allows the teacher to assess what a student can or cannot do in a particular role play and to adjust the interaction accordingly. This is important in the achievement of pedagogical goals.

Seedhouse (2004) categorized L2 classroom contexts into three types: form-and-accuracy, meaning-and-fluency, and task-based. He states that incorrect linguistic forms are frequently ignored in meaning-and-fluency contexts, unless they prevent the interaction from continuing. In the present study, all excerpts dealt with the role play activity – a student making a request of the teacher. Thus, a primary focus of the activity was on meaning, fluency and task completion. Despite this, as we have seen in Excerpt 1, the teacher inserted an exposed correction sequence where she corrected the student's incorrect forms inside a larger request sequence. The exposed correction sequence was nothing more than the form-and-accuracy type of activity. This shows that exposed correction can be inserted within the meaning-and-fluency type of activity. Considering the fact that Role plays 1 and 2 were performed right after students engaged in pair practice, we can speculate that the teacher wanted to make sure that the students used correct forms. And, this might have resulted in the exposed correction. In contrast, Role play 3 was performed approximately one week later after the students had more opportunities for practice with making request. Pedagogical focus here was placed more on meaning, fluency, and task completion than on accuracy. These differences in context and pedagogical focus within the role play activities, as well as spatial practices between the interlocutors, might have led to the specific repair trajectories we have observed here.

One pedagogical conclusion here is that it might be helpful for a teacher to balance the time for peer-completed repair and the student's self-repair in class. As we saw in Role play 2, teacher-initiated, peer-completed repairs are useful in terms of encouraging an entire class to participate in the repair process. However, what each student ultimately needs to develop is the ability to address problems of speaking, hearing, or understanding in real conversation because repair is an important component of one's interactional competence in ordinary conversation (Wong & Waring, 2010). As we saw in Excerpt 3, the fact that the teacher did not offer exposed correction here as she did in Role plays 1 and 2 might have actually contributed to more instances of self-repair in Role play 3. Van Lier (1988) suggests providing more wait time for self-repair instead of immediately providing other repair when a learner encounters trouble. This strategy might actually be very helpful.

Findings from the present study lend support to Rylander (2009) who also found exposed correction by the teacher in an activity that was primarily focused on meaning and fluency. However, it should be noted that the present study examined data collected from only one class. As Rylander suggests, we need to describe a variety of L2 activities and characteristics of repair organizations within each. Future studies should examine data collected from a variety of classes, including different target languages, different teachers, and learners at different proficiency levels. Further, examining data collected longitudinally from the same class will also contribute to understanding of the changes in repair trajectories and opportunities for L2 learning in the classroom (Hellerman, 2011).

References

Brouwer, C. E. (2004) Doing pronunciation: A specific type of repair sequence. In Gardner, R. and J. Wagner (eds) *Second Language Conversations* (pp. 93-113), London/New York: Continuum.

Brouwer, C. E., G. Rasmussen and J. Wagner (2004) Embedded corrections in second language talk. In Gardner, R. and J. Wagner (eds) *Second Language Conversations* (pp. 75-92), London/New York: Continuum.

Cook, H. M. (1996) The use of addressee honorifics in Japanese elementary school classrooms. In Akatsuka, N., S. Iwasaki and S. Strauss (eds) *Japanese/Korean Linguistics* Vol. 5 (pp. 67-81), Stanford, CA: Center for the Study of Language and Information.

Goffman, E. (1981) *Forms of Talk*, Oxford: Blackwell.

Hall, J. K. (2007) Redressing the roles of correction and repair in research on second and foreign language learning, *The Modern Language Journal* (91) 4: 511-526.

Hauser, E. (2010) Other-correction of language form following a repair sequence. In Kasper, G., H. Nguyen, D. Yoshimi, and J. Yoshioka (eds) *Pragmatics and Language Learning Vol. 12* (pp. 277-296), Honolulu, HI: University of Hawai'i, National Foreign Language Resource Center.

Hellermann, J. (2011) Members' methods, members' competencies: Looking for evidence of language learning in longitudinal investigations of other-initiated repair. In J. K. Hall, J. Hellermann and S. P. Doehler (eds.) *L2 Interactional Competence and Development* (pp. 147-172), Bristol: Multilingual Matters.

Heritage, J. (1984) A change-of-state token and aspects of its sequential placement. In Atkinson, J. M. and J. Heritage (eds) *Structures of Social Action* (pp. 299-345), Cambridge: Cambridge University Press.

Heritage, J. and G. Raymond (2005) The terms of agreement: Indexing epistemic authority and subordination in talk-in-interaction, *Social Psychology Quarterly* (68) 1: 15-38.

Hosoda, Y. (2006) Repair and relevance of differential language expertise, *Applied Linguistics* (27) 1: 25-50.

Hutchby, I. and R. Wooffitt (2008) *Conversation Analysis* (2nd edition), Cambridge, UK/Malden, MA: Polity Press.

Jefferson, G. (1972) Side sequences. In Sudnow, D. (ed) *Studies in Social Interaction* (pp. 294-338), New York: The Free Press.

Jefferson, G. (1987) On exposed and embedded correction in conversation. In Button, G. and J. R. E. Lee (eds) *Talk and Social Organization* (pp. 86-100), Clevedon: Multilingual Matters.

Jung, E. H. (1999) The organization of second language classroom repair, *Issues in Applied Linguistics* (10) 2: 153-171.

Kasper, G. (1985) Repair in foreign language teaching, *Studies in Second Language Acquisition* (2): 200–215.

Kasper, G. (2004) Beyond repair: Conversation analysis as an approach to SLA, *AILA Review* (19): 83-99.

Kasper, G. and Y-h. Kim (2007) Handling sequentially inapposite responses. In Hua, Z., P. Seedhouse, L. Wei and V. Cook (eds) *Language Learning and Teaching as Social Interaction* (pp. 22-41) Houndmills, Hampshire: Palgrave Macmillan.

Kasper, G. and J. Wagner (2011) A conversation-analytic approach to second language acquisition. In Atkinson, D. (ed) *Alternative Approaches to Second Language Acquisition* (pp. 117-142), London: Routledge.

Koshik, I. (2002) Designedly incomplete utterances: A pedagogical practice for eliciting knowledge displays in error correction sequences, *Research on Language and Social Interaction* (35) 3: 277–309.

Lee, Y-A. (2007) Third turn position in teacher talk: Contingency and the work of teaching, *Journal of Pragmatics* (39): 1204-1230.

Macbeth, D. (2004) The relevance of repair for classroom correction, *Language in Society* (33) 5: 703-736.

McHoul, A. W. (1990) The organization of repair in classroom talk, *Language in Society* (19) 3: 349-377.

Markee, N. (2000) *Conversation Analysis*, Mahwah, NJ: Lawrence Erlbaum Associates.

Mehan, H. (1979) *Learning Lessons*, Cambridge, MA: Harvard University Press.

Okada, Y. (2010) Learning through peripheral participation in overheard/ overseen talk in the language classroom. In Greer, T. (ed) *Observing Talk: CA Studies of L2 Interaction* (pp. 133-151), Tokyo: JALT.

Rylander, J. (2009) Repair work in a Chinese as a foreign language classroom. In Nguyen, H. and G. Kasper (eds) *Talk-in-interaction:*

Multilingual Perspectives, (pp. 245-280), Honolulu, HI: University of Hawai'i, National Foreign Language Resource Center.

Schegloff, E. A. (1997) Practices and actions: Boundary cases of other-initiated repair, *Discourse Processes* (23): 499–545.

Schegloff, E. A., G. Jefferson and H. Sacks (1977) The preference for self-correction in the organization of repair in conversation, *Language* (53): 361–382.

Seedhouse, P. (2004) *The Interactional Architecture of the Language Classroom: A Conversation Analysis Perspective*, Malden, MA : Blackwell.

Seedhouse, P. (2007) On ethnomethodological CA and "linguistic CA": A reply to Hall, *The Modern Language Journal* (91): 527–533.

Sidnell, J. (2011) *Conversation Analysis: An Introduction*, Malden, MA/Oxford, UK: Wiley-Blackwell.

Sinclair, M. and M. Coulthard (1975) *Towards an Analysis of Discourse*, Oxford: Oxford University Press.

Svennevig, J. (2004) Other-repetition as display of hearing, understanding and emotional stance, *Discourse Studies* (6): 489–516.

Tateyama, Y. and G. Kasper (2008). Talking with a classroom guest: Opportunities for learning Japanese pragmatics. In Alcón, E. Soler and A. Martínez-Flor (eds) *Investigating Pragmatics in Foreign Language Learning, Teaching and Testing* (pp. 45-71), Clevedon: Multilingual Matters.

van Lier, L. (1988) *The Classroom and the Language Learner*, New York: Longman.

van Lier, L. (2000) From input to affordance: Social-interactive learning from an ecological perspective. In Lantolf, J. P. (ed) *Sociocultural Theory and Second Language Learning* (pp. 245-259). Oxford: Oxford University Press.

Waring, H. Z. (2008) Using explicit positive assessment in the language classroom: IRF, feedback, and learning opportunities, *The Modern Language Journal* (92): 577-594.

Wong, J. and H. Z. Waring (2010) *Conversation Analysis and Second Language Pedagogy*, New York/London: Routledge.

Acknowledgements

I am grateful to Gabriele Kasper, the anonymous reviewer, and the editors of this volume for their insightful comments and suggestions. An earlier version of this chapter was presented at the Annual Conference of the American Association for Applied Linguistics in Chicago, Illinois (March 26 – 29, 2011).

Notes

[1]In his reply to Hall (2007), Seedhouse (2007) maintains the position that correction offered in the IRF sequence be considered a special case of repair in the institutional setting of classroom.

[2]Because the data were originally collected for a larger study with an entirely different purpose, the involvement of the author as an interlocutor should not have reduced the authenticity of the data. Actually, having a sound understanding of the classroom setting from which data have been drawn, as well as relevant membership competencies in the setting, might have helped in understanding the data (cf. Hutchby & Wooffitt, 2008).

[3]The present data were collected in the same class as reported in Tateyama & Kasper (2008), a few days after the Japanese guest's visit.

[4]In Japanese, expressions that show apology such as *sumimasen* [I'm sorry] are often used in thanking situations in order to show appreciation towards the interlocutor for the trouble that he or she has experienced.

[5]The video camera did capture Kent, so non-verbal features will be noted in Excerpt 2. (Brian in Excerpt 1 and Mary in Excerpt 3 were not captured in the video camera because the camera was fixed at the same spot in the classroom while class was in progress.)

Appendix

Transcription conventions

[	overlap
?	rising intonation
.	falling intonation
,	continuing intonation
:	elongated syllable
::	longer elongated syllable
↑	shift into especially high pitch in the next sound
↓	shift into especially low pitch in the next sound
H	audible breathing
.h	in-breath
h	out-breath
text	marked stress
TEXT	spoken loudly
<text>	spoken slowly
>text<	spoken rapidly
text	spoken softly

(1.5)	length of significant pause in seconds
(.)	micropause
=	latched talk
!	animated pronunciation
-	word cutoff
( )	unsure hearings
((behavior))	paralinguistic behavior

Abbreviations

AUX	Auxiliary
CP	Copula verb *be* in various forms
FL	Filler
LK	Linking nominal
N	Nominalizer
NEG	Negative morpheme
O	Object marker
P	Particle
Q	Question marker *ka*
QT	Quotation marker *to/tte*
S	Subject marker *ga*
TOP	Topic marker *wa*

Social perspectives on interaction and language learning in CLIL classrooms

Ana Llinares (Universidad Autónoma de Madrid)
Tom Morton (Universidad Autónoma de Madrid)

Content and language integrated learning (CLIL), an approach in which curriculum content and an additional language are taught together, has been identified by Graddol (2006) as one of the three major future trends in English language education, along with English as a lingua franca (ELF) and English for young learners (EYL). In Europe, CLIL has been considered a key strategy for the achievement of the EU's goals of increased plurungualism among its citizens. Much CLIL research takes a 'product' approach, in which CLIL learners' L2 learning achievements are measured, often in comparison with peers who did not participate in CLIL. However, there is a need for more studies which examine CLIL processes, specifically how the L2 is used for content and language learning in classroom interaction, and how learners' competences can be expected to develop.

This chapter argues that, in order to achieve greater understanding of interaction in CLIL classrooms, and how it can contribute to content and language learning goals, it is necessary to adopt social rather than individualistic perspectives on language, interaction and L2 development. To meet this need, the chapter examines two socially-oriented perspectives on L2 development and assesses their relevance for understanding interaction and language use in CLIL classrooms: a socio-interactionist approach which draws on conversation analysis and situated learning theory, and systemic functional linguistics (SFL). The chapter argues that these two social perspectives can be used separately or in combination to contribute to achieving two important goals in CLIL: a greater integration of content pedagogies and language learning; and a more specific identification of how the interactional organisation of CLIL classrooms may provide affordances for language development.

1 Introduction

In this chapter we examine two 'social' perspectives on language development and their relevance for understanding interaction and language use in CLIL classrooms: a socio-interactionist approach based on conversation analysis and situated learning theory, and systemic functional linguistics (SFL). We suggest how they might be combined in bringing about better understanding of two key issues in CLIL: a greater integration of content pedagogies and language learning; and a more specific identification of how the interactional organisation of CLIL classrooms may provide affordances for language development. These issues were identified by Leung (2005) as important in developing a more 'close-up' view of interaction and language use in bilingual classrooms, to complement the many existing studies which take a more 'macro' and product-oriented perspective. He argues that we don't only need to know *that* a particular type of bilingual education (such as CLIL) works, but "we also need to know *how* it works at the points where social and curriculum content meanings are communicated, and where opportunities for language development for the individual student may take place" (Leung 2005: 239. Emphasis added). If it is true, as the studies in Dalton-Puffer, Nikula and Smit (2010) suggest, that "CLIL contexts seem to offer students more, and more varied, opportunities for interaction than do traditional language classrooms" (p. 283), then it is important to know just what types of opportunities these are and how they can be enhanced. The main argument of this chapter is that the two social perspectives of situated learning theory and SFL can combine to enable a greater understanding of these processes.

The chapter is organised as follows. In section 2, we review how the notion of 'interaction' has evolved in SLA studies, showing how the concept of the 'social' has been expanded, not without controversy. We then focus on current research which adopts a strong socio-interactionist perspective, combining situated learning theory and conversation analysis (CA for SLA). In section 3 we show how these changing views of interaction have impacted on research on content-based learning contexts such as Canadian immersion and are beginning to emerge in studies of European CLIL. We highlight some problems and challenges that have to be faced by this strongly socially-situated approach, particularly the issue of how learning can be evidenced. Sections 4 and 5 change the focus by incorporating another strongly social perspective on language and interaction, Systemic Functional Linguistics (SFL), in which language is seen as a social semiotic. We show how this approach has been fruitful in studies of CLIL classroom discourse, particularly when combined with insights from another social perspective, neo-Vygotskian sociocultural theory. Section 6 brings the two main strands in the chapter together (the socially situated perspective embodied by CA for SLA and the language as social semiotic perspective of SFL), arguing that a much fuller picture of the relationships between CLIL classroom discourse and learning opportunity can be gained by combining both perspectives. We highlight some theoretical and methodological opportunities and challenges of such eclecticism.

2 Shifting perspectives on interaction and the social in studies of L2 learning

Interaction has for long been at the heart of attempts to build overarching theories of the process of second language acquisition. Perhaps the best known formulation of the role of interaction in language learning is Long's (1981; 1996) interaction hypothesis, in which he stated that input alone was not sufficient for second language acquisition, a necessary condition being that learners engaged in interaction with more competent speakers. It was through conversational modifications or negotiations that non-native speakers received the input they needed to drive forward the acquisition process. Swain (1985; 1995) added an emphasis on learner output; it was through the production of comprehensible output in interaction that learners could test hypotheses about how the foreign language worked, and thus move from semantic to syntactic processing. In fact, according to Block (2003), what he calls the 'input-interaction-output (IIO) model' as put forward by Gass (1997) became the 'biggest player on the SLA scene' (p. 26). It is this model that, as he explains, has come closest to providing for an overarching 'big theory' of SLA. In Gass's description of the model, the kind of social interaction a learner is participating in is seen as determining whether linguistic input is noticed, with conversational modifications playing a role in increasing the amount of input available. More recently, Gass and Mackey (2006) have claimed that SLA empirical research under the 'interaction' banner has provided enough evidence of the links between interaction and L2 learning to move beyond being either a 'hypothesis' or a 'model' to beginning to exhibit some characteristics of a theory. They suggest that the label could be changed to the 'interaction approach'. Whatever the terminology used, a common theme in interactional frameworks in SLA has been to link participation in interaction with learner-internal factors such as motivation, learning strategies, working memory, language aptitude, cognitive styles and social context (Gass & Mackey 2006: 14).

While the interaction approach recognises the role of social context in the acquisition process, over the past two decades there have been calls for a much fuller account of SLA as a social process. In fact, such has been the level of reassessment of the role of the 'social' in L2 studies, that Block (2003) claims that there has been a 'social turn' in the field of SLA, with the idea of the 'social' broadening out to include a much wider range of phenomena than before. While there had always been researchers on L2 learning who took a more 'social' or sociolinguistic' view (e.g. Aston 1993; Hall 1995; Rampton 1987; Trosset 1986), it was the publication of an article by Firth and Wagner in 1997 which sparked a reassessment among many in the SLA field of the role of the 'social' in learning additional languages. In this article, Firth and Wagner criticised the predominant view of discourse and communication in SLA for being "individualistic and mechanistic" and for failing "to account in a satisfactory way for interactional and sociolinguistic dimensions of language" (p. 285). The article questioned the individualistic cognitive assumptions underlying such prevalent notions in SLA as communicative strategies, the focus on the 'learner' as somehow a deficient native speaker, the ideas of 'interlanguage' as an underdeveloped version of native speaker competence, and the idea that conversational modifications are necessarily sparked by perceived deficiencies in non-natives' output. They called for a more holistic SLA which would see language as not only a individual cognitive phenomenon, but as also "fundamentally a social phenomenon, acquired and used interactively, in a variety of contexts for myriad practical purposes" (p. 768). Interestingly for the topic of this chapter, they also criticised SLA for a lack of attention to language use and learning outside instructed contexts, especially contexts in which English is used as a lingua franca for a wide range of purposes outside formal education. This raises important questions about language use and interaction in immersion and CLIL contexts, as they represent educational settings, but not in the way that is understood in instructed language learning in foreign language classrooms. Firth and Wagner also pointed out the need to develop the theoretical bases, research agenda and methodological approaches which would go along with their recommendations for a much more socially-informed SLA.

In part, Firth and Wagner's wishes have been met by the emergence of a burgeoning research field, CA for SLA, in which the metatheoretical and analytic resources of conversation analysis are brought to bear on the issue of how people use, and learn, additional languages in and through social interaction. In this perspective, it is claimed that fine-grained analyses of interaction as it unfolds, turn-by-turn, in real time, can be revealing of the competences and orientations displayed by speakers as they participate in situated action, whether inside or outside 'instructed' contexts. While there may be some differences between researchers in the extent to which internal cognition is seen as a factor in learning, there is a tendency to use a 'participation' metaphor (Sfard 1998) to explicate how learning takes place. Learning is thus claimed to be visible in the micro-processes of social interaction as opposed to being located 'inside the skull' (Kasper 2009). Extending the participation metaphor temporally, learning can be seen as changes in participation patterns, more specifically, in the ways in which people accomplish certain tasks that are important to the communities they are involved in. Pekarek Doehler (2010: 120) clearly states the broad questions addressed in this approach: "How does the accomplishment of L2 talk-in-interaction and L2 speakers' participation in talk change across time?

And how are changes in linguistic form and in other semiotic means embedded in (changes in) the accomplishment of talk and participation?"

A good example of work which takes this approach is Hellerman (2008), in which he describes how adult learners in an ESOL class open and disengage from task-based interactions. A strength of this approach is that it is able to trace the trajectories of individual students, showing how the ways in which they use the L2 to carry out such social actions as beginning a task change over time. Another example is Markee (2008), which introduces a methodology for the use of CA in tracking L2 learning over time. This consists of two types of analysis: learning object tracking (LOT), which involves documenting the appearance of learning objects (for example, vocabulary items, aspects of verb morphology or pronunciation) over a specified period of time, such as a term; learning process tracking (LPT), which involves analysing instances of interaction in which participants orient to, and possibly incorporate into their communicative repertoires, these objects.

Hellerman's and Markee's work are interesting as they highlight important differences in approach among researchers who take this quite radically 'social' approach to interaction and language learning. Hellerman's work is representative of an approach that establishes links with wider situated learning theories, particularly the concepts of 'legitimate peripheral participation' and 'communities of practice' (Lave & Wenger 1991; Wenger 1998). This is a view of learning in which cognitive abilities such as those involved in doing mathematical tasks are seen as deeply embedded in the situated activities people engage in (e.g. Lave 1988). People become 'full' members of groups which share joint activities (communities of practice) by beginning with 'legitimate peripheral participation' in which they engage, with the supervision of 'old-timers' in more low-risk tasks. Through time, they eventually are able to competently perform the full range of tasks relevant to their roles in the community.

Researchers such as Hellerman and Mondada and Pekarek Doehler (2004) have explicitly linked CA for SLA to these socially situated theories of learning, in what could be described as a 'strong socio-interactionist perspective' (Mondada & Pekarek Doehler 2004: 502). However, other researchers working in a CA for SLA perspective are reluctant to bring in what the see as 'exogenous theory' (Markee 2008). For them, theories from within SLA, such as the input-interaction-output model, or from without, such as situated learning and communities of practice, or, indeed, linguistic models such as systemic-functional linguistics, are seen as essentially 'etic' or theory-driven. This contrasts with CA's emic or participant-centred perspective, in which what participants are actually doing in social interaction can only be explained in terms of what they openly, publicly demonstrate in the ways in which they use talk-in-interaction to accomplish social actions. In these terms, even such 'cognitive-sounding' terms such as 'understanding' or 'knowing' can be respecified as 'displays of understanding and knowing', as in the recent work of Koole (2010).

Other researchers have pointed to problems in bringing together CA and situated learning theory. Hougaard (2009) claims that fine-grained CA for SLA studies of the type discussed here, while they are useful in showing how learners may increase the complexity of their interactional actions, cannot in fact demonstrate that 'learning' has taken place. This is particularly so when the participants themselves do not orient to having 'learned' anything in interactions described by analysts as evidence of learning having taken place. In Hougaard's view, learning can only be inferred from these interactions, and this approach in fact reduces learning to an epiphenomenon of social interaction. Hauser (2011) questions to what extent the concept of legitimate peripheral participation is relevant for L2 learning situations. He points out that this theory is designed to account for how people acquire competences in whichever activities are relevant to the communities they are a member of. It is not designed to explain how people learn linguistic or interactional competences. In fact, as he points out, a student in a language classroom, who shows only limited L2 linguistic or interactional competence, can be treated as a full member from the beginning, by participating in language learning activities appropriate to their level. As we discuss more fully in the next section, this raises very interesting issues for CLIL and immersion contexts, as the learners are apprenticed into being members of communities of school scientists, historians, mathematicians etc. What we need to understand is the role of social interaction in facilitating this process, and the likely consequences for L2 development itself.

To sum up, understandings of the roles of interaction in L2 learning have undergone significant transformations in the last 15-20 years. These shifts may be characterized as moving in two general directions: the first is a move from 'inner' to 'outer', that is, a shift from learning being seen as taking place 'inside the skull' to being seen as visible, publically displayed in the talk-in-interaction through which people accomplish social activities. The second is a broadening of focus - from dyadic interactions to participation in communities of practice (whether classroom ones or non-educational ones). This broadening of focus has allowed SLA to take in a much wider range of concerns than before, most notably a much deeper treatment of learner agency and identity (Block 2007). However, these shifts in perspective have not been shared throughout the SLA community, with the result that, in what might be described as the 'mainstream', the interaction approach (in Gass & Mackey's terms), with its integration of interactional and learner-internal factors, is still a powerful paradigm in L2 learning studies. In the next section, we look at how both of these broad frameworks for studying the effects of interaction in L2 learning have been used in immersion and CLIL contexts.

3 Research on interaction in CLIL and other content-based classroom contexts

SLA studies of content-based or CLIL classrooms using the interactionist framework are interested in the affordances that such environments provide for the kinds of negotiation associated with conversational modifications and with acquisition. Pica (2002) is sceptical that such classrooms always offer optimal conditions for the kinds of interactional negotiations in which learners can modify their output syntactically or receive feedback on their grammatical accuracy. She highlights one type of classroom activity, the discussion, as being less than effective for this purpose:

> Subject-matter content (…) provided a meaningful context for students' exposure to the form and meaning relationships they had yet to master. However, the discussion, as the most   frequently implemented interactional activity in these classrooms, did not promote the kinds of interaction that could draw attention to these relationships. Instead, it provided a context for the students to sustain lengthy, multi-utterance texts, whose comprehensibility of message meaning provided little basis for negotiation, form-focused intervention, and form-focused instruction (Pica 2002: 16).

Here, Pica highlights the positive nature of these content-based classrooms for providing exposure to input, but it seems that the participants in the interaction understood each other too well for any negotiation of form and/or meaning to occur. Musumeci, in an earlier study of an Italian content-based setting, noted other shortcomings related to the teacher's control of the classroom activity:

> The data reveal that the teachers in the third semester content-based Italian course speak more, more often, control the topic of discussion, rarely ask questions for which they do not have answers,

and appear to understand absolutely everything the students say, sometimes even before they say it! (Musumeci 1996: 314).

It seems, then, that in content-based classrooms, the participants understand each other too well for any real breakdowns in communication to occur. And, from an interaction approach standpoint, without these breakdowns and the resulting negotiation and modification, acquisition is unlikely to occur. More recent discourse studies of CLIL classrooms cast some light on the constraints on this type of negotiation happening. As Dalton-Puffer (2009) has shown, the CLIL lesson as a speech event can be characterized as having, among other things,

> a clear distribution of expert and novice roles entailing a specific turn-taking and topic nomination mechanism, idiosyncrasies in the realisation of repair and directives, *limits on meaning negotiation and conversational challenge*, quantitative and structural limits on student output, dominance of a small number of speech functions (...) (Dalton-Puffer 2009: 212, italics added).

If this is the case, then the CLIL lesson as a speech event may not be the optimum environment for the kinds of meaning and form negotiations seen by advocates of the interaction framework as crucial for SLA. In fact, given that this may be the case, one approach taken by SLA researchers has been to advocate teacher interventions which shift the interaction in content-based classrooms towards a greater focus on form. One such example is the 'counterbalanced' approach advocated by Lyster (2007). This approach recognises that, in interaction in immersion and content-based classrooms, learners' attention will be focused on the content-related meanings they are communicating. However, it is argued that this focus on meaning can be 'counterbalanced' by teachers pushing their students' attention towards features of the target language they may not otherwise notice. This can be done either by pre-selecting linguistic features for attention, in a 'proactive' approach, or by teachers providing corrective feedback in response to learners' output, a 'reactive' approach. Classroom interaction is crucial to this approach in which, as Lyster puts it,

> teachers and students need to negotiate language across the curriculum, as teachers exploit a range of interactional techniques that vary from the use of implicit feedback in the form of recasts that scaffold interaction in ways that facilitate students' participation, to feedback in the form of prompts and other signals that push

learners beyond their use of recalcitrant interlanguage forms (Lyster 2007: 135-6).

Apart from directing students' attention to language forms they might otherwise not attend to, recent studies on classroom interaction in CLIL and ESL contexts have highlighted other important roles of teacher feedback, such as expanding or elaborating feedback or functional recasts. Functional recasts have been linked with the systemic functional approach, and so are dealt with in section 1.4 below. Expanding or elaborating feedback occurs when teachers use their follow-up turn not to evaluate students' responses but to encourage them to elaborate their ideas, as exemplified in extract 1 below, from a CLIL history class:

Extract 1

> T: So for him the religion was something important?
> S: Important, yes. (   )
> T: Exactly
> S: And also he lost the part of Holland because of that.
>   ((mumbling)) (   )
> T: Why? Do you know why?
> S: Because we- they were starting to become Protestant because
>   in.. the Protestantism spread in north Europe.

In line 6, the teacher does not evaluate the student's response either positively or negatively. Instead, she asks him a 'question for reason', following Dalton-Puffer's (2007) typology of academic questions in CLIL classrooms, which encourages the student to elaborate his answer in line 4.

Research on interaction in CLIL classrooms (e.g. Dalton-Puffer 2007) has tended to confirm the ubiquity of the classic three-part pattern in classroom discourse, the IRF (initiation-response-follow-up) exchange, first described in detail by Sinclair and Coulthard (1975). Research on this pattern in CLIL classrooms has claimed that it can be restrictive as it does not encourage students' participation in extended talk (Nikula 2007). However, Llinares, Morton & Whittaker (2012) argue that the potential of the IRF pattern to encourage students' participation is not related to the pattern itself but to the purpose of the activity and the roles of the participants (also see discussion of IRF in classroom macrogenres in section 1.5 below).

Particularly interesting within the study of the IRF pattern are the chances for students to initiate interactions. As reported in Llinares et al. (2012) group work sessions can be a context with interesting potential for students to initiate their own interactions, as can be seen in the following extract on a CLIL group work lab session on chemistry:

Extract 2

S: So if you double the iodine, you should double the.. the lead also?
T: Yeah. But you don't double the iodine here
S: Yeah, you put
T: Here you have one.. one atom of lead and two atoms of iodine
S: Yes
T: So eh.. if you write a two here, the iodine is already balanced, so the iodine is okay now
S: Yeah, but not the, not the lead
T: Yes, the lead is one here, one here
S: But para, para (Sp. for, for) for joining the i- the iodine with the lead,   you may.. you may have one of.. two.. two of lead for two of iodine
T: No, this two only affects the iodine
S: Okay.

In lines 1 and 2, the student initiates the exchange with a question, with the teacher responding in line 3 and the student acknowledging the response with a follow-up move in line 4. There is evidence that group work sessions certainly allow for a wide variety of participating roles from the students. As seen in the example above, students do not act as mere "animators" (Goffman 1981), who are expected to display the knowledge that they have acquired, but they are also "principals" or generators of the ideas being discussed. In fact, in this extract, after the student's initiation in line 1, the teacher seems to dominate the floor, but the student takes the floor again in line 12: "But *para*, *para*, for joining the i- the iodine with the lead, you may.. you may have one of.. two.. two of lead for two of iodine". Apart from group work, student-initiated exchanges have also been found in teacher-fronted classrooms. As an example, Llinares' (2007) analysis of interaction patterns and communicative functions in young CLIL learners' discourse revealed that activities of the type 'Show and Tell sessions' triggered young learners' initiations in the L2. Nikula (2010) even argues that the CLIL classroom itself, independently of the activity, enourages students to participate more.

In her comparative study of the same teacher's performance in a CLIL and a first language content class she concludes:

> ...the teacher and the students seem to construct different understandings of their roles in CLIL classrooms and in classrooms taught in Finnish. While in the former the students are in a more equal footing with the teacher as far as the right to participate in classroom discourse is concerned, in the latter students are positioned in a rather passive as recipients of teacher talk (Nikula 2010: 119).

On the other hand, Dalton-Puffer's (2007) research in the Austrian context depicts an interactional context where teachers' questions for facts dominate and students do not seem to adopt an active role, rather like the Italian content-based classrooms described by Musumeci above. In sum, whether CLIL classes or specific activities trigger students' richer interactive participation is an area that has interesting potential for further research. It seems clear, however, that students should be encouraged to be active participants both for content and language engagement.

In a number of recent studies, the strongly socio-interactionist perspective, which was described above in the context of instructed L2 learning in the work of researchers such as Markee, Hellerman or Pekarek Doehler, has started to make inroads in research on interaction in immersion/CLIL classrooms. One such study is Pekarek Doehler and Ziegler (2007), which investigated interaction in a bilingual science classroom in German-speaking Switzerland, in which 15-16 year old students were studying biology in English. This study starts from a critique of assumptions underlying the binary distinction between 'content' and 'language' in immersion classrooms. The first assumption is one that reduces language learning to the acquisition of linguistic forms, ignoring the interactional competences necessary for any learning or language use to happen at all (see Macbeth 2011 and Hall, Hellerman & Pekarek Doehler 2011). The second assumption criticized is one in which communication is seen as the exchange of contents, that is, talk is *about* something, rather than being an activity, or part of an activity, itself. This study set out to explore how the participants themselves, in talk-in-interaction, sequentially organized the doing of science and language, and not only that, the doing of a range of other things, such as enacting identities as learners or experts, or teacher and students, and, in general jointly co-ordinating their mutual activities. The findings show the complex inter-relatedness of participants' orientations to language and to academic content. Orientation towards language form was embedded in and contributed to the work on specific scientific concepts, and this interplay between language and science was in itself closely related to the sequential organization of the classroom action as they moved from one activity to another. This interplay between language form and content was also seen in the ways in which students' contributions received certain grammatical formatting, such as the generic use of the definite article.

Another study which takes a socio-interactionist perspective on CLIL classroom interaction is that of Evnitskaya and Morton (2011). This study combines the situated learning framework of communities of practice with the analytic tools of multimodal conversation analysis to examine interaction and identity formation in two Spanish CLIL secondary science classrooms. The study's findings show how the use of a multimodal conversation analysis methodology can identify differences between the ways in which different CLIL classrooms are being constructed as communities of practice, and the different identities which emerge. In the study, a first year science class constructed learners as observers and reporters of phenomena actually seen in the lab under a microscope, while in a fourth year class, learners were positioned in the role of reinterpreting through scientific reifications phenomena they could observe in their everyday lives outside the classroom. The analyses show, in fine-grained detail, how a range of semiotic resources, including the three language codes in operation (English, Spanish and Catalan) and multimodal resources such as gesture, were used in the ongoing construction of these classroom communities of practice. The ways in which these resources were combined constructed the classroom communities in different ways and positioned the learners as members of these communities and language users in ways which created different types of learning opportunity. For example, in the fourth year class, the teacher built the interaction around different metaphors of 'seeing', or penetrating into a scientific reality beyond appearances, while in the first year class, the interaction and language use revolved around the observation of the behaviour of a cell under a microscope, and descriptions of its movements.

Another recent study of CLIL classrooms which uses a socio-interactionist and multimodal approach is that of Kupetz (2011). This study focuses on how a 10th grade German high school student studying geography in English uses a variety of multimodal resources such as pauses, facial expressions, pointing and gesture in carrying out the activity of explaining. The study shows in detail how the student used body position and gesture, and a sketch, in making subject-relevant meanings, and how he used other multimodal resources to involve other participants in solving language problems, particularly word-finding. The study highlights the importance of participants in CLIL classrooms' ability to navigate skillfully between different classroom micro-contexts, such as those in which there is an orientation to language form, and those in which there is a focus on content-related meanings. While, as we saw in the Pekarek Doehler and Ziegler paper above, the use of language forms is deeply embedded in the situated activity of the classroom, there may be times in which language form becomes the open object of attention for participants in the classroom. However, as Kupetz points out, it is "only where it is made relevant by the participants themselves, (that) there is an occasional change to focus on form" (p. 134).

Studies such as these suggest that studies of L2 development through interaction in CLIL contexts need to more strongly and explicitly take into account the classroom communities of practice in which language use is embedded. In these contexts, language use in CLIL classrooms may more profitably be seen as what Wells (2007) describes as 'discoursing', that is, "the use of language in interaction with others" (p. 160). As he points out, discoursing "always functions as a mediational means in achieving the goals of the action in which it occurs" (p.175). In this sense, we cannot separate instances of language use in CLIL classrooms from their role in achieving the goals of instruction, which in most cases, are the learning of the knowledge, understanding and skills related to the subject being taught. Binary distinctions between 'meaning' and 'form' may be less than helpful in gaining an understanding of language use and development in CLIL contexts. One view of language which provides a framework for overcoming these artificial distinctions is one in which language is seen as a social semiotic. This is the framework of Systemic Functional Linguistics, and to this we turn in the next section.

4 Systemic Functional Linguistics as a social perspective on language and learning

Systemic Functional Linguistics is a profoundly social theory of language and meaning. As Matthiessen, Teruya and Lam (2010: 101) explain, "Language is functional in the sense that it has evolved together with its "eco-social" environment (and develops in the individual together with this environment)". From its inception, Systemic Functional Linguistics was developed with the idea of creating a linguistic theory that could also have applications for language learning and teaching (Halliday, McIntosh & Strevens 1964). Halliday (1993) shows how the systemic framework can be seen as the basis for a language-based theory of learning itself. In the last two decades, the systemic functional notions of register and genre theory (first developed in studies such as Halliday & Hasan 1989 and Martin 1993) have been applied in different parts of the world in addressing linguistic problems in school contexts. Schleppegrell (2004) provides an SFL-based account of the role of language in learning school subjects, particularly the lexico-grammatical features of subject-specific language varieties, or registers.

In Australia, the concept of genre has been fruitful in studies on education, particularly on the role of literacy in learning school subjects (see Martin & Rose 2008 for state of the art account of the theory). In Martin and Rose's (2003) definition, a genre is a "staged, goal-oriented social process". Thus, the texts through which knowledge is construed in different subjects will reflect their different purposes, the ways in which meaning is made in different academic communities, and the ways in which activities are carried out in stages. Genre theorists in SFL have developed a framework for classroom pedagogy which aims to equip learners with the resources to use the different genres important in the subjects they are studying (see Martin 1999 for a description). In this model, teachers and learners 'deconstruct' critically examples of key genres, identifying their key stages and the lexicogrammar through which they are built. Learners and teachers can then jointly construct examples of the genre, before learners are asked to produce their own examples. At particulary the 'deconstruction' and 'joint construction' stages in this pedagogical model, classroom interaction plays a key role in how the teacher scaffolds learners' understandings of the features and roles of the genres.

Work on classroom discourse and interaction carried out in Australia using the systemic functional model can be divided into two broad lines of research associated with the work of Christie (2002) and Gibbons (2002, 2006). Drawing on Sinclair and Coulthard's early (1975) work, Christie (2002) conceives classroom discourse as a structured experience. There are many similarities between the two models. In Sinclair and Coulthard's model, there are several ranks arranged in hierarchical order and, thus, *lessons* include *transactions*, these include *exchanges*, *exchanges* include *moves* and moves include *acts*. Using the SFL work on genre theory highlighted above, Christie (2002) moves from a focus on larger units (*curriculum genre* and *curriculum macrogenre*) to smaller units (the *lexico-grammar* that characterises those genres). The difference between the two models, as Christie (2002: 5) puts it, referring to Sinclair and Coulthard's IRE (Initiation-Response-Feedback) model, is:

it has often neglected to look at the nature of the meanings in construction, the relative roles and responsibilities of teachers and students at the time of constructing those meanings, and the placement of those patterns in the overall larger cycle of classroom work.

Christie's work is a reminder of the need to consider classroom interaction patterns such as the IRF exchange in the context of the ongoing activity participants are involved in. In this sense, we can see links with the wider 'social' perspective on interaction as outlined in section 1.2 above. For example, interaction patterns such as the IRF exchange are better understood when seen in the context of the curriculum genres they are a part of. Thus, it makes little sense to isolate this (or any other) pattern as ineffective, as it may well have an important function in constructing a stage within a classroom genre. As Nassaji and Wells (2000) show, the IRF exchange or 'triadic dialogue' can have a range of positive functions within classroom genres.

Gibbons' (2006) analysis of classroom discourse is based on ESL (English as a Second Language) classrooms. As such, it is a context with some similarities with CLIL, in that learners are faced with the challenge of acquiring academic knowledge and academic language skills in an L2. Gibbons identifies patterns of classroom interaction which enable both of these learning objectives to be met. She applies the Vygotskian concept of scaffolding, which she defines as "the temporary assistance by which a teacher helps a learner know how to do something, so that the learner will later be able to complete a similar task alone" (2002:10). When this assistance is offered by the teacher in moment-by-moment classroom interaction, in response to learners' efforts to express content-related knowledge, it can be labelled 'contingent' or 'interactional' scaffolding. As we see in the examples of CLIL classroom interaction throughout this chapter, this is a crucial aspect of teachers' pedagogical repertoires.

Most of the work done on school registers and genres has been carried out in contexts in which the L1 is used as the medium of instruction, with some attention to contexts in which the students in the classroom may be English language learners (e.g. Schleppegrell 2002). However, as Martin (2009: 19) argues, "The practical power of a model of this kind has yet to be fully explored for L2 learning contexts." CLIL is in a unique position in this respect as both major justifications for an SFL approach are present. That is, not only will the rich accounts of the roles of register and genre in L1 subject learning be of interest to CLIL practitioners and researchers, but also the model's potential and practical power for understanding L2 learning can also be applied. In the following section, we turn our attention to the potential of

SFL as a social-semiotic account of the roles and functions of classroom discourse and interaction in CLIL

5 CLIL classroom discourse as social semiotic: a systemic functional perspective

In this section, we review some recent research on CLIL classroom discourse and interaction, which takes as its starting point the SFL perspective developed in the work by researchers such as Christie and Gibbons, among others. This work focuses on two broad areas of interest: in line with Christie, the lexico-grammatical features of subject-relevant registers and genres as used by students in CLIL classrooms and, following Gibbons, the role of activity type and interactional patterns in CLIL learners' use of the L2 as a possible correlate of classroom learning. This SFL-informed work, particuarly that of Gibbons, is social in a further sense. That is, it uses a neo-Vygostkian sociocultural framework, in which concepts such as mediation or scaffolding are key. This is not surprising, as researchers such as Wells (1999) have highlighted the affinity between Vygotsky's and Halliday's ideas about language and learning. It is an approach well placed to attend to the integration of content and language pedagogy, and it is able to take into account not only product, but also classroom processes. It thus contrasts with the generally cognitivist and product orientation of much research in bilingual education, and as such is very well placed to respond to Leung's (2005) call for a more close-up view of the connections between subject pedagogies and L2 learning opportunities. However, it is important to bear in mind that European CLIL presents a different context from the ESL and/or L1 contexts studied by SFL researchers such as Christie and Gibbons. As Lasagabaster and Sierra (2010) point out, it is important to distinguish between immersion contexts in which the L2 is spoken in the surrounding communities, and European CLIL, in which the L2 is a foreign language not used or spoken in the surrounding environment. Our focus here is on the latter, with English being the foreign language.

In their analysis of CLIL students' lexicogrammar when participating in CLIL classroom discussions, Whittaker and Llinares (2009) found that the students used different process types (material, relational, mental, etc...) depending on the academic subject or discipline. In their study the students mainly used material processes (action verbs) in geography while, in history, relational processes (verbs of being) increased. In their own words: "this result represents the way the Geography topic was constructed around natural events occurring and causing effects, whereas that of History was built around a description of civilizations at a particular moment in the past, and human activities then and now" (Whittaker & Llinares 2009: 230). The students' language also matched the prompt and expectations of the specific disciplines in their use of circumstances-mainly place and time. Interestingly, in another study comparing CLIL students' written and oral performance following the same prompt, it was found that the students used a higher proportion of possessive relational processes in the discussion, showing more personal involvement than in the compositions (Llinares, Dafouz & Whittaker 2007). This studies also showed that the teachers skillfully elicited the necessary language from the students without providing them with the right answer.

It is important not to forget that the CLIL classroom is an academic context and, in order for students to succeed, they need to master the appropriate academic language of the discipline. One key aspect of mastering the academic language of the subjects being studied is to be able to use, and produce, the genres through which knowledge is construed. The potential for the type of genre pedagogy described in the previous section for CLIL contexts is only beginning to be explored, but see Llinares, Morton and Whittaker (2012). Morton (2010) uses CLIL classroom data to show how already existing effective classroom practices could be enhanced by adopting aspects of a genre-based pedagogy. He argues that such a pedagogy in CLIL could help students to structure their linguistic output, and inform the processes of joint construction of knowledge and teacher feedback during classroom interaction.

Another area of interest in CLIL is related to the role of interactional scaffolding, defined by Gibbons (2006: 175) as "an outward manifestation of mediation in action, and its realization in practice". In their analysis of scaffolding in whole class discussions in CLIL classes, Llinares and Whittaker (2009) analysed the strategies used by CLIL teachers in order to scaffold the students' participation. One of the features observed was the teachers' use of 'message abundancy' (Gibbons 2006), where the teacher reformulates a question to make sure it is understood, as exemplified in extract 3 below:

Extract 3:

T: What do we have about the immediate effects? So there are lots of things happening around, ok? So, in the everyday life how did it affect?

In this extract, the teacher reformulates the nominal group in the question into two clauses, topicalising the cause in the first clause ("So there are lots of things happening around") and asking about the consequences in the second one.

Systemic functional linguistics also offers a rich perspective on the issue of instructional feedback. As we saw in section 1.3, feedback is seen as having a crucial role in interactionist SLA studies of classroom interaction which highlight 'focus on form'. Using the SFL model, Mohan and Beckett (2003) introduce the notion of 'functional recast', which provides new insight and complements the focus on form approach (e.g. Lyster 2007) and is particularly relevant for CLIL. In this study, Mohan and Beckett show how teachers' recasts can be used to upgrade or 'edit' students' output towards the more academically-acceptable language forms needed to express content-relevant meanings. The following example from Llinares et al (2012) exemplifies this type of recast:

Extract 4

S: Eh, yes because there was a lot of people in the countryside working and they have no place for everybody so they went to the cities and they went there.
T: … so that is the, em, the reason of the rebirth of cities.

Several studies within a broad systemic functional perspective have focused on the role of activity type in CLIL classes. We have already mentioned the study on young learners' initiated interactions in 'Show and Tell sessions' (Llinares 2007). This study also revealed that in these sessions the students used a wider variety of communicative functions compared to other activities. Two other activities have been compared in a number of studies on CLIL classrooms: whole-class discussions and individual interviews.

In their analysis of process types in secondary CLIL classrooms, Whittaker and Llinares (2009) found that the students used more mental processes (verbs of feeling, thinking, etc…) when they participated in individual interviews than in whole-class discussions on the same topic and following the same prompt. In addition, the students seemed to respond more fluently to questions that relate the topic to the students' personal experience (Llinares & Whittaker 2009: 81):

Individual interviews like these which invite more personal interaction should, if possible, be more frequent in the CLIL class: they motivate production of language and thus increase learning. This method of scaffolding helps students to understand something totally outside their experience, by comparing the new, or the unknown, with their personal experience, the known.

Another linguistic feature that was compared in whole-class discussions and interviews was the students' use of clause complexes. Paratactic extension was twice as frequent in the interviews as in the class discussions in the study carried out by Whittaker and Llinares (2009). The fact that, in the interviews, the students were allowed and encouraged to talk for as long as they wanted to might have led them to produce longer turns, whereas in class-discussions turns were controlled by the teacher and students' turns were more restricted to independent clauses.

Another study that compared class discussions and interviews is Llinares and Morton's (2010) analysis of explanations in different activities that constitute different participation frameworks. By combining a systemic-functional and a conversation analysis approach to the analysis of the data, results showed that the academic function of explanation was produced differently in the two contexts. In line with the studies reported above, in the interviews, CLIL students produced longer explanations andused a wider range of lexico-grammatical features. The study thus provided evidence that CLIL students' display of content and language knowledge in terms of register and genre features is shaped by the situated practices in which they participate.

The chances for CLIL students to be exposed to different activities which allow them to adopt different roles is key if we expect them to acquire full communicative competence that they can transfer to other situational contexts outside the classroom. Following Dalton-Puffer (2009: 212): "...CLIL also needs to start considering a further issue: namely whether teaching arrangements in CLIL lessons could perhaps be designed in such a way that they provide for a wider array of (assumed or played) roles". A systemic functional analysis of CLIL students' language in different activities can provide insights into ways in which the CLIL classroom can help students learn not only the genre and register features necessary to convey subject specific meanings, but also other interpersonal language features both related to the specific content and to participating socially in the classroom.

6   Combining 'social' approaches to interaction in CLIL: a necessary step towards establishing theoretical and methodological foundations

The two broad approaches to the 'social' in considering CLIL classroom discourse and interaction may be seen by some researchers as incompatible with each other. As mentioned in section 1.2, CA researchers such as Markee or Hauser may be resistant to the introduction of 'exogenous theory' in CA for SLA studies. However, a more open-handed approach would see the benefits of combining perspectives. This would be the approach advocated by Rampton et al. (2002), who argue that greater understandings of classroom discourse can be gleaned by combining approaches such as SFL and CA, rather than by using them in isolation. Young (2009) takes a similar approach, in which he proposes that CA and SFL can be combined with work such as Goffman's (1981) on participation frameworks in investigating discursive practices in L2 classrooms.

Such a combination of theoretical frameworks would go hand in hand with the strengthening of research within what Dalton-Puffer and Smit describe as the 'micro-process' approach to CLIL research (2007: 12-13). It would also contribute to a much-needed more integrative approach to content pedagogy and language learning, as called for by Leung (2005) in bilingual education in general. Within the CLIL field, Dalton-Puffer, Nikula and Smit (2010) argue that a challenge for CLIL is to move towards a 'fusional' perspective on content and language rather than a combinatorial one. They suggest that a suitable theoretical base for such a move is the use of approaches "that emphasize the social, discursive and contextually situated nature of learning" (p. 289). This is exactly the approach that has been advocated in this chapter, and we believe that a combination of such 'social' approaches is necessary to confront the complexity of CLIL classroom communities, where subject pedagogies, L2 use, interaction and learning opportunites are so intimately intertwined. Analysing what is going on in the actual setting where learning takes place is key in order to be able to obtain results that can inform CLIL practitioners and open up new lines of research.

Such new lines of research would necessarily combine both theoretical and methodological aspects of the social approaches described in this chapter. For example, a lexico-grammatical approach to data in which linguistic features can be quantified in line with the methodology used in corpus linguistics could be combined with a more qualitative CA-based approach. This would enable us to examine how CLIL students use these language items along with other modes in moment-by-moment interaction. One example of a step in this direction is Llinares and Morton's (2010) study in which qualitative analysis was combined with a systemic functional analysis of CLIL students' lexicogrammar used in the specific history genre of explanation (see Coffin 2006). This approach enabled them to relate the students' different language production to two different interactional situations they were participating in: class discussions and interviews.

Another, perhaps more challenging, line of research would be the combination of 'focus on form' with 'functional' SFL approaches. Llinares, Morton and Whittaker (2012) suggest integrating Lyster's (2007) model of corrective recasts with Mohan and Beckett's (2003) model of functional recasts. That is, the linguistic features focused on in either a proactive or reactive approach could be linked to the registers and genres of the subjects being studied. Another possible link is with Markee's (2008) idea of learning object tracking (LOT), as described in section 1.2. The 'objects' in Markee's paper are rather loosely described, which perhaps meets the purposes of that study. However, in CLIL, it would be possible to use SFL to identify more precise register and genre-related learning objects, which could then be tracked and their incorporation explored using the second of Markee's concepts, learning process tracking (LPT).

7 Conclusion

In this chapter we have argued that research on language use and interaction in CLIL classrooms needs to be informed by theoretical approaches that consider the social context as having a key role in students' learning process. Our main focus has been on the constraints and affordances of the CLIL classroom for L2 development. The examples of work in the two 'social' traditions, as well as work in the more mainstream interactionist tradition in SLA, individually provide rich insights into what happens in classrooms when an L2 is used for academic content learning. However, combining these perspectives, if theoretical and methodological problems can be overcome, would allow for even greater insights. Whatever the practical issues or specific research questions addressed, we believe that combining the resources of these two 'social' approaches to classroom discourse and interaction in CLIL can provide a more complete picture of the challenges and opportunities of content and language learning in CLIL contexts than that which each on its own can provide. We do not only need a 'fusional' perspective on content and language in CLIL classrooms, but a fusional and eclectic approach to investigating what goes on inside them, and its possible consequences for content and language learning.

References

Aston, G. (1993) Notes on the interlanguage of comity. In Kasper, G. & Blum-Kulka, S. (eds) *Interlanguage Pragmatics*, Oxford: Oxford University Press.

Block, D. (2003) *The Social Turn in Second Language Acquisition*, Edinburgh: Edinburgh University Press.

Block, D. (2007) The rise of identity in SLA research, post Firth and Wagner (1997), *The Modern Language Journal*, *91*, 863-876.

Christie, F. (2002) *Classroom Discourse Analysis: A Functional Perspective*, London: Continuum.

Coffin, C. (2006) Learning the language of school history: The role of linguistics in mapping the writing demands of the secondary school curriculum, *Journal of Curriculum Studies*, *38*(4), 413-429.

Dalton-Puffer, C. (2007) *Discourse in Content and Language Integrated Learning (CLIL) Classrooms*, Amsterdam, Philadelphia: John Benjamins.

Dalton-Puffer, C. (2009) Communicative competence and the CLIL lesson. In Ruiz de Zarobe, Y. & Jiménez Catalán, R.M. (eds) *Content and Language Integrated Learning: Evidence from research in Europe* (pp. 197-214), Bristol: Multilingual Matters.

Dalton-Puffer, C., Nikula, T., & Smit, U. (2010) Language use and language learning in CLIL: Current findings and contentious issues. In Dalton-Puffer, C., Nikula, T. & Smit, U. (eds) *Language Use and Language Learning in CLIL Classrooms* (pp. 279-91), Amsterdam; Philadelphia: John Benjamins.

Dalton-Puffer, C., Nikula, T., & Smit, U. (2010) *Language Use and Language Learning in CLIL Classrooms*, Amsterdam, Philadelphia: John Benjamins.

Dalton-Puffer, C., & Smit, U. (2007) Introduction. In Dalton-Puffer, C. & Smit, U. (eds) *Empirical perspectives on CLIL classroom discourse* (pp. 7-23), Frankfurt/Vienna: Peter Lang.

Evnitskaya, N., & Morton, T. (2011) Knowledge construction, meaning-making and interaction in CLIL science classroom communities of practice, *Language and Education*, *25*(2), 109-127.

Firth, A., & Wagner, J. (1997) On discourse, communication, and (some) fundamental concepts in SLA research, *The Modern Language Journal*, *81*(3), 285-300.

Gass, S. M. (1997) *Input, Interaction, and the Second Language Learner*, Mahwah, NJ: Lawrence Erlbaum.

Gass, S. M., & Mackey, A. (2006) Input, interaction and output: An overview, *AILA review*, *19*(1), 3–17.

Gibbons, P. (2002) *Scaffolding Language, Scaffolding Learning: Teaching Second Language Learners in the Mainstream Classroom*, Portsmouth, NH: Heinemann.

Gibbons, P. (2006) *Bridging Discourses in the ESL Classroom: Students, Teachers and Researchers*, London: Continuum.

Goffman, E. (1981) *Forms of talk*, Philadelphia: University of Pennsylvania Press.

Graddol, D. (2006) *English Next*. London: British Council.

Hall, J. K. (1995) "Aw, Man Where You Goin'?": Classroom interaction and the development of L2 interactional competence, Issues in Applied Linguistics, 6(2), 37-62.

Hall, J. K., Hellermann, J., & Pekarek Doehler, S. (2011) *L2 Interactional Competence and Development*, Bristol: Multilingual Matters.

Halliday, M. A. K. (1993) Towards a language-based theory of learning, *Linguistics and Education*, *5*(2), 93-116.

Halliday, M. A. K., & Hasan, R. (1989) *Language, Context, and Text: Aspects of Language in a Social-Semiotic Perspective,* Oxford: Oxford University Press.

Halliday, M. A. K., McIntosh, A., & Strevens, P. (1964) *The Linguistic Sciences and Language Teaching*, London: Longman.

Hauser, E. (2011) On the danger of exogenous theory in CA-for-SLA: A response to Hellermann and Cole (2009), *Applied Linguistics*. doi:10.1093/applin/amr015

Hellerman, J. (2008) *Social Actions for Classroom Language Learning*, Clevedon, UK: Multilingual Matters.

Hougaard, G. R. (2009) Legitimate peripheral participation as a framework for conversation analytic work in second language learning, *Forum:Qualitative Social Research*, *10*(2). Retrieved 4 July 2011 from http://www.qualitative-research.net/index.php/fqs/article/viewArticle/1280

Kasper, G. (2009) Locating cognition in second language interaction and learning: Inside the skull or in public view?, *IRAL - International Review of Applied Linguistics in Language Teaching*, *47*(1), 11-36.

Koole, T. (2010) Displays of epistemic access: Student responses to teacher explanations, *Research on Language & Social Interaction*, *43*(2), 183-209.

Kupetz, M. (2011) Multimodal resources in students' explanations in CLIL interaction, *Novitas ROYAL*, *5*(1), 121-142.

Lave, J. (1988) *Cognition in Practice: Mind, Mathematics, and Culture in Everyday Life*, Cambridge: Cambridge University Press.

Lave, J., & Wenger, E. (1991) *Situated Learning: Legitimate Peripheral Participation,* Cambridge: Cambridge University Press.

Lasagabaster, D., & Sierra, J. M. (2010) Immersion and CLIL in English: More differences than similarities, *ELT Journal*, *64*(4), 367-375.

Leung, C. (2005) Language and content in bilingual education, *Linguistics and Education*, *16*(2), 238-252.

Llinares, A. (2007) Classroom bilingualism at an early age: Towards a more natural EFL context. In Pérez Vidal, C. et al. (eds), *A Portrait of the Young in Multilingual Spain* (pp. 185-199), Bristol: Multilingual Matters.

Llinares, A., Dafouz, E., & Whittaker, R. (2007) A linguistic analysis of compositions written by Spanish learners of social sciences in CLIL contexts. In Wolff, D. & Marsh, D. (eds), *Diverse contexts, Converging goals. Content and Language Integrated Learning in Europe* (pp. 227–236). Frankfurt: Peter Lang.

Llinares, A., & Morton, T. (2010) Historical explanations as situated practice in content and language integrated learning, *Classroom Discourse*, *1*(1), 46-65.

Llinares, A., Morton, T., & Whittaker, R. (2012) *The Roles of Language in CLIL*, Cambridge: Cambridge University Press.

Llinares, A., & Whittaker, R. (2009) Teaching and learning history in secondary CLIL classrooms: From speaking to writing. In Dafouz, E. & Guerrini, M. (eds) *CLIL across educational levels: Experiences from Primary, Secondary and Tertiary Contexts.* (pp. 73-89), London/Madrid: Richmond /Santillana.

Long, M. H. (1981) Input, interaction, and second - language acquisition, *Annals of the New York Academy of Sciences*, *379* (1), 259-278.

Long, M. H. (1996) The role of the linguistic environment in second language acquisition, *Handbook of Second Language Acquisition* (pp. 413-468), San Diego: Academic Press.

Lyster, R. (2007) *Learning and Teaching Languages through Content: A Counterbalanced Approach*, Amsterdam, Philadelphia: John Benjamins.

Macbeth, D. (2011) Understanding understanding as an instructional matter, *Journal of Pragmatics*, *43*(2), 438-451.

Markee, N. (2008) Toward a learning behavior tracking methodology for CA-for-SLA, *Applied Linguistics*, *29*(3), 404 -427.

Martin, J. R. (1993) A contextual theory of language. In Cope, B. & Kalantzis, M. (eds) *The Powers of Literacy- A Genre Approach to Teaching Writing* (pp. 116-36), Pittsburgh: University of Pittsburgh Press.

Martin, J. R. (1999) Mentoring semogenesis. In Christie, F. (ed) *Pedagogy and the Shaping of Consciousness.* (pp. 123–55), London and New York: Cassell.

Martin, J. R. (2009) Genre and language learning: A social semiotic perspective, *Linguistics and Education, 20*(1), 10-21.

Martin, J. R., & Rose, D. (2003) *Working with Discourse: Meaning beyond the Clause*, London: Continuum.

Martin, J. R., & Rose, D. (2008) *Genre Relations: Mapping Culture*, London: Equinox.

Matthiessen, C. M. I. M., Teruya, K., & Lam, M. (2010) *Key Terms in Systemic Functional Linguistics*, London: Continuum.

Mohan, B., & Beckett, G. H. (2003) A functional approach to research on content-based language learning: Recasts in causal explanations, *The Modern Language Journal, 87*(3), 421-432.

Mondada, L., & Pekarek Doehler, S. P. (2004) Second language acquisition as situated practice: Task accomplishment in the French second language classroom, *The Modern Language Journal, 88*(4), 501-518.

Morton, T. (2010) Using a genre-based approach to integrating content and language in CLIL: The example of secondary history. In Dalton-Puffer, C., Nikula, T. & Smit, U. (eds) *Language Use and Language Learning in CLIL Classrooms*, Amsterdam: John Benjamins.

Musumeci, D. (1996) Teacher-learner negotiation in content-based instruction: Communication at cross-purposes?, *Applied Linguistics, 17*(3), 286-325.

Nassaji, H., & Wells, G. (2000) What's the use of "triadic dialogue"?: An investigation of teacher-student interaction, *Applied Linguistics, 21*(3), 376-406.

Nikula, T. (2007) The IRF pattern and space for interaction: Comparing CLIL and EFL classrooms. In Dalton-Puffer, C. & Smit, U. (eds) *Empirical Perspectives on CLIL Classroom Discourse - CLIL: empirische Untersuchungen zum Unterrichtsdiskurs* (pp. 179-204), Frankfurt: Peter Lang.

Nikula, T. (2010) Effects of CLIL on a teacher's classroom language use. In Dalton-Puffer, C., Nikula, T. & Smit, U. (eds) *Language Use and Language Learning in CLIL Classrooms* (pp. 105-123), Amsterdam: John Benjamins.

Pekarek Doehler, S. (2010) Conceptual changes and methodological challenges: on language, learning and documenting learning in conversation analytic SLA research. In Seedhouse, P., Walsh, S. & Jenks, C. (eds) *Conceptualising Learning in Applied Linguistics* (pp. 105-126), Basingstoke: Palgrave MacMillan.

Pekarek Doehler, S., & Ziegler, G. (2007) Doing language, doing science and the sequential organization of the immersion classroom. In Hua, Z., Seedhouse, P., Wei, L. & Cook, V. (eds) *Language Learning and Teaching as Social Inter-action,* Basingstoke: Palgrave MacMillan.

Pica, T. (2002) Subject-matter content: How does it assist the interactional and linguistic needs of classroom language learners?, *The Modern Language Journal, 86*(1), 1-19.

Rampton, B. (1987) Stylistic variability and not speaking "normal" English: Some post-Labovian approaches and their implications for the study of interlanguage. In Ellis, R. (ed) *Second language acquisition in context* (pp. 47–58), Englewood Cliffs, NJ: Prentice Hall.

Rampton, B., Roberts, C., Leung, C., & Harris, R. (2002) Methodology in the analysis of classroom discourse, *Applied Linguistics, 23*(3), 373 - 392.

Schleppegrell, M. J. (2002) Challenges of the science register for ESL students: Errors and meaning-making. In Schleppegrell, M.J. & Colombi, C. (eds) *Developing Advanced Literacy in First and Second Languages: Meaning with Power* (pp. 119–142), Mahwah, NJ: Lawrence Erlbaum Associates

Schleppegrell, M. J. (2004) *The Language of Schooling: A Functional Linguistics Perspective*, Mahwah, NJ, London: Lawrence Erlbaum.

Sfard, A. (1998) On two metaphors for learning and the dangers of choosing just one, *Educational Researcher, 27*(2), 4 -13.

Sinclair, J. M., & Coulthard, R. M. (1975) *Towards an Analysis of Discourse: The Language of Teachers and Pupils*, London: Oxford University Press.

Swain, M. (1985) Communicative competence: Some roles of comprehensible input and comprehensible output in its development. In Gass, S. & Madden, C. (eds) *Input in Second Language Acquisition* (pp. 235-253), New York: Newbury House.

Swain, M. (1995) Three functions of output in second language learning. In Cook, G. & Seidlhofer, B. (eds) *Principle and Practice in Applied Linguistics: Studies in Honour of HG Widdowson* (pp. 125–144), Oxford: Oxford University Press.

Trosset, C. S. (1986) The social identity of Welsh learners, *Language in Society, 15*(2), 165-191.

Wells, G. (1999) *Dialogic Inquiry: Towards a Socio-cultural Practice and Theory of Education*, Cambridge: Cambridge University Press.

Wells, G. (2007) The mediating role of discoursing in activity, *Mind, Culture, and Activity, 14*(3), 160-177.

Wenger, E. (1998) *Communities of Practice: Learning, Meaning and Identity*, Cambridge: Cambridge University Press.

Whittaker, R., & Llinares, A. (2009) CLIL in social science classrooms: analysis of spoken and written productions. In Ruiz de Zarobe, Y. & Jiménez Catalán, R.M. (eds) *Content and Language Integrated Learning: Evidence from research in Europe* (pp. 215-234), Bristol: Multilingual Matters.

Young, R. F. (2009) *Discursive Practice in Language Learning and Teaching*, Chichester: Wiley-Blackwell.

On the role of peer discussions in the learning of subject-specific language use in CLIL[1]

Tarja Nikula (University of Jyväskylä)

Content and language integrated learning (CLIL) contexts, i.e. classrooms where the medium of instruction is a foreign language, have become increasingly popular throughout Europe. Earlier research on CLIL classroom discourse has mainly explored teacher-fronted situations and the effect of teacher-student interaction on target language competence, with less attention to subject-specific aspects of language learning and use. Talk among peers and its role in language and subject learning has not been researched much, either. This paper draws on a discourse-pragmatic framework and focuses on Finnish students' peer discussions during group-work activities in CLIL history lessons conducted in English. The purpose is to explore students' joint processes of meaning-making and the extent to which their discursive practices reveal awareness of subject-specific language use. The focus is thus on the very notion of subject and language integration and how student co-construct an understanding of a subject-specific activity and the type of language it requires. The findings show that the intertwined nature of language and content knowledge often becomes salient in students' group-work activities, especially in phases that involve meaning negotiations. It will also be argued that a close look at situations that require joint meaning-making by the students can provide some useful insights for CLIL pedagogical practice as regards raising students' awareness of subject- and genre-specific language use.

1 Introduction

Language learners' discourse, the theme of this volume, is approached in this chapter from the viewpoint of content and language integrated learning, known as CLIL (e.g. Coyle, Hood & Marsh 2010). The context is Finland, with data from secondary level history classes taught in English. More specifically, this chapter explores learner discourse in a hitherto underexplored context: group-work situations where students are involved in peer discussions without the presence of the teacher. While reaching a research-based understanding of the dynamics of teacher-student interaction in CLIL settings continues to be important for the whole CLIL enterprise and a goal worth pursuing further, it is also worthwhile to direct an analytical gaze at group-work situations and at learners' joint processes of negotiation and interaction, because we know less about the value of these contexts for learning.

What further characterizes this chapter is that rather than focusing on how students learn or how well they master the target language as a system (i.e. paying attention to the correctness of formal aspects of language), the purpose is to explore what students' group-work interaction reveals about content and language *integration*, a crucial concern in CLIL given its dual and overlapping goals. In so doing, it seeks to investigate students' joint processes of meaning making and the extent to which their discursive practices reveal any orientation to subject-specific language use. The focus is thus on the very notion of subject and language integration, how students co-construct understanding of a subject-specific activity, and the type of language this requires.

Theoretically, the study is based on a discourse-pragmatic orientation to interaction which emphasizes both the necessity of situated exploration of the details of talk and attention to the social-interpersonal dimensions inherent in any communicative encounter (for more details, see Nikula 2005, 2008). As regards the approach to learning, the study draws on socio-constructivist understandings of learning, according to which it is useful to see learning as social accomplishment and meaning making as a joint construction rather than a process undertaken solely by individuals (e.g. Lantolf & Poehner 2008).

2 Language and content integration

Content and language integrated learning (CLIL) is an educational approach that aims at the simultaneous learning of language and subject; it has steadily gained ground in Europe especially since the 1990s (for overview, see Dalton-Puffer, Nikula & Smit 2010b). Research on CLIL is also flourishing, and we now know a great deal both about the benefits of CLIL and about areas needing further development (e.g. Ruiz de Zarobe & Jiménez Catalan 2009, Coyle, Hood & Marsh 2010, Dalton-Puffer, Nikula & Smit 2010a). Learning outcomes, especially as regards target language learning, have been extensively explored, and there is also a growing number of studies that have investigated various aspects of CLIL classroom discourse (e.g. contributions in Dalton-Puffer and Smit 2007).

Recently, researchers have also highlighted the need to conceptualize language learning and competence in CLIL in ways that take better into account the notion of integration, i.e. that the objective in CLIL is for learners to acquire subject-specific language in the target language rather than 'generic' foreign language knowledge. For example, Gajo (2007: 564) argues that in CLIL research today, "a firm basis of reflection on the very concept of integration is missing". Accordingly, Dalton-Puffer et al. (2010c: 288-289) suggest that the fusion of language and content deserves more research attention than has until now been the case; they suggest that tackling the question of integration to the full will probably also require a transdisciplinary research construct. In a similar vein, Coyle (2007: 548) argues for the need for "critical analysis and discourse of emergent CLIL theoretical principles at both macro and micro levels" that would account for the essence of CLIL, i.e. that it combines learning to use language and using language to learn.

Focusing on what language and content integration in essence means is important because it has implications for different levels of CLIL practice. For example, in terms of pedagogy, teachers need to consider how instruction can maximally support the successful learning of language and content. The same applies to CLIL materials development. In terms of assessment, there is plenty of scope for research to determine the intertwined nature of content and language and how to take this duality into account when evaluating student performance (cf. Coetzee-Lachmann 2007).

When writing about bilingual education, Leung (2005: 239) highlights the importance of "close-up knowledge" based on classroom research by arguing that "claims for or against bilingual education of any form ring hollow when there is not a clear sense of what happens inside the classroom". In this spirit, this chapter brings the question of content and language integration to the level of classroom discourse because it is at the concrete level of classroom activities and practices that integration is brought into being by teachers and students.

That language has an important role in learning any school subject is not a novel idea; it has been investigated extensively in earlier research. Lemke's (1990) book on the role of language in science education is a pioneering work that has influenced the thinking of many researchers. Researchers working within the systemic functional paradigm have been particularly active in exploring the language of school subjects and language use in classrooms (e.g. Christie 2002, Schleppegrell 2004, Coffin 2006). Mortimer and Scott (2003), for their part, adopt a socioculturally and dialogically oriented approach to investigate meaning making in secondary school science classrooms.

While the intertwined nature of language and content concerns all learners, the simultaneous challenge of learning them both is highlighted when instruction takes place through languages other than the learners' native language. Most of the research referred to above on subject-specific language use and learning has dealt with participants who are operating in classrooms in their L1. However, the popularity of immersion education and various forms of bilingual education (see e.g. Fortune & Tedick 2008, García 2009) and the fact that classrooms all over the world today, especially in urban contexts, are becoming increasingly multilingual (Creese & Martin 2003) make it necessary to consider the effects that operating in languages other than L1 has on learning subject-specific literacies. As regards CLIL, its rapid spread in Europe during the last couple of decades has directed researchers' attention to questions of subject-specific speaking and writing. For example, a relevant study from the perspective of this paper, which focuses on history classrooms, is the study by Llinares and Whittaker (2010 which shows that learning the appropriate language of history in speaking and writing poses problems for both CLIL students and for those studying in their L1. Järvinen (2010) comes to similar conclusions when investigating Finnish lower secondary learners' written essays on historical subjects. Lim Falk's (2008) study on science classrooms shows that CLIL students taught through English used less relevant subject-based language in speech and writing than control students taught in Swedish. Other CLIL research specifically focusing on subject-specific competence includes Coetzee-Lachmann's (2007) study on the assessment of subject-specific task performance in geography and Nikula's (2010) case study on the ways in which a biology teacher makes subject-specific language salient in his classroom talk when teaching biology in Finnish and, during CLIL lessons, in English.

Earlier research has thus made clear the importance of studying the realisations and implications of content and language integration. As pointed out above, this chapter addresses this question from the perspective of secondary level CLIL history classrooms, with particular attention to what students' peer discussions in group-work situations reveal about subject-specific language use.

3 Data and analytic approach

The data for the paper derive from a larger set of CLIL classroom recordings made in secondary schools in Finland. The data under scrutiny here are from 7th grade history lessons with a class of 14 students aged 13. The students are part of a group which receives extensive CLIL, with all other subjects apart from Finnish being instructed through English. Most of the students have had all the six years of their elementary education from grades 1 to 6 in Finnish, with the exception of one boy who is a native speaker of English.

In the history lessons studied in this chapter, students are working in pairs or small groups, with the teacher (a native speaker of English) circling round the classroom, providing assistance when groups need it but otherwise leaving responsibility for the work to the learners. There are 4 groups altogether, each with a tape recorder on the table. However, this paper is based on audio recordings of only three groups because the contribution of one of the groups was unavailable due to technical problems in the recording. There are two 90-minute sessions from each of the groups, recorded on consecutive days, i.e. altogether 9 hours of recorded group-work data.

The topics dealt with in the group-work sessions concern the Industrial Revolution and the American Civil War. More specifically, the class has been told by the teacher to discuss and work through the causes and consequences of the Industrial Revolution and the American Civil War, and through that discussion both to come to an overall understanding of 'the big picture' of these phenomena and to pick out the most important aspects of the two events, 'the nutshell', the issues presented concisely. Students have prepared for the group-work sessions partly during previous lessons, when their teacher has led them through the topic areas, partly through their homework. The materials they are using when working in the classroom include handouts and reference books in English, dictionaries, and history textbooks in Finnish, which they are using (as in most other CLIL subjects in the school) as support material to give them an idea of how the content area is handled in Finnish. They may have used the internet when doing their homework but computers are not available in the classroom.

The working language during the group work is English and students keep to it almost all the time; very little Finnish is used. This may be due to the teacher as well as one of the students in the class being native speakers of English. However, it is notable that even in groups where everyone has Finnish as their L1, the use of English prevails.

As pointed out above, the analysis aims at exploring instances where subject-specific language becomes an issue, whether explicitly or implicitly. However, defining subject-specific language is not an easy task. Firstly, there are certain features of language use that belong to academic and educational contexts in general rather than being confined to particular subjects. According to Dalton-Puffer (2007:128), typical academic language functions include, for example, analysing, defining, explaining, hypothesising, narrating; even though such functions also exist in everyday talk, their high frequency and co-occurrence are typical of educational and academic contexts. Each school subject and disciplinary area also tends to have its own special terminology. History, the focus in this chapter, may not be as rich in special terminology as, say, biology or chemistry, but it does have its agreed-upon labels and phrases for given phenomena and periods in time (e.g. the Industrial Revolution in the present data). School subjects also differ from one another in terms of the discourse patterns through which knowledge gets constructed. Typical discourse patterns in history include narratives, causal explanations, recording, explaining and arguing (e.g. Schleppegrell, Achugar & Oteíza 2004, Coffin 2006, Llinares & Morton 2010).

In this study, the analysis is informed by the points above in that the search for instances of talk that reflect students' awareness of subject-specific language is guided, firstly, by any explicit references the participants may make to how things are said or done in history, as these are valuable indicators of participants' perceptions. Furthermore, subject-specific terms and expressions and subject-specific discourse patterns and language functions are considered to be important indeces of language use typical of history. In addition, as an overarching frame, instances of subject-specific talk will in this study be approached as an interactional phenomenon rather than in isolation, with attention to how the participants jointly construct and negotiate their understanding of subject-specific use of language and/or ways of constructing knowledge. As Llinares and Morton (2010:47) argue, it is important to realize that subject-specific language and knowledge also involve interactional competence.

4 Findings

Before focusing on how the students talk about historical events during their peer discussions, a few words are in order about the group-work situations generally. The groups under observation here concentrate on their given tasks remarkably well, and there is very little off-record talk. In essence, then, almost everything they say during the group-work situations can be regarded as constructing their understanding of the topics they were given, the causes and consequences of the Industrial Revolution and of the American Civil War. However, as already stated above, attention will be focused on those instances of talk that seem to reflect their awareness of the subject of history requiring particular types of language use, indicated either by explicit reference to matters of terminology or by negotiations over relevant ways of constructing and/or displaying their knowledge of history.

4.1 Explicit references to history

Explicit references to history by the students are extremely rare during the peer discussions studied. In all the group sessions analysed, the word 'history' is only used ten times by the students. These few occurrences, however, reveal in an interesting way students' awareness of different subjects requiring specific types of talk. Furthermore, all the explicit references to history seem to relate to a certain type of policing of the group task by the students, because what seems to be the issue in both extracts, 1 and 2, below is one of the participants wishing to stop what s/he perceives as either a distraction or a digression from history related talk, prompting the group to 'talk about' or 'concentrate on' history.

In Extract 1 Laura and Minna, who are working in their group with two boys, are discussing the Industrial Revolution when Minna feels distracted by Richard, a boy in another group who is talking in a loud voice about something unrelated to the task at hand. Minna makes the distraction explicit in line 7, but when she receives no reaction from Richard, she catches his attention by calling his name in line 9 (none of the names in the transcripts are participants' real names). In lines 11-16 Minna demands that Richard stops what he is doing and concentrates on history because *this is history lesson.* Although the episode as a whole has probably more to do with playful teasing between teenage girls and boys than subject-specific language use, it suggests that Laura and Minna are oriented to subject-specific talk and have a clear understanding of the kind of behaviour expected in history classrooms – no doubt a result of years of socialisation into classroom cultures.

Extract 1 (Group 3)

1	Laura	okay new source of energy there's coal
2	Minna	new sources of energy (.) coal (.) steel (1.5) new ways of
3		making (.) iron
4	Laura	no new ways of- new ways of making iron into steel that's like
5		a new-
6		((unclear talk for 14 seconds))
7	Minna	excuse me↑ you're distracting me
8		((a pause for 12 seconds, talk in the background))
9	Minna	Richard Jenkins
10	Richard	yeah↑
11	Minna	see that worked (.) can you stop talking about this and
12		concentrate on history
13	Laura	((inaudible))
14	Minna	no: no no (.) this is history lesson (.) is history
15		(3.1)
16	Minna	okay that's history (1.7) you're distracting

Extract 2 from the early stages of one group's work similarly shows awareness that school work involves shifts between everyday and subject-specific language. Matti first seems to make a move from commenting on the recording equipment (lines 1-2) to talking about history (lines 4-7), with Ville taking up the suggestion (lines 9-10). However, when Matti, from line 12 onwards, starts using an artificial, high-pitched voice and seems to be pretending to be assuming the role of the teacher when praising Ville's performance in the other group, it becomes obvious that he is play-acting and having fun – probably for the sake of the researchers, who he knows will later listen to the recordings. His skilful language performance shows his awareness of characteristics of the institutional talk of school and Ville's reactions (lines 16, 30, 33) show that he is trying to stop Matti's roleplaying as it is out of line with what they have been instructed to do.

Extract 2 (Group 1)

1	Matti	((laughter)) look at this (.) wow (1.0) it's a sony
2		((inaudible))
3	Ville	(xxx)=
4	Matti	=okay (.) let's talk about history (2.4) let's talk about history
5		and the paper thing (xx)
6		(4.0)
7	Matti	okay what have you guys been doing with your other group Ville↑
8		(1.6)
9	Ville	a- well something about industrial revolution and we read
10		something about (.) north american
11		(1.4)
12	Matti	((in an altered, high-pitched voice)) good Ville (.) what else has
13		your group been doing because mister (teacher's name) said your
14		group was the best and now I'm with you so we must be the best
15		((laughter)) (5.2)
16	Ville	don't don't don't
		[… 13 lines of transcript of Matti continuing his playacting deleted]
30	Ville	don't play any roles
31	Matti	((speaking in an altered, high-pitched voice)) what roles am I
32		playing↑ like ridge forrester in the bold and the beautiful↑ no.
33	Ville	you are ruining our group work

The extracts above serve to illustrate that when history is explicitly mentioned by the students, reference is usually being made to context-specific behaviour in general – the need to keep to the task and topic of group talk and to talk about history – rather than to subject-specific language as such. However, as illustrated in the following sections, there are other ways in which the language of history is made salient.

4.2   Awareness of subject-specific terms and concepts

One of the groups has only two participants, Matti and Ville, two boys who seem to be at slightly different levels in terms of their fluency in English. In this group in particular there are several instances of the boys negotiating and coming to an agreement about terms and concepts. Some of the terms are more specific to history than others but in every case the question is about expressions that are more typical of formal, academic registers than of everyday spoken language. In other words, there is a clear sense in the extracts below of Ville in particular being aware of the existence of a subject-specific language repertoire that is rather formal in style, and of their need to work towards acquiring it. In other words, even though in CLIL classrooms the role of the teacher is often crucial in providing students with opportunities to come to an understanding of concepts, as shown for example by Alanen et al. (2008), in peer discussions a more knowledgeable classmate may also effectively support the process of advancing towards subject-specific language use.

Extract 3 shows Ville and Matti discussing the American Civil War. Line 3 already gives a hint of Ville attuning to the formal register of the school subject when he repeats, laughingly, Matti's formulation *more everything;* the laughter indexes the expression as somehow problematic, in this case probably as too colloquial. In line 8 Ville more explicitly orients to appropriacy of expression when he recasts Matti's word *people* as *population,* a more technical and formal word. Matti acknowledges the recast by immediately repeating it (line 9) before continuing with his account. There is thus a sense of the boys, through joint meaning negotiation, gradually moving towards a more formal register of academic genres.

Extract 3 (Group 1)

1	Ville	okay (2.7) so what was the reason why northern union won
2	Matti	they had more people and more everything
3	Ville	((laughing)) more everything
4	Matti	they had more-
5	Ville	more guns
6	Matti	they had more trains they had more factories they had more
7		fields they had more production they had more people
8	Ville	population
9	Matti	or population (.) they even had (x)
10		(3.0)
11	Ville	(xx) southern confederation had no (area)
12	Matti	southern's more like (.) more (1.0) eh how do I say (.) they were
13		racist (xxx)
14	Ville	inside the confederation

Another example of Matti and Ville negotiating over the meaning of a word concerns the word *serf* in Extract 4. Again, Ville is the more knowledgeable one and he is also clearly willing to assist Matti in meaning construction. That Matti is having some problems with the term is indicated by his apparent search for words in lines 1-2. Instead of reacting to Matti's problem, Ville at this stage initiates a joking exchange (lines 3-6). Matti's *okay* in line

8 signals the closure of joking and *so* a transition to more serious talk about the Industrial Revolution (lines 8-9). In this connection, he uses the word *service*, which Ville corrects to *servants* (lines 10-12) and a meaning negotiation, partly in Finnish, ensues (lines 12-18). Importantly, once agreement has been reached, interaction continues in English.

Extract 4 (Group 1)

1	Matti	do you got these (.) these (people) serfage (.) surface (.) service
2		servants
3	Ville	they're rich
4	Matti	no they're not ((laughing))
5	Ville	they're rich in beards
6	Matti	okay ((laughing))
7	Ville	no they're poor
8	Matti	okay (.) so (.) people (in the) industrial revolution those people
9		were service mostly
10	Ville	servants
11	Matti	(huh↑)
12	Ville	servants
13	Matti	servants (2.4) some kind of-
14	Ville	palvelijoita 'servants'
15	Matti	mitä 'what'
16	Ville	(x) (niissä oli) palvelijoita *'among them were servants'*
17	Matti	maaorja (.) serf (.) s e r f ((spells the word)) (1.4)
18		some kind of slaves
19	Ville	they were (xx)
20	Matti	yeah okay

Finally, Extract 5 from another group shows Samuli and Richard discussing what they are expected to do during the group work. The extract also involves negotiating about terminology when the boys are searching for a shared understanding of what *advent* means in this context. The extract illustrates well the boys' awareness of the need to define the central concepts they are using (e.g. lines 4, 17-18), defining being very much a language function typical of academic genres. Furthermore, in lines 11-13 and 14-15 it is worth noting how the boys play with word pairs that include both a more everyday and a more academic version (*things* vs. *events* and *coming* vs. *arrival*). This seems to reflect their awareness of subject-specific language.

Extract 5 (Group 3)

1	Samuli	erm (1.5) I don't know if the question means this (.)
2		erm or the coming of industrial age (1.3)
3		could it mean that↑

4	Richard	I don't know (.) I'll have to check the (.) advent
5	Samuli	erm yeah (1.7) this is the dictionary
6	Richard	°yeah°
7	Samuli	this is the big dictionary (x) here
8	Richard	yeah I need the (.) big dictionary (.) this said nothing
9	Samuli	okay (.) about what
10	Richard	coming or arrival or something
		[ca. 2 mins cut during which the boys consult dictionaries and engage in some off-topic talk]
11	Samuli	what were the things (.) what (1.9) events (2.5) et cetera
12		were necessary (1.0) for the coming of industrial
13		revolution (1.0) what events-
14	Richard	I think it's arrival not the coming
15	Samuli	doesn't matter (.) the coming (1.0) slash (1.7) arrival (2.0)
16		arrival of the industrial revolution (.) erm (1.5) what
17		conditions (.) what events conditions (xx) (1.7) define
18		(xx) (.) define conditions (xx)
19	Richard	what
20	Samuli	define conditions
21	Richard	okay (x)

Two points thus seem to emerge as regards subject-specific terms and expressions. On the one hand, the students display some level of awareness of the need to move from everyday words to more abstract and academic expressions to capture the phenomena under discussion. On the other hand, the extracts also show that meaning negotiation is very much a shared, interactional undertaking among the participants.

4.3   Use of subject-specific discourse patterns

As Morton (2010: 86-67) points out, according to secondary level history curricula students are expected to gradually progress from 'recording genres' that retell events via 'explaining' genres that involve explanation and identification of cause and consequences to 'arguing' genres that require balancing different points of view of historical events. The 7th graders in the present data are directed towards the explaining genre in that the teacher has specifically asked them to work through the causes and consequences of the two historical phenomena in question. In other words, they are expected to produce historical narratives and causal explanations and to forge connections between events, which are discourse patterns that are common in constructing knowledge in the school subject of history (e.g. Coffin 2006, Llinares & Morton 2010). However, interestingly from the viewpoint of content and language integration, the teacher does not make any explicit references to whether the students might benefit from using some specific type of language to discuss these causes and consequences. It is therefore worth exploring what kind of resources students are able to use to forge causal connections in English.

Table1 provides an overview of the lexical means specifically geared to expressing cause-effect relationships during the group-work sessions. As the table shows, the students mostly tackle the task by creating a narrative of a sequence of events, linking propositions most often with conjunctions such as *(and) then,* or *and.* As regards expressing what the events lead to, the conjunction most often used is *so,* followed by *because.* The more academic vocabulary used to express cause-effect relationships such as nominalisations and verbs (e.g. 'consequence', 'effect', 'to result'), which Schleppengrell at al. (2004: 73, 84) refer to as typical ways of expressing cause-effect relations in history textbooks, are practically not used at all in the students' spoken language. The few occurrences of the nouns 'consequence', 'connection' and 'result' are all from a single occasion when a student refers to the written instructions given to the class by the teacher (*we haven't read this yet, about conseq- (.) consequences (.) results (.) connections*).

Conjunctions and nouns	Number of occurrences
(and) then	46
and	45
so	30
because	26
that's why	6
therefore	2
consequence	2
connection	1
result	1

Table 1 Lexical elements used to express cause-effect relationships

As pointed out above, the teacher has asked students to work through the causes and consequences of the two historical events in question; this may be considered an indirect way to lead them towards producing discourse typical of the school subject of history. Although the variety of linguistic means to express cause and effect relationships is rather small, the fact that students use them while engaged in shared meaning negotiations shows that they have at least some level of understanding of what kind of discourse they are expected to produce.

Extract 6 is an example of how students are engaged in producing subject-specific discourse. It is from a situation in which two girls, Minna and Laura, are discussing the consequences of industrialisation for craftspeople. The extract illustrates, firstly, the use of *so* (lines 2, 4, 13, 14), *and* (lines 6, 17) and *because* (line 10) to connect different observations and to show relationships between them. Secondly, it shows that meaning making is a joint accomplishment, as Minna first brings in the fact of machines taking over in line 1, with Laura from line 2 onwards elaborating on the consequences this had for craftspeople. Minna first acts as a listener, providing supporting feedback (lines 3, 5, 8), but soon also contributes to the historical narrative initiated by Laura (lines 10, 13, 17-19). The shared construction of the narrative shows the girls as agentive and responsible discourse participants, a state of affairs that may be more difficult to attain in whole-class situations where the social pressures related to speaking in public combined with the teacher's powerful role as the gatekeeper may hinder such active student participation.

Extract 6 (Group 2)

1	Minna	machine takes over
2	Laura	yeah but erm so the crafts like- people erm go out of business
3	Minna	yeah=
4	Laura	=so they go to factories
5	Minna	mhm
6	Laura	and they're like you know their skills they had and- (.) like
7		(xx) work (xx) you know
8	Minna	yeah
9	Laura	and then like-
10	Minna	because they need new skills- they need [new skills]
11	Laura	[machine-] yeah but
12		with machines you don't need that many skills (.) do you
13	Minna	yeah (.) so then their skills are pretty much useless
14	Laura	yeah (.) (xx) like that (.) so they go like out of business and
15		they go to factories (.) to work in the factories (.) and the
16		factories like take over the whole thing
17	Minna	yeah (.) and they don't have-=
18	Laura	=yeah
19	Minna	that much time
20	Laura	but there is like positive things about factories like you know
21		all the products become cheaper

While the extract above showed students engaged in the discourse pattern of causal explanations, in Extract 7 the students are engaged in another type of discourse typical of history, that of drawing connections between different phenomena, in this case between increasing population and the Industrial Revolution. The extract is partly from the same group as above but it involves inter-group talk with Richard from Group 3 participating as well. Before this extract, Laura has tried to explain to her group how and why there is a connection between increasing population and the Industrial Revolution, talking about people from the countryside moving to towns because factories needed more workers. Her explanation is apparently not successful, judging from Minna's reaction: *Laura's just trying to explain something to me that I don't (xx)*. Laura pursues her efforts but when no mutual understanding seems to ensue, the girls turn to Richard, a member of another group, to check whether he understands the connection. Extract 7 begins with this appeal to Richard by Laura (lines 1-7). Minna's turns in lines 8 and 12 reveal that she doubts the connection between increasing population and the Industrial Revolution and regards them as *two completely different things*. Laura's reaction to this is to offer to explain the connection again to Richard (line 13), and she begins her explanation in line 19. Unfortunately the explanation itself could not be captured in the transcript because the poor quality of the recording combined with students' overlapping speech made deciphering impossible, but Minna's *I understand it now* a bit later suggests that they managed to reach a shared understanding. The extract shows the importance of the speech function of explaining (see Dalton-Puffer 2007:139-142) for history and also hints at the difficulties that CLIL students may encounter in realising this function in a foreign language. As Llinares and Morton (2010:49) point out, CLIL students do not necessarily have much experience of using language to express causality.

Extract 7 (Group 2)

1	Laura	just come here [speaks to Richard] do you understand (the fact)
2		((unclear talk for 7 seconds))
3	Richard	the increase of what
4	Laura	population
5	Richard	population
6	Minna	yes
7	Laura	how did the increase of population
8	Minna	what did it have to do with industrial revolution
9	Richard	(xx) (you wanna link it)
10	Laura	yes
11	Richard	okay (.) erm
12	Minna	they are two completely different things
13	Laura	I'll explain to you and say if you understand
14	Richard	[sure]
15	Minna	[no no] no no no
16	Richard	let her
17	Laura	okay

18	Minna	it's gonna take a while
19	Laura	(okay when there's) more people there's more people trying to
20		get the job and erm bosses (xx) trying to make (xxx) (1.0) (xx)
21		more people more workers [continues explanation which is
		uninterpretable due to overlapping speech]]

Extract 8 serves as the final example of the students' apparent awareness of what kind of discourse and language functions are required from them to complete the group work. The extract comes from a point at which Matti and Ville have discussed the causes and consequences of the American Civil War and are now in the process of wrapping up the discussion and attempting to produce a concise account, with Ville describing the essence of the war and Matti supporting him in this. In line 3, Ville explicitly states *that's the nutshell* to characterize the function of his talk. It has been clear throughout this pair's work that Ville is better positioned to take charge of the situation, both linguistically and because he seems to have prepared for the lesson better. Interestingly, towards the end of the extract (lines 11-12) Ville resorts to ironic self-appraisal, as if to mockingly play down his knowledgeability for reasons of solidarity. This seems to be well received by Matti, who joins the fun by roleplaying (line 13); shared laughter closes off the situation.

Extract 8 (Group 1)

1	Ville	southern con- confederation wanted to (.) slave those
2		p- black people and northern union was against (x)
3		(1.9) that's the nutshell (.) and the northern union won (.)
4		because of (xx)
5	Matti	(xx) northern union was against the slavery
6	Ville	yeah (4.7) northern union was about ten million people
7		and in southern confederation was about (0.8) sorry (.)
8		northern union was about sixteen million people and in
9		then (1.0) southern confederation was about
10	Matti	I can see (xx)
11	Ville	ten million (.) yeah (.) I found it from the internet (.) I'm
12		a good boy
13	Matti	he is a good ((in an altered, high-pitched voice))
14		(1.4)
15	Ville	stop
16		((laughter))

What the extracts above have highlighted is that the students are actively using English during their group-work sessions to construct a shared understanding of the tasks at hand and the historical phenomena involved. More importantly from the viewpoint of the focus of the present chapter, they employ discipline and subject-relevant language in their peer discussions. No doubt the teacher's instruction to focus on causes and consequences has had an important role in steering the students' work and language use. The following extract from a situation where the teacher briefly discusses the subject with one of the groups shows, moreover, how the teacher motivates the learners to search for links between the causes and consequences:

> T   this is just that you (x) are learning history in a patchwork quilt (.)
>   type way so you learn all these details but it's difficult to step back and
>   see how yeah you'll see all that happens on the quilt but you gotta step
>   away from the quilt and see how the quilt is all made which is very
>   difficult but if you get practice in that (.) all the details should
>   start making sense in the grander design (.) the bigger picture (.)
>   so it'd be easy for me to ask you for example what different
>   inventions (x) industrial revolution (1.0) and I could ask you
>   something about the social effects (.) but I'm hoping you can
>   start understanding how all these things are related (.) manufacturing
>   textiles (.) industrialization (.) social effects (.) these inventions
>   how they all work together all these details

Such meta-level descriptions are important in steering students' attention to how things are done and how understanding is achieved in specific subjects. However, from the viewpoint of content and language integration and awareness of subject-specific language use in CLIL, the next step could be to explicitly draw students' attention to language functions that are involved in presenting knowledge in subject-specific ways.

5   Concluding remarks

According to Llinares and Morton (2010:47), CLIL is about developing L2 academic literacies, and "[p]articipating in CLIL lessons entails using spoken language to carry out a range of academic language functions through which relevant subject-related meanings are expressed". The purpose of this chapter has been to explore Finnish secondary-level CLIL history students' language use in group-work situations from the perspective of subject-specific language use, an essential yet relatively underexplored aspect of CLIL education.

Even though the data sample is limited and obviously cannot be used for making broad generalisations, some observations can be made that are worth taking further. Firstly, the present data seem to show that subject-specific language use is very rarely explicitly discussed. Admittedly, there are some references to the need to 'talk about history' during the group-work sessions but they seem to relate to the topics of talk rather than their linguistic and/or discoursal realisation. Nevertheless, through their language use when carrying out group work and pair work, the students display at least some level of awareness that history requires a particular type of language use. Above, this was shown to be realized on two levels. Firstly, during their group work the students were engaged in meaning negotiations over terms, showing in this process some sensitivity to the difference between everyday and academic language use. Noteworthy in this process was how the students strove towards a shared understanding and joint meaning-making through very involved interaction in ways that are often absent in whole-class situations, which reminds one of Moore's (2011) observation that CLIL students' participatory patterns are more often collaborative than those of their mainstream peers.

Secondly, and even more significantly from the perspective of subject-specific language use, the students were shown to be actively engaged in discourse patterns typical of history: providing explanations, seeking causal connections, attempting syntheses through providing 'the big picture' and teasing out the essence from the multitude of factors involved through identifying what the teacher had referred to as 'the nutshell'. They were clearly aware of what they were expected to do in their group work. However, it is unclear to what extent they associate these activities with specific academic speech functions and particular ways of using language.
As regards the role of peer discussions in supporting the learning of subject-specific language use, the findings of this study seem encouraging. Group-work situations in CLIL lessons are often suspected of both discouraging the use of the target language and encouraging off-topic talk. In the present data, the students use English throughout and keep to the tasks and topics at hand very well. It may well be that this can largely be explained by their awareness of being recorded for research purposes. Yet the data undeniably show that 13-year-old students are fully able to negotiate their way through group-work tasks in English and to engage in complex and purposeful meaning negotiations around historical events and concepts. It is hence likely, as Llinares and Morton (2010:62) argue, that "CLIL students may be able to do more than we think, if we provide them with the interactional space to articulate their understandings". It seems that group work among peers forms a safe environment, provided that students have a clear understanding of what activities they are expected to perform.

Mondada and Pekarek Doehler (2004:515), when studying task accomplishment in second language classrooms, argue that it "necessarily involves various embedded linguistic, interactional, institutional competences". Judging from the present data, joint meaning construction in group-work situations also involves a complex range of competences, and it seems that one fruitful avenue for future CLIL research would be a more comprehensive account of content and language integration than has been achieved to date as a phenomenon relating not only to language and content but also to (subject-specific) patterns of discourse and the choreography of interaction involved when participants are striving towards shared understandings. Gajo (2007:564) is thinking along similar lines when he argues that integration is "a complex interactional and discursive process relevant to both the language(s) and the subject". This study, although small in scale, has hopefully provided some insights into the complexities involved and into both explicit and implicit ways in which students' peer discussions index their awareness of subject-specific language use.

References

Alanen, R., A.-K. Jäppinen and T. Nikula (2008) "But big is a funny word": A multiple perspective on concept formation in a foreign-language-mediated classroom, *Journal of Applied Linguistics* 3(1)/2006: 69-90.

Christie, F. (2002) *Classroom Discourse Analysis. A Functional Perspective.* London: Continuum.

Coetzee-Lachmann, D. (2007) Assessment of subject-specific task performance of bilingual geography learners: Analysing aspects of subject-specific written discourse. PhD Dissertation, Universität Osnabrück. http://repositorium.uni-osnabrueck.de/bitstream/urn:nbn:de:gbv:700-2009030617/2/E-Diss864_thesis.pdf

Coffin, C. (2006) Learning the language of school history: the role of linguistics in mapping the writing demands of the secondary school curriculum, *Journal of Curriculum Studies* 38(4): 413–429.

Coyle, D. (2007) Content and language integrated learning: Toward a connected research agenda for CLIL pedagogies, *The International Journal of Bilingual Education and Bilingualism* 10: 543-562.

Coyle, D., P. Hood and D Marsh (2010) *CLIL. Content and Language Integrated Learning.* Cambridge: CUP.

Creese, A. and P. Martin (2003) *Multilingual Classroom Ecologies: Inter-Relationships, Interactions and Ideologies.* Clevedon: Multilingual Matters.

Dalton-Puffer, C. (2007) *Discourse in Content and Language Integrated Learning (CLIL) Classrooms.* Amsterdam: John Benjamins.

Dalton-Puffer, C. and U. Smit (eds.) (2007) *Empirical Perspectives on CLIL Classroom Discourse*. Frankfurt: Peter Lang.

Dalton-Puffer, C. T. Nikula and U. Smit (eds.) (2010a) *Language Use and Language Learning in CLIL Classrooms*. Amsterdam: John Benjamins.

Dalton-Puffer, C., T. Nikula and U. Smit (2010b) Charting policies, premises and research on content and language integrated learning. In Dalton-Puffer, C., T. Nikula and U. Smit (eds.) 2010a, 1-19.

Dalton-Puffer, C., T. Nikula and U. Smit (2010c) Language use and language learning in CLIL: Current findings and contentious issues. In Dalton-Puffer, C., T. Nikula and U. Smit (eds.) 2010a, 279-291.

Fortune, T. W. and D. J. Tedick (eds.) (2008) *Pathways to Multilingualism: Evolving Perspectives on Immersion Education*. Clevedon: Multilingual Matters.

Gajo, L. (2007) Linguistic knowledge and subject knowledge: How does bilingualism contribute to subject development? *The International Journal of Bilingual Education and Bilingualism* 10(5): 563-579.

García, O. (2009) *Bilingual Education in the 21st Century: A Global Perspective*. Malden, MA and Oxford: Wiley-Blackwell.

Järvinen, H.-M. (2010) Language as a meaning making resource in learning and teaching content. Analysing historical writing in content and language integrated learning. In Dalton-Puffer, C., T. Nikula and U. Smit (eds.) 2010a, 145-168.

Lantolf, J. P. and M. E. Poehner (eds.) (2008) *Sociocultural Theory and the Teaching of Second Languages*. London: Equinox Publishing.

Lemke, J. (1990) *Talking Science: Language, Learning, and Values*. Norwood, NJ: Ablex.

Leung, C. (2005) Language and content in bilingual education, *Linguistics and Education* 16: 28-252.

Lim Falk, M. (2008) *Svenska i engelskspråkig skolmiljö. Ämnesrelaterat språkbruk i två gymnasieklasser.* (Swedish in an English-language School Environment. Subject-based Language use in two upper secondary classes.) Acta Universitatis Stockholmiensis. Stockholm Studies in Scandinavian Philology.

Llinares, A. and T. Morton (2010) Historical explanations as situated practice in content and language integrated learning, *Classroom Discourse* 1(1): 46-65.

Llinares, A. and R. Whittaker (2010) Writing and speaking in the history class. A comparative analysis of CLIL and first language contexts. In Dalton-Puffer, C., T. Nikula and U. Smit (eds.) 2010a, 125-143.

Mondada, L. and S. Pekarek Doehler (2004) Second language acquisition as situated practice: Task accomplishment in the French second language classroom, *The Modern Language Journal* 88: 501-518.

Moore, P. (2011) Collaborative interaction in turn-taking: a comparative study of European bilingual (CLIL) and mainstream (MS) foreign language learners in early secondary education, *International Journal of Bilingual Education and Bilingualism* 14 (5): 531-549.

Mortimer, E. F. and P. H. Scott (2003) *Meaning Making in Secondary Science Classrooms*. Maidenhead, UK: Open University Press.

Morton, T. (2010) Using a genre-based approach to integrating content and language in CLIL. In Dalton-Puffer, C., T. Nikula and U. Smit (eds.) 2010a, 81-104.

Nikula, T. (2005) English as an object and tool of study: interactional effects and pragmatic implications, *Linguistics and Education* 16 (1): 27-58.

Nikula, T. (2008) Learning pragmatics in content-based classrooms. In E. Alcón and A. Martinez-Flor (eds.) *Investigating Pragmatics in Foreign Language Learning, Teaching, and Testing*. Clevedon: Multilingual Matters, 94–113.

Nikula, T. (2010) On teachers' interactional resources to make subject-specifc language use salient in CLIL. A paper presented in AILA CLIL Network Research Symposium, University of Jyväskylä, June 10-11 2010, University of Jyväskylä.

Ruiz de Zarobe, Y. and R. M. Jiménez Catalán (eds.) (2009) *Content and Language Integrated Learning. Evidence from Research in Europe*. Bristol: Multilingual Matters.

Schleppegrell, M. (2004) *The Language of Schooling. A Functional Linguistics Perspective*. Mahwah, NJ: Lawrence Erlbaum.

Schleppegrell, M., M. Achugar and T. Oteíza (2004) The grammar of history: Enhancing content-based instruction through a functional focus on language, *TESOL Quarterly* 38 (1): 67-93.

Notes

[1] This study is part of a research project 'Language and content integration: towards a conceptual framework' funded by the Academy of Finland (2012-2014).

Appendix

TRANSCRIPTION CONVENTIONS

overlapping [speech] [text]	overlapping speech
(.)	a short pause that is not timed, less than a second
(2.5)	a pause, timed in seconds
text= =text	latching utterances
exte:nsion	noticeable extension of the sound or syllable
cut off wo-	cut off word or truncated speech
°high circles°	spoken more silently than surrounding utterances
.	falling intonation
↑	rising intonation
((text))	transcriber's comments
(text)	transcriber's interpretation of unclear word(s)
(x)	unclear speech, probably a word
(xx)	unclear speech, probably a phrase
(xxx)	longer stretch of unclear speech

English as a Lingua Franca (ELF) and its role in integrating content and language in higher education. A longitudinal study of question-initiated exchanges

Ute Smit (Universität Wien)

Given the increasing popularity amongst mainland European higher educational institutions to offer some of their classes and courses in English, this paper addresses the roles English plays in such classroom discourse. By focussing on one specific English-medium hotel management programme, it is argued that English functions, on the one hand, as language of the learners' future expertise and, on the other, as their only shared medium of communication, i.e., their lingua franca. A detailed analysis of question-initiated exchanges taken from critical phases throughout the programme accompanied over its whole duration illustrates the realities of this multifunctionality of English as revealed in teachers and students raising, and responding to, different kinds of question at different points in time. On the basis of these discourse-pragmatic findings it is suggested that (language) learning processes depend in their complexity and dynamics on English in its roles as lingua franca and as professional language, but also on how these roles are conceptuald within a generally content-focussed teaching programme.

1 Introduction

Especially in the European context, 'Bologna' has become almost synonymous with 'internationalising tertiary educational institutions'. The structurally clearest consequence is most likely the three-level architecture of study programmes into bachelor/master/doctorate, but an arguably equally obvious result is the burgeoning use of English as medium of instruction at universities in mainland Europe, which have had a tradition in lecturing in the respective national language. This popularity of university teaching in English is fuelled by internationalisation on two levels: as regards the exchange of information, i.e. academic knowledge and thought, and of lecturers and students as relevant social agents.

Understandably, this recent development of offering study programmes or, at least, individual classes in English, has attracted a considerable amount of applied linguistic research interest (e.g. Wächter and Maiworm, 2008;

Wilkinson, 2004; Wilkinson and Zegers, 2007). As regards the micro-level of the classroom language itself, the conceptual frame tends to be the one of English for specific purposes (ESP). Put somewhat crudely, it pictures and describes classroom discourse in relation to language norms established either in works of language codification or by the expert community of the specialisation in question (e.g. Fortanet-Gómez & Räisänen, 2008). This underlying prescriptive orientation seems compatible with the educational setting at stake and its central focus on formal learning. Inspired by the modelling of primary and secondary education in an additional language as 'CLIL' (content and language integrated learning), the learning process is argued to include the respective knowledge content area as well as the additional language used (Coyle, Hood and Marsh, 2010), giving it the label 'integrating content and language in higher education' (ICLHE) (Wilkinson and Zegers, 2007). In other words, English as classroom language is modelled as object of learning itself.

While such a conceptualisation has its clear merits – the range and variety of publications and their insights provide ample proof of that – the emphasis placed on ESP arguably sidelines the fact that English has yet another function, and at that a very crucial one. In view of the internationalisation of academia in research and teaching it is used as the multilingual social actors' common medium of communication, which permits direct exchange of information and construction of knowledge across language borders. In other words, English is the lecturers' and students' lingua franca (e.g. Björkman, 2009; Smit, 2010a). Recently, research into ELF has been booming, resulting in an impressive array of findings and insights with the underlying endeavour to describe English as it is used in communication, rather than in contrast with what *ought to* be the case in comparison with norms and expectations, reflecting language learning outcomes.[1]

When turning back to English-medium tertiary education in mainland Europe, the situation is rather complex in that it actually combines all these functions of English: it is the participants' lingua franca, but it is also an additional language partially in need of improvement, especially as regards the linguistic resources necessary for the respective area of expertise (Smit, 2010b, pp. 406–407). In an attempt to give credit to this multifunctionality of English, this contribution argues for enriching the conceptualisation of ICLHE by recognising that the 'L' also functions as the participants' lingua franca.

In order to substantiate this claim, the paper reports on a longitudinal study of classroom discourse in an ICLHE setting and on how the lecturers and students construct their interactions by relying on English as their lingua franca. More precisely, the focus will be on question-initiated exchanges as a prototypical discursive site of constructing classroom talk in traditional lessons, constituted largely by teacher-whole class interaction. By discussing the dynamics with which question-initiated exchanges develop over time, the analysis will offer insights into the workings of English as a lingua franca in such a tertiary educational context as well as its implications for integrating content and language (see section 5). Before turning to the study itself (section 4), however, the argumentative focus will be placed on the relevance and specificities of questions in the classroom (section 3) and, to begin with, on some important aspects of internationalising tertiary classroom discourse.

2 Internationalising tertiary classroom discourse – conceptual considerations on integrating content and English

While 'internationalisation' is heralded as a recent driving force behind the changing landscape of especially European tertiary education, the landmark of using English as medium of instruction has been part and parcel of tertiary education elsewhere for quite some time. Universities set in Kachru's (1996) 'Outer Circle'[2] have relied mainly or solely on English since their inception and have thus had to face the implications of using an additional language for the central processes of teaching and learning (e.g. Banda, 2009; Ferguson, 2006; Lin & Martin, 2005). Similar bi- or multilingual realities have reached many institutions in the 'Inner Circle', given the increasingly growing numbers of foreign students in the 'MESDCs' (major English speaking destination countries) (Graddol, 2006, p. 76) and the resulting groups of learners and partly also lecturers to whom English is not the first language. In other words, employing English as an additional language at tertiary level is nothing new; and yet, it is new to mainland Europe. While long ago universities used to rely for many centuries on Latin as an additional language for tertiary education, the highly influential nationalist ideology of the 18th to the 20th century placed the respective national languages as main, and later on exclusive, languages of tertiary education. In the light of such historically grown language practices, it seems fair to recognize the European situation as qualitatively different from other settings (Smit, 2010b, p. 61). This novel situation is also reflected in recent quantitative surveys (Ammon, 2001; Wächter and Maiworm, 2008), which generally support the impression that an increasing number of tertiary institutions offer English-medium classes and courses, mainly with the explicit aim to attract or accommodate international students and lecturers, occasionally also to prepare their local students for their future international careers.

Additionally, such surveys provide information on the diversity of implementation to be found: In Germany, for instance, some institutions introduced English-medium classes for the first year of studies with the aim that non-German speakers improve on their German skills in separate language classes and then change over to German-medium education (Motz, 2005). In Spain, on the other hand, English-medium programmes at the tertiary level tend to focus on local students equally strongly. As described in Ruiz-Garrido and Palmer-Silveira (2008), the English language requirements of the surrounding industry helped in devising an English-medium programme in Castellon with the explicit aim to prepare Spanish students for an international work market. To give a third, rather different example, an overwhelming number of MA, but also BA programmes at many Dutch universities is offered exclusively in English. In an attempt to prepare mainly international students for such programmes, the universities run preparatory English language courses and/or offer short-term, highly focussed language teaching tightly integrated with the content classes (Wilkinson, 2008). These different cases already illustrate that European tertiary educational programmes pursue different policies when it comes to teaching in English and, correspondingly, engage in different practices in relation to English functioning as an additional language for the students and usually also for the lecturers.[3]

Despite potentially fundamental differences in how programmes integrate English as medium, what they all share is that their perceived success hinges fundamentally on what is going on in the classroom itself, i.e. on classroom discourse, which, clearly of central relevance also to the present paper, has attracted interest not only as the site of meaning making, but, interpreted within sociocultural theorising (e.g. Wertsch, 1992), as the locus of constructing learning opportunities. One rather obvious, but only rarely researched prerequisite for such opportunities to take place is degree of understanding reached. Classroom talk in general and lecturing in particular are such that students cannot easily make public their problems in understanding the lecturer. This means that classroom talk alone does not suffice as indicator of how understandable a lecture is perceived to be. Based on a questionnaire-based survey amongst Norwegian students, Hellekjær (2010) finds that, while lecturing can pose problems of understanding irrespective of the medium of instruction, it is considered more difficult when undertaken in English. Students identified problems on all three levels of reaching understanding (cf. Kachru, 2008), i.e. intelligibility, comprehensibility and interpretability.[4] By tackling the issue from the perspective of teacher talk, Dafouz-Milne and Núñez-Perucha (2010) analyse lecturing behaviour in Madrid and, by comparing aeronautical engineering lectures given by the same lecturers in English and Spanish, identify a considerable degree of similarity between lecturing styles in both languages, but less explicitness when it comes to signalling transitions between lecturing phases in English. Further findings relate to the readiness of students to take on active participatory roles. Here, it seems that the foreign language might hinder some students from contributing during class, thus reducing their chance to express potential problems of understanding (Airey, 2009).

As regards the roles English plays in higher education, the brief literature review has already indicated that, on the one hand, English is the international language of most academic disciplines and thus essential for producing and reading relevant publications. Thus, English is employed so that students can participate in the up-to-date research scene and improve on their language skills in addition to their discipline-specific competences. On the other hand, tertiary programmes in Europe increasingly cater for international groups of students and lecturers, using English as the only linguistic means to make direct exchange possible. The correspondingly explicit focus on highly situated language in use is central to research into English as a lingua franca (ELF), which has foregrounded that such multilingual interactants aim mainly to make communication work, sidelining concerns of exonormative linguistic correctness (e.g. Kaur, 2009).
While each research approach has yielded valuable results and insights, the particularities of ICLHE suggest that a more comprehensive conceptualisation of English might do credit to the complexity of its functions and roles. Given that English is lingua franca and language of the discipline, it seems necessary to aim for a conceptual frame that allows and caters for both, English as only shared medium of communication *and* as one of the learning aims of the students. As indicated above, one methodological stepping stone into this direction is to focus on classroom discourse as locus of communication as well as of learning. Such a perspective suggests itself when, as argued in Smit (2010a, pp. 77–81), 'ELF as classroom language' is conceptuald in a multilayered and dynamic way, drawing on the central notion of community of practice (Wenger, 1998), with the multilingual participants jointly engaged in their common educational enterprise and, by doing so, developing their shared repertoire (cf. also Meyerhoff, 2002). In view of the constitutive role discourse plays in formal education, classroom talk in ELF amounts to the central practices, which are shaped by the individual members' repertoires, the established practices of the content subjects in question and, most centrally, by the fully contextuald communicational needs that arise within the community itself (for a detailed discussion see Smit, 2010b). In short, the nexus of analysing the dynamics of ELF and its relevance to learning arguably lies in a detailed analysis of classroom discourse.

Given the complexity and situatedness of discursive practices, the research take proposed so far will be exemplified in the following by analysing the classroom discourse of one specific educational setting. As it is my intention to sketch discursive dynamics at the micro-level at certain interactional moments, but also over time, a mixed-methods approach is applied (Dörnyei, 2007, p. 43): within a fundamentally qualitative frame, some quantification is embedded so as to substantiate typical discursive patterns as well as to trace their relevance and changing nature longitudinally. Such a research interest squares well with discourse-pragmatics (Blum-Kulka, 1997; Nikula, 2005) and its empirical focus on specific discursive patterns. The one expanded on in the following is of central relevance to what Cazden (2001, p. 56) calls so aptly traditional lessons: the question-initiated exchange.

3   Question-initiated exchanges in the classroom

As argued in many seminal works (Mehan, 1979; Marton & Tsui, 2004; Richard & Lockhart, 1994; van Lier, 1988) and confirmed in various studies (e.g. Dalton-Puffer & Nikula, 2006; Lee, 2008; Morell, 2004), classroom talk is centrally characterd by the use of questions, with which the social players "carry out their [professional] practices" (Lee, 2006, p. 238). This centrality of questions is also reflected in their ubiquity: while actual frequencies differ according to factors such as interactional style or educational level, studies agree on questions as highly frequent and central discourse move (e.g. Dalton-Puffer, 2007, p. 100; Musumeci, 1996). In other words, the empirical findings confirm what we know from personal experience: classroom talk is pointedly structured by the use of questions. Equally obviously, questions do not stand alone, but – and here especially conversation analytical research has provided us with detailed descriptions – are integral to classroom talk in general, by being embedded in and/or directing ongoing exchanges (Markee, 2000). It is for this central, but integrated role that questions play in any institutionald discourse, and especially in classroom talk, that the analytical focus lies here on 'question-initiated exchanges'.

Following Edmondson (1981, pp. 80–81), an 'exchange' is understood as a structural unit with an interactional outcome.[5] While there are various moves that trigger exchanges, questions are the prototypical ones in educational settings as they seek "a response that facilitate[s] the transmission of information in line with the overall goal" (Schiffrin, 1994, p. 182). Lastingly conceptuald by speech act theory, a question is defined as a directive, i.e., "an attempt to get someone to do something" (Searle, 1976, p. 11), with the 'doing something' being specified as a verbal act. The intrinsic distinction between verbal and non-verbal is substantiated theoretically by the language system itself, which distinguishes structurally between demanding information from demanding goods-and-services (cf. Halliday, 2004, p. 187). Additionally, knowledge-focussed education places language into a constitutive role of the learning process, with non-verbal skills remaining ancillary to the undertaking (cf. Christie, 2002, pp. 129–152). Giving and demanding information is thus at the heart of classroom talk, which most likely explicates why questioning is "the most distinctive feature of classroom discourse" (Tsui et al, , 2004, p. 113). With the help of questions teachers act out their role as organrs of classroom talk (Widdowson, 1990, pp. 181–191) and make the respective content more accessible to their learners. In the best case, questions help teachers and students engage in the joint construction of knowledge. As far as classroom talk is concerned, questions also play an important conversational role in identifying and sorting out instances of potential mis/non-understanding. By stimulating repair (e.g. Schegloff, Jefferson, & Sacks, 1977; Markee, 2000), questions often help participants to keep their communication going.

Besides such a positive assessment of the roles questions can play in class, a sizable amount of research has assessed their potentially negative impact on learning possibilities and processes. Firstly, criticism has often been heard as regards the wide-spread use of 'display question', i.e. questions to which teachers know the answers already (e.g. Long & Sato, 1983; Mehan, 1979; Morell, 2004). Instead, so the argument goes, teachers should rather raise referential questions to which they do not know the answer yet, thus asking 'real' questions. While display questions are interpretable as perpetuating the quasi omniscient status teachers tend to take on in class, their employment can also be seen as revealing new information as regards the students' state of knowledge (Dalton-Puffer, 2007, p. 95). Reflecting their different participatory roles in class, students tend to formulate referential questions. Furthermore, research has shown that the frequency with which display questions appear is not a mere coincidence: when employed context-sensitively, display questions can play an important and supportive pedagogical role in helping learners along (Lee, 2006, p. 708; Smit, 2010a, p. 240); as, for instance, when they aid the teacher in scaffolding new information. Given the repeatedly confirmed relevance of these two categories of questions, they will also be considered in the present analysis (see Table 1).

Secondly, questions have been categord according to the degree of cognitive demand they pose on the respondent and criticism has been raised regarding a heavy use of less demanding, usually fact-oriented questions that can be replied to in short answers. It is argued that such so-called 'lower-order questions' do not foster the discursive construction of more complex ways of thinking (Edwards & Westgate, 1994, p. 144). Additionally, by refraining from giving extended answers, learners do not have the chance to elaborate on their productive academic language skills, which has been identified as particularly problematic in the case of additional language speakers (Zwiers, 2007). At the same time and as already commented on in the 1980s (summard in Edwards & Westgate, 1994, p. 144), it would be overly simplistic to try and equate type of question asked with either kind of cognitive processing or student response length. In an attempt not to presuppose degree of cognitive demand, this paper follows others (cf. Zuengler & Brinton, 1997; Dalton-Puffer, 2007) and distinguishes question types by the kind of information enquired about. While many more categories are possible and worthy of analysis (cf. Smit, 2010a, pp. 254–255), Table 1 contains the most frequently used objects of questions in the study reported on here, namely facts, and reasons and explanations. Reflecting the nature of the questions and responses analysed, the latter two are grouped together.

Category	Example (taken from the HMP data set)
A) Status of information	
display question	TON: Why do suppliers suffer if I go bankrupt?
	XEN: first principle the will of the people and it's the principle of ?
referential question	
	AKL: any question to this organization chart ?
	Anki: if the chambers of commerce do they have to belong to a special party ?
B) Object of question	
fact	
	TON: but what happens if (.) I'm making (2) a chip this big (.) for a machine that you make ,
	Lula: le meridien is opening soon?
reason + explanation	
	TON: why would I expect a bigger divid:end from intel than I would from wallmart
	Jens: what is (EEO) .

Table 1. Typologies of questions (adapted from Smit 2010a: 255)

Apart from the kinds of question involved, the following analysis of classroom talk will take into account the participatory roles teacher and students enact in class. A revealing distinction in this context is the one between those phases that focus on instructional discourse furthering curricular content and the complementary phases that are structured by regulative discourse managing the lesson and the participants (e.g. Christie, 2002). As will be elaborated on in the next section, these distinct phases are particularly relevant in view of the fact that the students were adults and highly experienced learners in formal contexts.

4 The study and data base[6]

The longitudinal dataset subjected to detailed discourse-pragmatic and ethnographic study was collected during the whole duration of a four-semester post-secondary programme in international hotel management, HMP for short (Smit, 2010a).[7] This certificate-bearing programme is run by a Viennese hospitality educational centre and aims to prepare newcomers to this business sector for managerial jobs in the service industry. At the same time, it is acknowledged as the first part of bachelor programmes at various universities in Austria and abroad. From its very beginning in the late 1980s, the programme has been offered in English and has catered for the international, upper-class hotel market in terms of attracting international students and at the same time preparing local ones for employment abroad. The student cohort observed in this ethnographic study is a case in point: it consisted of 28 students of 14 different nationalities, using 22 languages for daily communication. Reflecting this impressive degree of multilingualism, English was the only language they all shared, but German played a special role as well in that about 80% of the students had some proficiency in the language of the environment. The students ranged in age between 18 and 36 and came with little to no prior knowledge or experience in the field of hospitality.

The teachers, on the other hand, were mainly Austrian, but, fitting to the range of subjects taught, equipped with diverse professional backgrounds. Reflecting the international character of hospitality in general, practically all had spent some years in international businesses abroad, which means that they had used English not only for private, but also for professional purposes. As far as their teaching expertise is concerned, some lecturers were professional teachers, others had gained considerable practical experience in teaching, while a minority were newcomers to teaching on the whole. The programme itself was structured intensively in that it could only be done full-time and entailed a weekly work-load of approximately 34 contact hours throughout the four semesters. Between year 1 and 2, the students were given a break of four months which they were required to use for an internship in an international hospitality business, thus gaining work experience in addition to the theoretical and practical knowledge of the classes.

Given the research interest in studying one tertiary educational setting relying on English as a lingua franca as their classroom language, the investigation accompanied the HMP from the first to the last day of classes, collecting classroom discourse as well as the participants' views on using English as classroom language throughout the four semesters of the programme. This has led to a rich database of about 50 semi-structured interviews, regular informal conversations with the stakeholders (students, teachers, administrators) and 33 audio-recorded and transcribed lessons. The lessons chosen involved ten teachers and eleven subjects, spread over three phases of the HMP that were identified as critical by the participants themselves: T1 or the introductory first two weeks, T2 or the second half of the first semester and T3 or the third semester following on the practical internships all students had to do.[8]

In view of the present research interest in question-initiated exchanges, the main focus in the following is placed on the classroom discourse data set. More precisely and in accordance with comparable studies (Dalton-Puffer, 2007; Morell, 2004), a subset of nine lessons was analysed in detail (Smit, 2010b, chapter 6). This data-set, consisting of 6.5 hours or almost 60,000 words (see Table 2), is balanced in terms of critical phases, subjects and teachers. The three lessons per phase, which cover the subjects of finances, hotel management, human relations and law, were given by teachers of diverse backgrounds: TON, the only man in this selection, was a native Briton, an accounting expert with an extended practical experience in teaching. The four female teachers were Austrian. XEN, the only trained teacher, had double qualifications with law, but relatively little experience in using English for professional purposes. AKL and MER had extensive careers in their fields – hotel management and public relations respectively – and solid practical experience in training and lecturing in pre- and in-service settings. OPP, on the other hand, was a newcomer to pre-service teaching, but had done in-service training before. In sum, the classes chosen allow for comparisons across the three points in time (T1, T2 and T3) and, at the same time, offer points of contrast in terms of subject, teachers' teaching background as well as English language proficiency.

	Subjects	Lecturers	Mins	Turns	Words
T1	Financial Management	TON	39	199	4408
(sem 1,	Front Office Management	AKL	41	204	7022
wks 1&2)	Austrian Law	XEN	45	379	6064
T2	Financial Management	TON	43	372	6575
(sem 1,	Austrian Law	XEN	45	401	5985
mths 3&4)	Human Resources	OPP	48	241	7856
T3	Financial Management	TON	45	365	5991
(sem 3,	Food & Beverage	AKL	34	313	6622
	Management				
mths 1&2)	Public Relations	MER	50	370	9347
Total			*390*	*2844*	*59870*

Table 2. Lessons analysed

In accordance with the considerations voiced above as regards question-initiated exchanges in the HMP classroom discourse, the data analysis has been undertaken in response to the following research questions:

1) What types of question are used by whom and when?
2) Which roles do questions play in the development of curricular content?
3) In what ways do question-initiated exchanges reveal (language) learning processes?

In an attempt to approach these questions, a mixed-methods approach has been applied in that quantitative and qualitative steps are understood as complementary (cf. Smit, 2010a, p. 188). Therefore, and in pursuit of research question 1, the analysis will start with a quantitative sketch of question usage and will then approach research question 2 by analysing typical question-initiated exchanges from various lessons given at different points in time. On the basis of these findings, it will then be possible to approach the third, more interpretative research question regarding learning, especially language learning.

5 An analysis of question-initiated exchanges

5.1 The quantitative basics

The detailed identification of questions within the data base of 9 lessons or 6.5 hours of class time has revealed a sum total of 575 questions. Purely statistically speaking, this relates to almost two questions per minute, thus confirming the previously established all-pervasiveness of questions in teacher-whole class interaction. While the actual distribution of questions varies quite remarkably from lesson (phase) to lesson (phase), it is not directly dependent on point in time. As summard in Table 3, the totals of questions during the three emically established critical phases are roughly comparable, with the lessons from T2 containing somewhat more questions than those of the other two phases. The 3:1 distribution of teacher to student questions, on the other hand, shows quite clearly the predominant role teachers play. While these two numerical cornerstones identify the HMP lessons as typically traditional classrooms, the third general statistic contrasting questions in regulative vs. instructional register underlines the advanced level of the learner group analysed here. In contrast to primary and (lower) secondary education (e.g. Dalton-Puffer, 2007, p. 100; Musumeci, 1996), tertiary classroom discourse reveals considerably less need to deal with regulative issues, thus focussing predominantly on the instructional register.

Points in time		Speaker		Register	
T1	182	teacher	424	regulative	58
T2	211	student	151	instructional	517
T3	182				

Table 3. Overall distribution of questions (total: 575)

Given the numerical preponderance of instructional questions, they can be subjected to a quantitative sketch. As regards the distribution of questions according to status of information, i.e. previously known to the teacher or not, Table 4 (see appendix) reveals, firstly, that referential questions outnumber display questions (307 vs. 208). This is interesting insofar as other studies report on a reversed distribution (e.g. Long & Sato, 1983; Musumeci, 1996) or on a balanced one (Dalton-Puffer, 2007, p. 101). One reason for this distributional difference might be the different age of learner groups involved, with the one investigated here being a highly experienced one.

When it comes to the subcategories of questions raised, the quantitative findings point at interesting preferences and processes. There is, firstly, the relation between teacher display vs. referential questions, which changes in a statistically highly significant way between the three critical phases (see appendix, Table 4).[9] As illustrated in Figure 1, teachers started into the HMP by asking twice as many display than referential questions. Already a few weeks later they raised both kinds of question almost equally often. In the third semester, the relationship was turned around with almost double as many referential as display questions recorded.

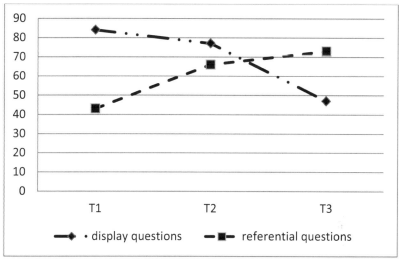

Figure 1. Instructional teacher display and referential questions (absolute frequencies) according to points in time (for statistics see Appendix, Table 4)

This developmental pattern gains in clarity when drawing on the distinction of questions according to objects asked for, i.e. questions for fact vs. for reason and explanation. As discernable from Table 5, these amount to 386 or 75% of all questions asked. When analysed in combination with the distinction into display vs. referential questions, the temporal perspective reveals an interesting and statistically significant shift in prevalence from display questions for facts at T1, display questions for reason and explanation, and referential questions for fact at T2 and, at T3, a clear preference for referential questions. The percentages highlighted in the table identify the phase in which the respective category is the strongest. Additionally, almost two thirds of all referential questions for reason and explanation were asked at T3.

Question types	T1		T2		T3		Total
	N	%	N	%	N	%	
display qus. for fact	73	**41,7**	61	*34,9*	41	*23,4*	175
display qus. for reason and explanation	12	*35,3*	16	**47,1**	6	*17,6*	34
referential qus. for fact	29	*23,6*	50	**40,7**	44	*35,8*	123
referential qus. for reason and explanation	8	*14,8*	12	*22,2*	34	**63,0**	54
Total	122	*31,6*	139	*36,0*	125	*32,4*	386

Chi-square = 40.58; df = 6; p < .0001

Table 5. Display and referential questions for facts and reasons

Overall, the search for answers to research question 1 *(What types of question are used by whom and when?)* has led to findings that underscore a few widely-found aspects of classroom discourse: teachers ask the majority of questions and practically all display questions, thus acting out the traditional teacher role of classroom manager. Furthermore, the most favoured communicational topics seem to be factual in nature. More unexpectedly maybe, the distribution of regulative to instructional questions can be seen as reflecting the age and maturity of the learners who are so experienced in formal learning scenarios that issues of classroom management or procedures need relatively little discursive attention. At the same time, the quantitative sketch points towards a dynamic development during the HMP towards more questions raised for previously unknown information and to more exchanges dealing with reasoning and explaining besides the generally strong conversational focus on factual knowledge.

5.2   Insights into developing curricular content

By building on these initial quantitative findings, the following detailed description of selected examples of question-initiated exchanges will approach the second research question (*Which roles do questions play in the development of curricular content?*). Given the long-term nature of any educational setting as well as the longitudinal research approach pursued in this study, I will proceed chronologically, tracing the participants' questioning and responding behaviour from the first to the third semester. In the interest of space, the discussion will omit the critical phase T2, but will focus on illustrating the development in interactional patterns from the introductory days (T1) to the third semester (T3).

The large number of display questions especially at T1 (see Table 5) hints at their particular relevance during the first days of class. Besides the widely acted upon need to scaffold new content, thus making it accessible to the learners, the HMP teachers also rely on display questions for fact to help create a friendly and collaborative atmosphere. In Extract 1, for instance, the Front Office Management teacher appeals to common knowledge first before raising a display question for explanation (lines 1-2). When no student offers a reply, the teacher chooses to rephrase the question into a yes-no question, whose answer has already been presupposed in her original question. This simplification has its intended effect and allows many students to affirm it (line 4). Now, the teacher can restate her original question, and this time Suka, a student with previous knowledge in hotel management, volunteers an answer (line 6). The moment the student seems stuck, AKL rephrases her question again into one for fact and, by offering supportive minimal feedback (lines 9, 11) and a useful phrase (line 14), helps the student formulate her answer.

Extract 1. Front Office Management (T1)[10]

1	AKL	you've seen organization charts before , **why is it important to have an**
2		**organization chart for a property that's three hundred rooms for**
3		**example** ? (1) **is it important to have one** ?
4	SS	yes
5	AKL	yes , **why** ?
6	Suka	in er
7	AKL	**what does it show**
8	Suka	the duties like everything is (really) separated for each person
9	AKL	right
10	Suka	er it's not possible that each person can handle everything .
11	AKL	yeah
12	Suka	there er a person should be specialized in a particular department and there
13		should be department head , very very (xx)
14	AKL	the lines of authority
15	Suka	yeah

During these early days of the course, students raise relatively few questions themselves. One of them is captured in Extract 2. In line 1 Jins, who is a Korean student with some background in mathematics, but a relatively low proficiency in English,[11] requires further explanation in relation to a financial problem the teacher has started to work on in class. Interestingly, this question follows on a three-second period of silence and is introduced by the preparatory *excuse me*, which is used very seldom on the whole and if so, then only during the first few days. The teacher is immediately highly collaborative in that he first helps formulate the question (line 2) before he offers an explanation in lines 4 and 6. Similar to Suka's affirmative minimal response finishing off the question-initiated exchange in Extract 1, Jins makes her level of understanding explicit (lines 7, 9).

Extract 2. **Financial Management (T1)**

1	Jins	(3) excuse me ? **how could you get that re:- ?**
2	TON	retained profit . so=
3	Jins	**=in again**
4	TON	(1) we decided , we wanted to keep
5	Jins	uhu
6	TON	about half to reinvest . (.) this is a decision .
7	Jins	I understand no calculate
8	TON	no
9	Jins	no calculate @

These two extracts illustrate, firstly, that during the first few days teachers aimed mainly at establishing a friendly and supportive atmosphere by either raising questions that allowed for easy answers or helping students along in formulating their questions and contributions. Students, on the other hand, remained relatively silent, restricting contributions to a handful of linguistically marked referential questions and to teacher prompted and supported contributions, with the overall aim to co-construct understanding. This generally shared aim to make understanding possible was also an issue talked about in the one-to-one interviews (see Quote 1).

Quote 1. **Interview (1st sem, 4th mth)**

Anns: yes there are differences, some people are it is hard for them to understand because the way they have learnt English , is different. […] when they speak sometimes yes the others don't understand . but we yes we try to communicate with each other.

While the differences in interactional behaviour between teachers and students can be observed throughout T1, they are restricted to the instructional register, i.e. the long lesson phases dealing with the content matter of the various classes. During the much shorter and less frequent regulatory exchanges focusing on administrative matters, question-answer sequences display a different interactional pattern right from the start of the HMP. As illustrated in Extracts 3 and 4, the few regulatory questions can be formulated by teacher or student, do not require any teacher prompt, neither any preparatory moves, nor do they necessarily lead to lengthy confirmatory exchanges.

Extract 3. **Front Office Management (T1)**

1	AKL	good so we talked about the difference er between a (.) chain hotel and an
2		independent hotel ? (1) **so what time do we finish did you say now**
3	SX-m	<1>six minutes earlier</1>
4	AKL	<1>**eleven fi** </1> **forty five hu ? or eleven yeah**

5   SX-m   forty four (2)

Extract 4. Financial Management (T1)

1   TON   <TON hands books out (10)> okay
2   Clap   **and so we keep this book ?**
3   TON   yes you could , you should keep these books for the length of your stay here
4   and do not, hm: ?
5   Clap   **after(wards) we'll have to return the book ?**
6   TON   it's not a new book , you have to give them back at the end .

To sum up, question-initiated exchanges at T1 reveal clearly different patterns for the two main registers – instructional and regulatory – in that the latter seems to place the participants at an interactionally more equal level, while the former and much more widely used register is discursively constructed in such a way that it is dominated by the teachers wanting to offer their learners a smooth introduction to their diverse content areas. This is attempted by, firstly, a concentrated use of display questions for fact, secondly, explicit acknowledgement of (student) understanding and, thirdly, elaborate use of minimal feedback on behalf of the teachers.

A year later, question-initiated exchanges look fundamentally different. First of all, students take on considerably more active roles. Extract 5 comes from a Food and Beverage (F&B) Management class. Triggered by a discussion of strategic vs. operational planning in F&B management, the teacher raises a question that appears to be of a display nature: she asks for operational steps to be taken when a bar is not doing well enough (lines 1-2). In a remarkably smooth flow of contributions, various students suggest different reasons for too low a revenue and possible solutions to solve such a problem. Starting off with too high costs, Jenz suggests lowering prices of drinks (line 5) before bringing up the issue of staff costs (lines 7-8). This leads on to two students and the teacher suggesting illegal acts employees might commit by either offering free drinks, taking beverages home or drinking them themselves. Finally, Kosk mentions a further potential problem, namely low numbers of customers. Here, the teacher repeats her question of what could be done to change such a situation (line 21) to which two students add latching contributions, offering planning steps, which the teacher's supportive comments identify as well-informed (lines 22-28).

Extract 5. Food and Beverage Management (T3)

1   AKL   **if a bar (.) is not doing very well in a five star hotel, what could you do**
2   **with this bar ,**
3   Jenz   if the er (.) costs , too high ?
4   AKL   the cost could be too high because of too much staff=
5   Jenz   =then you have to: for example er I just say the beverage is too high ,
6   AKL   yeah ,

7,	Jenz	then you have to find a reason ? maybe is too many staff , we just have to
8		make sure ,
9	AKL	that's right . <3> look at the staff . yes ?</3>
10	Jenz	<3> o:r maybe somebody </3> give free drink (.) **you know what I mean ?**
11	AKL	fraud you mean maybe yeah
12	Jenz	so they they're not very high and the revenue very low , so you have to find
13		(reason) .
14	AKL	so you have to evaluate and investigate if the staff is taking , (.) you know
15		drinks home ?
16	SS	@@@
17	Kosk	or they drinking them themselves ,
18	AKL	liquor or spirits home ? (.) so this is (then) the fraud . er the other thing (.)
19		could happen that you have to too many staff , (.)_
20	Kosk	or too less guest- customers ,
21	AKL	not enough customers . in the case of not enough customers , **what could you**
		do ?
22	Kama	outsource =
23	Kosk	=you promote =
24	AKL	= outsource , (.) that's one (.) option .
25	Kosk	or you promote the bar to do: well with the=
26	AKL	=you promote the bar you might=
27	Kosk	=In cooperation with the f- the f- the front office department ,
28	AKL	right . <T continues by bringing the example of a Viennese hotel bar that
29		applied such operational planning successfully>

When contrasting with question-initiated exchanges in the first semester, the third semester reveals a clearly higher readiness amongst students to contribute to the ongoing conversation. This readiness comes to the fore in two ways in Extract 5: firstly, there are all in all three students willing to respond to the teacher's question. Their immediate and varied contributions reveal that, in contrast to T1, they can bring in their own content-related expertise and also practical experience. Admittedly, their contributions are rather short and highly contextuald (for a discussion see below). Secondly, Jenz's confirmation check in line 10 illustrates the general readiness to make potential problems of understanding explicit. After a year of having communicated in English as the community's lingua franca, all participants act upon their awareness of the relevance of signalling understanding. Quote 2, in which a student comments on the communicational need to raise clarification requests, supports the general relevance given to communicational strategies within the HMP.

Quote 2. **Interview (4th sem, 1st mth)**

> Lura: I think erm whenever somebody doesn't understand a word , everybody will help them , but as long as people don't ask nobody will actually then translate each word they say , so I think if somebody doesn't understand something , he or she should ask and yeah .

In addition to their interest in signalling understanding and responding to teacher questions, students also raise instructional questions unpromptedly and without any preparatory moves. Extract 6 is taken from the public relations class that followed on a visit to the studios of the largest Austrian radio station. Kosk, a Greek student, initiates this exchange by asking for an explanation of the high frequency of weather reports on Austrian radio. By drawing on his cultural knowledge and formulating follow-on questions (lines 3, 9) he directs the teacher in offering an explanation by drawing on her expert knowledge (lines 13-16).

Extract 6. Public Relations (T3)

1	Kosk	**why do you have so much information about weather , (every fifteen minutes)**
2	MER	erm .
3	Kosk	**I mean like (.) if it's snowy outside we see it , yeah** ?
4	SS	<4> @@@. </4>
5	MER	that's <4> right @@ </4> can you know how it is in greek Kosk , (.) but the
6		Austrians are eager (.) to get to know what the weather will be (.) and they are
7		also interested in the weather situation right now . (.) even if they can look out
8		of the window .
9	Kosk	**every fifteen minutes , isn't it too much ?**
10	MER	<1> every thirty yeah . </1>
11	SS	<1> @@@. </1>
12	Kosk	<1> overload @@ every thirty </1> **isn't that overload ?**
13	MER	erm (.) there exist researches (.) where erm (1) they try to find out which
14		programs are the most interesting ones for listeners and viewers . (.) and the
15		weather forecast (.) is on top position , I don't know the exact ranking , (.) but
16		it's on top position actually .

Besides instigating topics and thus influencing the curricular content discussed, students also display their heightened level of active participation in response to a teacher question. In Extract 7, the Financial Management teacher, who has been discussing the general growth potential of modern technological markets, raises a seemingly rhetorical question, which he answers himself after a second's pause (line 2). Interestingly, one student displays a different interpretation of the question, and uses it in order to voice her own ideas, which differ from the teacher's (lines 11 and 13). By doing so she extends the argument, which leads to a further teacher question, this time a referential one (line 15). By now, various students contribute to the exchange, first to the teacher's question, but then also in response to each other. While the teacher still has a special role, as his long turn in lines 25-27 shows, students feel free to offer their contributions unpromptedly.

Extract 7. Financial Management (T3)

1	TON	once you got two P Cs that really IS enough . **do you need a third one ?** (1)
2		not really .
3	Cana	no but they rely on ,
4	TON	replacement . (3) but it's not the exciting business where (.) the demand is

5		doubling , (2) every six months or anything . (1) it's not as <1> exciting </1>.
6	Cana	<1> not yet .</1>
7	TON	no , we- we've been through there .
8	Cana	yeah but still . (1) there're (.) are so many new things coming up , (.) that (x) are
9		gonna change .
10	TON	yes .
11	Cana	it's the same thing like <GERMAN> handies </GERMAN>
12	TON	**like what sorry ?**
13	Cana	like cell phones . (1) same thing ,
14	TON	(3) yes , although it's interesting I think because cell phones , (.) they keep trying
15		to add new options . (.) **what more can you put into a P C** . (1) you can only ,
16		you only really need =
17	Anki	=smell.
18	SS	@@@@.
19	Jins	they have that already . <2> yeah (some) smell </2>.
20	Zuyz	<2> (oranges x) </2>
21	Jins	(xxxx) <3> </3>> (xxx) </3>
22	Flor	<3> **what** (.) **really ?** </3>
23	Zuyz	(you can smell them .)
24	Flor	he he ,
25	TON	it's getting more and more difficult to find these . isn't it . (.) because (1) they
26		they they've got (lot) of graphics , (.) the computer's very fast , (.) erm they've
27		got sounds now . (.) they just have to get bigger (.) and in this respect , (1) there erm
28	Jins	**do we have a robot ?**
29	Anle	no we haven't got one
30	Jins	just a-
31	Anle	(xxx)
32	TON	no , yeah (.) but for- **that would be rather more than a PC , wouldn't it .**
33	Sx-f	yes .

In summary, the latter three extracts have shown how differently students and teachers interacted in question-initiated exchanges in the third semester. While teachers were clearly still in charge of classroom management and overall topic development, students took a more active role in responding to questions, raising their own and introducing new subtopics. Additionally, students engaged in collaborative talk with each other, thus adding sequences of multiparty communication to the bipolar constellations of teacher-whole class or teacher-one student, exclusively observable at the beginning of the HMP. This increased readiness of students to contribute to a topic is also reflected in the fact that more students took their turns at talk, such as Zuyz in Extract 7, who did not make himself heard at T1 at all.

While the findings described so far already imply a developmental process within the HMP, research question 2 (*Which roles do questions play in the development of curricular content?*) requires a more direct and detailed discussion of the dynamics to be witnessed in the data set. At the beginning of the HMP, the intensive use of display questions on behalf of the teachers clearly reflects their role as organizers of classroom talk in terms of turn allotment as well as topic development. In other words, display questions make possible a teacher-directed, but student-oriented development of curricular content. The teachers' role of classroom manager remains completely uncontested during the first semester in that students raise questions for facts or reasons and explanations mainly to solve issues of vague or non-understanding that arise from the teacher-led ongoing interaction (Extracts 1 and 2). While the instructional question-initiated exchanges thus portray the teachers as generally acknowledged 'primary knowers' (Berry, 1981) ready to introduce novices to their fields of expertise, the regulative exchanges (Extracts 3 and 4) picture interactants that communicate on a more equal footing, reflecting their common base of extensive educational expertise. As can be expected from this initial scenario, the participatory pattern of regulative exchanges does not change throughout the HMP. This contrasts markedly with the instructional exchanges in the third semester. As indicated above, students do not only respond to teachers' questions by drawing on their own growing professional expertise, they also raise their own questions, thus pushing the discursive topic introduced by the teacher into a new direction (e.g. Extracts 5 and 7) or introducing a completely new topic as in Extract 6. In terms of the research question this means that students' questions for facts, but even more so those for reason and explanation seem to indicate their more active involvement in developing topics.

In conclusion, the quantitatively established change from more display to more referential questions, slowly asking also for reasons and explanations in addition to the generally central questions for facts (see Tables 4 and 5) can now be interpreted as revealing a qualitatively observable change in question-initiated exchanges towards what might be referred to as more interactional equality in developing curricular content.

5.3   Implications for (language) learning

Research question 3 (*In what ways do question-initiated exchanges reveal (language) learning processes?*) necessitates a rather interpretative research step from interactional exchanges, i.e. observable language in use, to learning processes, i.e. unobservable cognitive changes. While thus further removed from the data itself, the longitudinal methodology makes it still possible to substantiate the interpretative claims made by extrapolating from the long-term findings of classroom talk, triangulated with the participants' views voiced during the interviews.

As argued by Tsui et al. (2004, p. 4) the actual learning process of acquiring knowledge is intricately linked to the 'space of learning', which "is constituted by linguistic means in the interaction between teacher and students" (Tsui et al., 2004, p. 24), i.e. in classroom discourse. While such a sociocultural understanding of learning is so widely shared in present-day research that explicit mentioning might seem superfluous, the crucial link between classroom talk and learning underlines, firstly, that learning is complex and dynamic, including intentional and incidental, social and individual processes (e.g. Hulstijn, 2003), and secondly, that in view of the heightened relevance of the teacher in class, it remains contingent on teaching.

The latter point is particularly obvious in traditional lessons which are largely organised by the teacher because even when the HMP students increasingly influence the construction of class topics, it clearly remains the teachers' role to decide on curricular content. As regards intentional and incidental learning, the extracts discussed above allow for glimpses into the discursive space for both kinds of learning: Many teacher questions aim for intentional learning by, for instance, opening a fitting space for learning on operational planning (Extract 5); the same can be said for a good many of the students' questions (e.g. Extract 2). When comparing examples across phases and subjects, some questions or responses reveal that students benefited from such spaces of learning, such as in Extract 5 (line 22) when a student suggests "outsourcing", a strategy explicitly taught and discussed in relation to hotel management in the first semester.

At the same time, the question-initiated exchanges of T3 when compared to those at T1 reveal incidental learning in terms of an increased ability to react quickly to questions, to add contributions or to apply communicational strategies in order to make oneself understood. Such increased fluency, however, seems to go hand-in-hand with little concern for accuracy. As the contributions in all extracts show, grammatical correctness does not seem to feature strongly; a disregard which is clearly an important characteristic of English functioning as the community's lingua franca and also identified as communicationally necessary by community members (see Quote 3).

Quote 3. Interview (1st sem, 3rd mth)

> Flor: and for every sentence I was just thinking of erm is it right , is it grammatically right , and then just express it , I mean just say the sentence and then afterwards , er did I say it right or not , so you have to think about it and that's why the sentences are coming very slow . and right now I just don't think about it just keep on talking and maybe sometimes it's wrong , but ja […] ja you feel very good .

In other words, the function of English as their lingua franca comes to the fore in the interactional data, but is also topicald as such in the participants' reflections. This contrasts with English functioning as their (future) professional language, where the data do not offer a similarly homogeneous picture. Some students commented on their self-evaluation of having gained a more professional English (see Quote 4); others, however, commented on their own proficiency having suffered in the course of the HMP (see Quote 5).

Quote 4. **Interview (4th sem, 1st mth)**

> Elig: I think it [= English] did improve in a more professional way , because as you know I've been to the U S for a year and I had this typical kind of American high school English and I think it improved a lot , so I can also use it in hotels , you know it is like we don't have a room , @@ you shouldn't say that in this way .

Quote 5. **Interview (2nd sem, 2nd mth)**

> Lula: I think I'm losing it [= English] here in Vienna a little bit @ [...] I mean before I used to have like my friends who'd say come on , we'll elaborate on that and we used to have discussions and all these things and then you come here and nobody's gonna tell you elaborate on that then I go okay (xx) enough thanks .

These diverse self evaluations find their reflection in the classroom discourse data. The extracts discussed earlier contain some student expressions that seem to reflect professional language use (e.g. "revenue [is] very low", line 12 in Extract 5), but the overall impression is a different one: most of the frequent instances of teachers recasting student contributions into more professional language in Extracts 1, 2 and 5 are not taken up; a finding which suggests that the immediate communicational needs of constructing mutual understanding might have overruled the longer-term aims of language learning. At the same time, this interpretation might need a broader data base. At present, the data consist exclusively of classroom talk and, given the fundamental institutional difference between the hotel and the classroom and the contingencies of the latter on the students' discursive behaviour in class, their largely unprofessional language use might actually be motivated by the setting rather than their language proficiency. For a more reliable evaluation of their professional language abilities it would therefore be necessary to complement the present data base with either hotel-based interactions or other specific discourse, such as in the written mode.

Even if the impression on limited learning in terms of English as a professional language might be biased due to the limited data-base, the sheer absence of any teaching focus on professional discourse arguably reveals that English in its function as a professional language was not paid attention to in the HMP content classrooms. This claim finds support in the participants' generally shared beliefs on language proficiency and learning, revealed in the many interviews. First of all, 'learning (English)' tended to be identified as (intentional) vocabulary learning (see Quote 6), while gaining fluency and appropriacy in using the language was referred to by 'improving (English)' (see Quote 7), thus revealing a strong belief in naturalistic language acquisition as so lastingly formulated in the 1980s by Stephen Krashen (e.g. 1982).

Quote 6. Interview (4th sem, 1st mth)

Elig: I think every field has their specific vocabulary and you just [...] have to learn it , I don't think it's the English , just special terminology .

Quote 7. Interview (4th sem, 1st mth)

Lura: yeah erm when I came here I erm knew some English , I knew how to speak and everything , but it wasn't fluent and didn't understand a lot of words and I think now when- wherever I go in the world , I can use my English , [...] I think it's no problem to communicate for me and I think I speak pretty fluent so .

Such lay modelling of language learning reflects a lexically explicit distinction between intentional and incidental learning: 'learning' is reserved for the intentional processes of acquisition, while 'improving' captures the incidental ones. At the same time, the quotes illustrate a fairly simplistic view on language proficiency insofar as the object of intentional learning is limited to vocabulary only, while general fluency and communicational ability are seen as the outcome of incidental learning. In other words, intentional learning is reduced to lexical inventories ('terminology'), considerations of appropriate register, discursive aims and their textualisations are left unattended; pushed back to the realm of incidentally 'picking it up'. This conceptualisation is clearly reflected in the structure of the HMP – content classes and content-wise independent ESP classes in the first two semesters – but also in the classroom data: the focus is exclusively on content and, if identified as necessary, terminological clarification (for a detailed analysis cf. Smit, 2010a, pp. 384–389). In other words, what is markedly absent from the way proficiency is constructed in this context is an understanding of generic competences (e.g. Bhatia, 1997) and that they can, and should be taught explicitly (e.g. Hüttner, Smit & Mehlmauer-Larcher, 2009).

To conclude, the analysis of question-initiated exchanges has unearthed their relevance for teachers and students creating 'spaces for learning'. Additionally, the more actively students participate the more likely it is that they can draw on their own learning, thus engaging in the dynamic process of knowledge construction. At the same time, the analysis has also made clear that the potentialities of learning are contingent on teaching aims. As argued above, if teachers do not aim for professional language use, they will not include it in their teaching programme, with the result that students' language learning is left to the incidental level.

6 Conclusions

The analysis of question-initiated exchanges presented in this paper has confirmed previous research in identifying the question as highly central speech act for formal educational settings in terms of frequency as well as relevance to structuring classroom talk. In the present context of a tertiary, English-medium hotel management educational programme (HMP) set in Vienna, Austria, the longitudinal study has revealed that questions are ubiquitously used, generally more often by teachers, but with the programme progressing also more centrally by students. The initial preference teachers reveal for known-answer or display questions is soon abandoned for a mix of display and referential questions, raised by teachers and students alike. The more active participatory role students take on in the third semester is also witnessed in the increased use of referential questions for reason and explanation, thus engaging in longer exchanges co-constructing curricular content together with their teachers. As regards language use and learning, the most interesting finding surely is the explicit and implicit modelling of their classroom language as lingua franca, thus catering for the communicational realities of their community, but at the same time hampering the realisation and enactment of English as the learners' (future) professional language.

Additionally, the research focus on question-initiated exchanges has proven to be methodologically fruitful. As an operationalisable concept, it leads to a transparently identified selection of discursively relevant exchanges. Given their frequency, the resulting set of exchanges can then be thoroughly analysed in a mixed-method approach, combining the strengths of both, quantification and qualification.

In an attempt to move beyond the individual study, the findings are arguably also relevant for other tertiary institutions offering English-medium courses, especially in mainland Europe. On the reassuring side, the HMP shows that English-medium tertiary education can work even when it is an additional language to all participants. The HMP teachers and students interviewed all evaluated their programme and doing it in English as generally successful. Their subjective evaluations find an objective counterpart in the fact that the programme has been going strong for more than twenty years, and prides itself in the successful professional placements of many of its graduates. On a more cautious note, this study also shows that the employment of English as classroom language would necessitate a pedagogical approach that takes on board the complexity of English as the group's lingua franca as well as their future professional language. As argued above, what is at stake are the participants' highly contextuald communicational as well as their future professional discursive needs. Supported by in-service teacher education, such programmes should aim for a conscious and explicitly integrative approach of teaching content and English in its complexity as lingua franca and professional language.

References

Airey, J. (2009) *Science, Language and Literacy. Case Studies of Learning in Swedish University Physics*, University of Uppsala: Acta Universitatis Upsaliensis.

Ammon, U. (ed.). (2001) *The Dominance of English as a Language of Science. Effects on Other Languages and Language Communities*, Berlin: Mouton de Gruyter.

Banda, F. (2009) Critical perspectives on language planning and policy in Africa: Accounting for the notion of multilingualism, *SPIL (Stellenbosch Papers in Linguistics) Plus. Special Issue: Multilingualism and Language Policies in Africa* (38*)*: 1–11.

Berry, M. (1981) Systemic linguistics and discourse analysis: a multi-layered approach to exchange structure. In Malcolm Coulthard (Ed.), *Studies in Discourse Analysis*, London: Routledge: 120–145.

Bhatia, V. K. (1997) Introduction: genre analysis and World Englishes, *World Englishes* (16*)* 3: 313–319.

Björkman, B. (2009) From code to discourse in spoken ELF. In A. Mauranen & E. Ranta (eds.), *English as a Lingua Franca. Studies and Findings*, Cambridge: Cambridge Scholars Publishing: 213–232.

Blum-Kulka, S. (1997) Discourse pragmatics. In Teun A. van Dijk (ed.), *Discourse as Social Interaction. Discourse Studies: a Multidisciplinary Introduction. Volume 2,* London: Sage Publications: 38–63.

Cazden, C. B. (2001) *Classroom Discourse: The Language of Teaching and Learning* (2nd ed.), Portsmouth, NH: Heinemann.

Christie, F. (2002) *Classroom DiscourseAanalysis: A Functional Perspective*, London, New York: Continuum.

Coyle, D., Hood, P., & Marsh, D. (2010) *CLIL. Content and Language Integrated Learning,* Cambridge: Cambridge University Press.

Dafouz-Milne, E., & Núñez-Perucha, B. (2010).,Metadiscursive devices in university lectures: a contrastive analysis of L1 and L2 teacher performance. In C. Dalton-Puffer, T. Nikula, & U. Smit (eds.), *Language Use and Language Learning in CLIL Classrooms AILA*

Applied Linguistics Series: Vol. 7, Amsterdam [u.a.]: Benjamins: 213–232.

Dalton-Puffer, C., & Nikula, T. (2006) Pragmatics of content-based instruction: Teacher and student Directives in Finnish and Austrian classrooms, *Applied Linguistics*, (27) 2:, 241–267. Dalton-Puffer, C. (2007) *Discourse in Content and Language Integrated Learning (CLIL) Classrooms*, Amsterdam ; Philadelphia: John Benjamins Pub.

Dörnyei, Z. (2007) *Research Methods in Applied Linguistics: Quantitative, Qualitative and Mixed Methodologies* (1. publ). *Oxford applied linguistics*, Oxford: Oxford University Press.

Edmondson, W. (1981) *Spoken Discourse: A Model for Analysis. Longman Linguistics Library: Vol. 27*, London: Longman.

Edwards, A., & Westgate, D. (1994) *Investigating Classroom Talk* (2nd edition), London and Washington D.C.: Palmer press.

Ferguson, G. (2006) *Language Planning and Education*, Edinburgh: Edinburgh University Press.

Fortanet-Gómez, I., & Räisänen, C. A. (eds.) (2008) *ESP in European Higher Education: Integrating Language and Content*, Amsterdam: Benjamins.

Graddol, D. (2006) *English Next. Why Global English Might Mean the End of 'English as a Foreign Language'*, British Council: The English Company (UK) Ltd.

Halliday, M.A.K. (2004). *An Introduction to Functional Grammar* (3rd edition), London: Arnold.

Hellekjær, G. (2010) Assessing lecture comprehension in English-medium higher education: A Norwegian Case Study. In C. Dalton-Puffer, T. Nikula, & U. Smit (Eds.) *Language Use in Content-and-Language Integrated Learning (CLIL)*, Amsterdam: Benjamins: 233-258.

Hüllen, W. (1982) Teaching a foreign language as 'lingua franca'. *Grazer Linguistische Studien*, (16): 83-88.

Hulstijn, J. (2003) Incidental and intentional learning. In C. Doughty & M. Long (eds.) *The Handbook of Second Language Acquisition* , Oxford: Blackwell: 349–381.

Hüttner, J., Smit, U., & Mehlmauer-Larcher, B. (2009) ESP teacher education at the interface of theory and practice: Introducing a model of mediated corpus-based genre analysis, *System* (37)1: 99–109.

Kachru, B. B. (1996) English as lingua franca. In H. Goebl, P. H. Nelde, Z. Stary, & W. Wölck (Eds.), *Kontaktlinguistik. Contact Linguistics. Linguistique de contact*, Berlin: Walter de Gruyter: 906–913.

Kachru, B. B. (2008) Symposium on intelligibility and cross-Cultural communication in world Englishes: Introduction. The first step: the Smith paradigm for intelligibility in world Englishes, *World Englishes* (27)3/4: 293–296.

Kaur, J. (2009) *English as a Lingua Franca: Co-constructing Understanding*, Saarbrücken: VDM Verlag Müller.

Krashen, S. D. (1982) *Principles and practice in second language acquisition* (1st edition), Oxford/New York: Pergamon.

Lee, Y.-A. (2006) Respecifying display questions: Interactional resources for language teaching, *TESOL Quarterly* (40)4: 691–713.

Lee, Y.-A. (2008) Yes-no questions in the third-turn position: Pedagogical discourse processes, *Discourse Processes*(45) 3: 237–262.

Lemke, J. L. (1990) *Talking science: Language, Learning, and Values. Language and EducationalProcesses*, Norwood, NJ: Ablex Publ.

Lin, A., & Martin, P. (eds.) (2005) *Decolonisation, Globalisation. Language-in-education Policy and Practice,* Clevedon: Multilingual Matters.

Long, M., & Sato, C. J. (1983) Classroom foreigner talk discourse: forms and functions of teachers' questions. In H. G. Seliger & M. H. Long (Eds.), *Classroom Oriented Research in Second Language Acquisition*, Rowley: Newbury House Publishers: 269–286.

Markee, N. (2000) *Conversation Analysis. Second LanguageAacquisition Research*, Mahwah, NJ: Erlbaum.

Marton, F., & Tsui, A. B. M. (eds.) (2004) *Classroom Discourse and the Space of Learning*, Mahwah, NJ: Lawrence Erlbaum.

Mehan, H. (1979) *Learning Lessons: Social Organization in the Classroom*, Cambridge Mass: Harvard University Press.

Meyerhoff, M. (2002) Communities of practice. In J. K. Chambers, P. Trudgill, & N. Schilling-Estes (Eds.), *The Handbook of Language Variation and Change* , Malden, M.A.: Blackwell: 521–548.

Morell, T. (2004) Interactive lecture discourse for university EFL students, *English for Specific Purposes*, (23): 325–338.

Motz, M. (2005) Internationalisierung der Hochschulen und Deutsch als Fremdsprache. In M. Motz (Ed.), *Englisch oder Deutsch in Internationalen Studiengängen?*, Frankfurt: Lang: 131–152.

Musumeci, D. (1996) Teacher-learner negotiation in content-based instruction: communication at cross-purposes? *Applied Linguistics* (17*)*: 286–325.

Nassaji, H., & Wells, G. (2000) What's the use of 'Triadic Dialogue'? An investigation of teacher-student interaction, *Applied Linguistics*, (21*)*3: 376–406.

Nikula, T. (2005) English as an object and a tool of study in classrooms: interactional effects and pragmatic implications, *Linguistics and Education* (*16*)1: 27–58.

Richard, J. C., & Lockhart, C. (1994) *Reflective Teaching in Second Language Classrooms*, Cambridge: Cambridge University Press.

Ruiz-Garrido, M. F., & Palmer-Silveira, J. C. (2008) Content learning in business communication: a teaching experience within a new European framework. In I. Fortanet-Gómez & C. A. Räisänen (Eds.), *ESP in European Higher Education. Integrating Language and Content* , Amsterdam: Benjamins: 147–164.

Schegloff, E. A., Jefferson, G., & Sacks, H. (1977) The preference for self-correction in the organization of repair in conversation, *Language*(53*)*2: 361-382.

Schiffrin, D. (1994) *Approaches to Discourse. Blackwell Textbooks in Linguistics: Vol. 8*, Oxford: Blackwell.

Searle, J. (1976). A classification of illocutionary acts, *Language in Society* (5): 1-23.

Smit, U. (2009) Emic evaluations and interactive processes in a classroom community of practice. In A. Mauranen and E. Ranta (eds) *English as a Lingua Franca: Studies and Findings*, Newcastle upon Tyne: Cambridge Scholars Publihsers: 200-224.

Smit, U. (2010a) Conceptualising English as a lingua franca (ELF) as a tertiary classroom language, *Stellenbosch Papers in Linguistics* (39): 59–74.

Smit, U. (2010b) *English as a Lingua franca in Higher Education: A Longitudinal Study of Classroom Discourse. Trends in Applied Linguistics: Vol. 2*, Berlin [u.a.]: De Gruyter Mouton.

Smith, L., & Nelson, C. (1985) International intelligibility of English: directions and resources. *World Englishes*, 4 (3): 333–342.

Smith, L. E. (1984) Teaching English as an international language. *Studium Linguistik* (15): 52–59.

Tsui, A. B. M., Marton, F., Mok, I. A., & Ng, D. F. (2004) Questions and the space of learning. In F. Marton & A. B. M. Tsui (Eds.) *Classroom*

Discourse and the Space of Learning, Mahwah, NJ: Lawrence Erlbaum: 98–118.

Unterberger, B., & Wilhelmer, N. (forthcoming) English-medium education in economics and business studies: capturing the status quo at Austrian universities .van Lier, L. (1988) *The Classroom and the Language Learner*, London and New York: Longman.

Wächter, B., & Maiworm, F. (2008) *English-taught Programmes in European Higher Education. The Picture in 2007*, Bonn: Lemmens.

Walsh, S. (2006) *Investigating Classroom Discourse*, London and New York: Routledge.

Wenger, E. (1998) *Communities of Practice: Learning, Meaning, and Identity. Learning in Doing*, Cambridge, U.K, New York, N.Y: Cambridge University Press.

Wertsch, J. V. (ed.) (1992) *Culture, Communication and Cognition: Vygotskian Perspectives*, Cambridge: Cambridge University Press.

Widdowson, H. G. (1990) *Aspects of Language Teaching*, Oxford: Oxford University Press.

Wilkinson, R. (Ed.). (2004) *Integrating Content and Language: Meeting the Challenge of a Multilingual Higher Education ; Proceedings of the ICL Conference, October 23-25 2003*, Maastricht: Universitaire Pers Maastricht.

Wilkinson, R. (2008) Locating the ESP space in problem-based learning. English-medium degree programmes from a post-Bologna perspective. In I. Fortanet-Gómez (Ed.), *ESP in European Higher Education. Integrating Language and Content AILA Applied Linguistics Series: Vol. 4.*, Amsterdam [u.a.]: Benjamins: 55–73.

Wilkinson, R., & Zegers, V. (eds.) (2007) *Researching content and language integration in higher education*, Nijmegen [u. a.]: Valkhof Pers.

Zuengler, J., & Brinton, D. M. (1997) Linguistic form, pragmatic function: relevant research from content-based research. In M. A. Snow & D. M. Brinton (eds.) *The Content Based Classroom. Perspectives on Integrating Language and Content*, White Plains, NY: Longman: 263–273.

Zwiers, J. (2007) Teacher practices and perspectives for developing academic language, *International Journal of Applied Linguistics* (17) 1: 93–116.

Appendix
Transcription conventions

3-letter pseudonyms (in capitals)	refer to teachers
4-letter pseudonyms	refer to students
SS	students
SX-m	unidentified male student
SX-f	unidentified female student
(.)	pause shorter than a second
(2)	pauses, timed in seconds
exte:nsion	noticeable extension of a syllable or sound
cut off wo-	cut off word or truncated speech
text=	latching utterances
=text	
@	laughter (in syllable length)
<1>, </1>	overlapping speech
xxx	inaudible speech
(text)	unclear speech
.	falling intonation
?	rising intonation
,	level intonation
[...]	deletion of text
<text>	added explanations
text (in excerpts)	material which is currently under discussion

Instructional teacher questions	T1		T2		T3		Total
	N	%	N	%	N	%	
display	84	40,4	77	37,0	47	22,6	208
referential	43	23,6	66	36,3	73	40,1	182
Total	127	32,6	143	36,7	120	30,8	390

Chi-square = 18.06; df = 2; p = 0.0001.

Table 4. Instructional teacher display and referential questions according to points in time

[1] While the first macro-level considerations concerning ELF go back to the 1980s (Hüllen, 1982; Smith, 1984), the last 15 years have witnessed an explosion in empirical research, as reflected in the impressive number of special ELF issues of international journals (e.g. English Today, 2008; Intercultural Pragmatics, 2009; International Journal of the Sociology of Language, 2006;

Nordic Journal of English Studies, 2006) as well as in the recently founded Journal of English as a Lingua Franca

[2] The Outer Circle'contains the countries in which English has functioned as one of the official or national languages since the times of British or American colonization. The Inner Circle'on the other hand comprises the countries in which English is the majoritys first language, such as the UK, Ireland, USA, Canada, Australia or New Zealand.

[3] Reflecting the diversity of practices as regards English-medium higher education, Unterberger and Wilhelmer (forthcoming) suggest a model of five instructional types of inte grating content and language at tertiary level that takes into consideration the interplay of various factors, such as teaching aims, pedagogical approach, the role of language or kinds of assessment.

[4] Originally conceptualised in Smith and Nelson (1985) intelligibility refers to recognizing words and phrases and is a precondition for comprehensibility, or recognizing their meaning, and interpretability, i.e. recognizing the speakers intention.

[5] A prototypical exchange structure in the classroom is the well-described 'Triadic Dialogue' (Lemke, 1990) with its three-part structure of (teacher) initiation, (student) response and (teacher) follow-up (cf. also Walsh, 2006, p. 46); for succinct overviews of the ongoing discussion on its value to the teaching and learning process cf. Dalton-Puffer (2007, pp. 72–75); Nassaji and Wells (2000).

[6] This study has been made possible by a research grant of the Austrian Science Fund; the transcriptions have in part been financed by a grant of the Wiener Hochschuljubiläumsstiftung.

[7] In order to respect the participants'anonymity, indications of time are given in relative terms only, by specifying the semester and month within the tertiary educational programme investigated. Furthermore, the students are referred to b y arbitrarily chosen pseudonyms consisting of four-letter combinations, while upper -case three -letter ones are reserved for the teachers.

[8] For a brief description of the data base cf. Smit (2009: 205 -206); for a detailed discussion cf. Smit (2010a: ch. 3).

[9] Statistical tests were undertaken with the help of the chi-square test for rows by columns contingency tables on the VassarStats Website for Statistical Computation (http://faculty.vassar.edu/lowry/VassarStats.html).

[10] For the transcription conventions see the Appendix.

[11] Information on the students'linguistic and educational backgrounds was collected in the questionnaires, interviews and informal conversations. For a detailed summary cf. Smit (2010b, chapter 4)

Identity and face in institutional English as Lingua Franca discourse[1]

Juliane House (University of Hamburg)

In this paper I examine interactions in institutional and intercultural pedagogic discourse in English as a lingua franca (ELF) between international students of various L1s, faculty members and assistants in both German and Danish university contexts. Of particular interest in institutional ELF interactions are potentially face-threatening acts such as requests for information or action (Edmondson 1981; Blum-Kulka et al 1989) addressed by students to status superiors in the context of advising and examining sessions. Issues related to face and identity construction in the realization of requests arise from the ELF inherent phenomenon that there is often a remarkable imbalance in interactants' demonstrated oral competence in EL. And this imbalance may be responsible for creating precarious situations of potential embarrassment, face loss and necessary negotiations of professional identity. On the basis of three 30-minute ELF interactions complemented by post-hoc collaborative reflections on rich points in the interactions, the paper investigates emergent issues of face threat and face maintenance as well as strategies of saving and re-enacting institutionally sanctioned identity both from a micro interactional and a macro-contextual perspective. Based on the findings of the analyses, I will also make several suggestions as to how interactants' pragmatic fluency might be improved.

1 Introduction

In this paper I will examine institutional pedagogic interactions in English as a lingua franca between international students of various L1s and German professors and assistants in a German university context. Of particular interest in institutional English as a lingua franca discourse are identity- and face related issues. The small case-study presented in this paper will look at issues of identity and face-threat and face-maintenance that emerge from interactions in academic advising sessions as one type of institutional pedagogic discourse.

In the first part of the paper I briefly define English as a lingua franca and describe some important strands in the field of English as a lingua franca; secondly I describe the present study, and thirdly I draw some conclusions.

1.1   English as a Lingua Franca (ELF)

English as a lingua franca (ELF) is a relatively new field of inquiry but it is of great importance given the continuing spread of English over many geographical and cultural areas and its enormous functional and formal flexibility. A major characteristic of ELF is its multiplicity of voices. ELF is a language for communication, and a medium that can be given substance with different national, regional, local, and individual cultural identities. ELF speakers can be said to use ELF primarily as a language of communication, not as a language for identification (Hüllen 1992; House 2003). Native L1 pragmatic norms are therefore often maintained in the medium of the English language. When ELF is used in interactions between, say, German, Spanish and French speakers, the differences in interactional norms, in standards of politeness, directness, values, and feelings of cultural and historical tradition will often remain unchanged underneath, as it were, the English surface. So we can say that ELF speakers are developing their very own discourse strategies, speech act modifications, and communicative styles in their use of the English language.

As long as a threshold of understanding is achieved, ELF speakers appear to adopt the so-called   "let-it-pass" principle, an interpretive procedure that makes the interactional style "robust", "normal" and consensual (Firth 1990) One might think that the adoption of such a strategy would endanger effective communication, since the sort of superficial consensus achieved may well mask deeper sources of trouble arising, for instance, from great differences in linguaculturally-based knowledge frames. However, ELF talk was found to be basically meaningful and "ordinary" (Firth 1996; House 2002). This ordinariness is a joint achievement of interactants, who successfully engage in their interactional and interpretive work in order to sustain the appearance of normality despite being exposed to each other's often idiosyncratic linguistic behavior. Achieving ordinariness is the direct outcome of the "let it pass" procedure, which interactants resort to whenever understanding threatens to become difficult. Unclear talk is then routinely "passed" over on the common sense assumption that, as the talk progresses, it will either eventually become clear or end up as redundant and thus negligible. ELF talk's "ordinariness" is achieved via a "make-it-normal" orientation, which implies that, faced with their interactants' marked lexical and phonological selections, morphological vagaries and idiosyncratic syntactic structuring, ELF speakers tend to behave in such a way as to deliberately divert attention from these infelicitous forms. Standards of native English are thus no longer operative.

An important general characteristic of ELF talk that has come to the foreground more recently is its inherent variability (Dewey 2009; Firth 2009). This variability is not to be equated with ELF speakers' "failure" to fulfil native norms, and their differential levels of competence in English. Rather it lies at the core of ELF discourse, where speakers creatively exploit, intentionally appropriate, locally adapt and communicatively align the potential inherent in the forms and functions, items and collocations of the virtual English language they take recourse to in their performance as the need arises (cf. Widdowson 2003).

Since ELF speakers do not seek to adjust to some real or imaginary native speaker norm, they do not conceive of themselves as learners of English as a foreign language, rather as individual ELF users united in a specific "community of practice" in the sense of Wenger (1989) and Eckert and McConnell-Ginet (1992). The notion "community of practice" is most appropriate for ELF (House 2003) in that the constitution of a community of practice is governed by a joint purpose, in this case to communicate efficiently in English as the agreed and chosen language of communication without, however, being constrained by English native norms (cf. House 2010, 2011). The relevance of the concept of "community of practice" for ELF has recently also been taken up by Seidlhofer (2007) and Dewey (2009).

A project specifically concerned with discourse pragmatics is the Hamburg ELF project (cf. e.g., House 2002, 2008; Baumgarten and House 2007, 2010). Here we have collected different sets of data from international students of various disciplines at the University of Hamburg: L1 English interactions, interactions between L1 English speakers and ELF speakers, ELF interactions between speakers of different L1s as well as retrospective interviews for collaborative interpretation. Subjects were involved in 5-30 minute interactions on the basis of a written textual trigger.

In a separate study funded since 2008 by the Volkswagen Foundation and conducted jointly at the universities of Siegen, Kassel and Hamburg, we have focussed on ELF interactions during academic advising sessions or office hours which takes place between international students and their academic advisors, professors and assistants. (cf. also House and Lévy-Toedter 2009; 2010). The results of analyses of this ELF data as well as ELF users' reflections about their own productions have revealed a number of characteristics of ELF use that point to strategies of expressing identity as well as maintaining face in the presence of face threats. These will be described in what follows. Some of the data presented below were discussed under a different research question in House and Levy-Toedter 2010.

2.1   Code-switching as an Expression of ELF Speakers' Identity

One means of expressing identity is switching from ELF into L1. Excerpts 1 and 2 show how the academic advisor, a German professor (P), makes use of code-switching during office hours to express his identity and to get his meaning across to the other two participants who both know German. WM-his assistant is a native speaker of German, and the Spanish Erasmus student (S) has at least a working knowledge of German.

Excerpt 1

P: (reads softly) Yeah then just take this off
S: Yes
P: We´ll do it by quickly its
S: So I need to (0.5) write=
P: =**Ja ja** [yes yes]
S: This office for uh (1sec) they approve the new
P: **Ja ja ja [yes yes yes]**
S: Without
WM: Without
P: Without this application always it it it it it is easily you can design a
       a a a a a cantilever slab within one week (0.5) not more to do it=
WM: =Or a shorter time
P: (fast) For a shorter everything (…)
S: Erm
P: **Joh ja können wir mal ruhig machen** (to WM) [yes yes we can
       certainly do this] it should be no problem

By using the German discourse marker *ja*, the professor also reassures the student about the ease with which he will be able to change the title of his thesis. This is done automatically, quickly and subconsciously. In the last move, the professor again resorts to German - the usual mode of communication between him and his assistant– in order to give a brief instruction.   Consider also excerpt 2, in which another lengthy code-switching sequence occurs:

Excerpt 2

P: Statements are sometimes **aber** [but] in general you just say here for example the code something something like this and then you you don't say (0.5) basis is maybe about this one they made some tests or whatsoever or from the other equation you cannot read I I think somewhere did did you cho this one is ok (fast) in principle (fast) but the other equation the next one the cc equation cc equation you

to your code so there must be some similarity there is literature available about this (0.5) mister [name3] has made some publication in Germany about this how he comes to this number this is for example the big discussion the be the debate about this number it is something which must be in your thesis

S: (fast) **Ja[yes]**

P: Okay? for this YES and erm **haben sie noch was nee des is der erste Teil war fertig**

      [anything else no this is the first part is finished]

WM: **Ja [yes]**

In excerpt 2, P's switch into his native German is followed by WM's uptake with the German *ja*. P's code-switching occurs at a critical point in the talk in that it marks the end of one part of the advising session, where P asks whether the session should go on or not. We can characterize P's utterance as an organisational move and liken it to the type of "management talk" which occurs in other instructional settings such as foreign language classrooms. Here, as in the above academic advising talk, switching to a shared L1 tends to occur with great frequency (cf. Edmondson and House 1981; 2011) Code-switching often involves the use of discourse markers or gambits, in particular "uptakers" such as *yes/ja* (Edmondson 1981). They usually occur as second-pair parts of an exchange, and are often characterized by a speaker's reduced monitoring of her own production, i.e., automatically, "off-guard" and with little conscious control. That switching into one's mother tongue should occur in this particular interactive slot is thus easily explained. Despite the relatively automatic switch into L1, this relapse can also be interpreted as a powerful assertion of a speaker's identification with his L1, and it supports the hypothesis that alongside ELF as a language for communication, speaker's L1s remain co-activated (Grosjean 2001), omnipresent and intact for identification.

A similar finding of the use of L1 in code-switching is presented in Pölzl and Seidlhofer (2006), where the authors document the use of Arabic gambits and other L1 discourse phenomena in ELF talk.

2.2   Re-interpretation of the Discourse Markers *I think* and *I mean* as Expressions of Identity in ELF Talk

The discourse markers *I think* and *I mean* tend to be re-interpreted in ELF talk to express identity and subjectivity. As compared to their conventional use by native speakers of English, ELF speakers tend to use of the construction I *think* in its prototypical meaning: they prefer formal structures (main clause complement structures) over the more grammaticalized structures and pragmaticalized meanings of *I think* used as a verbal routines (cf. Baumgarten & House 2007; 2010). The construction *I think* in ELF talk is thus often chosen when an ELF speaker wants to express her subjective opinion and, with this, her identity. This use indicates that ELF speakers have re-interpreted the standard native speaker usage of *I think* as an empty routine (see here already Edmondson & House 1981 for a discussion of the overrepresentation of *I think* in German users' English).

The expression *I mean* is often employed with an evaluative element in ELF talk over and above its function of reformulation and clarification (Baumgarten and House 2007). *I mean in ELF* talk functions as a focalizing device in the speaker's own contributions. It serves as a point of departure for an explicit expression of a subjective evaluation, indicating affective involvement in the topic as well as the speaker's identity. Here are some examples of the use of *I think* and *I mean* in our Hamburg ELF office hours data:

Excerpt 3

P: erm (6s) in which company do you want to do it?
S: erm that was (company 1)
P: (Company1) ohh ja ja (1s) **but I think** they can wait
S: okay because I told them to wait till Monday I will get it
P: till Monday? Hmm **but I think** erm we can do it erm

Excerpt 4
S: they are investigating most pumps that work in the same er let's say principle
WM: okay

S: because what you see HERE in these er let's say formulas are let's say the stage (?) er

the input current and these are common for all [pumps]
WM: yeah
S: I mean if you just change the the way it is dis defined then you will have er the right

formula **but er in our case I think** we don't have to change anything

Excerpt 5
S: but I try I try to to calculate V times I to make using the calculator and and average it it

was minus some[thing]
WM: [no no no] **but I mean**
S: **I mean** you know from the device parameters I can go to the results and check the

device

Excerpt 6
WM: and erm of course it's not as comfortable as
S: (unintelligible)
WM: yes exactly simply like a trimmer or so **but at least I think** that's the most reliable

source we have **soo first I mean** I will I would see if the delta source it will work

We can see in data excerpts (3) to (6) that there is an interesting co-occurrence of the markers *I think* and *I mean* with the adversative conjunction *but. I think* and *I mean* seem to act as reinforcing strategies making the idea initiated by the conjunction *but* more expressive, more salient, more affective and subjective. A similar co-occurrence pattern was found in the present author's investigation of the behaviour of the discourse maker *you know* in ELF talk (House 2009). Here *you know* was found to co-occur with the conjunction *but, because* and *and* with surprising frequency. The conjunctions *but, because* and *and* tend to signal what is called in systemic-functional linguistics 'externally operating relations", i.e. they are oriented to the proposition and to the subject-matter related category FIELD in systemic-functional theory (cf. the discussion in Martin 1992). So we may assume that *I think* and *I mean* in their comparable co-occurrence with *but* also function not as a semantically empty routine, but rather as an expression of a speaker's opinion vis a vis externally operating relations or states of affairs. At the same time, *I think* and *I mean* are used to express a speaker's subjectivity and identity through the presence of the first person pronoun *I*.

2.3   Handling potential face-threats in ELF academic advising sessions

In our Hamburg ELF office hours data we found a number of interruptions, corrections, and reformulations of utterances produced by the person of highest rank: the professor (P). In excerpts (7), (8) and (9), it is the student who interrupts the professor and sometimes finishes his utterances for him. Given the status difference between a professor and a student in the institution 'university' – at least in a German university context- the student can be said to potentially threaten the professor's face.

Excerpt 7

P:	so the next would be: so if this MAN who is working erm in [town3] for [company1] if he would have an interesting subject in in [town3] itself (.) would=
S:	=this is again on the topic of composites or?=
P:	=yes composites
S:	okay that's good

Excerpt 8

S:	I think it's okay
P:	yes you should erm erm attached that also but erm erm people KNOW that er
S:	this is required

Excerpt 9

P:	so if you follow the the river [river1] er towards
S:	to the sea
P:	to the sea then it's approximately fifty
S:	okay i think i know the place
P:	yah it's not fifty it's it's
S:	on the way to [town6]?
P:	yes mhm so there is a big erm plant [company1] plant and so they are the the centre of er composites

S: and researches also probably
P: yes and THEY have a special research centre (.)

In excerpts (7) and (8) the student interrupts the professor and finishes his moves for him. In (9) the student cuts the professor's utterances short stating that he already knows what the professor is going on about ("okay I think I know the place") – a potential face-threat as it is implied that the professor's statement is quite unnecessary and useless. The professor, however, does not seem to interpret these interruptions as threats to his face, rather he benignly agrees with the student's interventions.

In excerpts (10) and (11), it is the professor's assistant who interrupts the professor

Excerpt 10

P: like like a beam once er a beam yeah more or less but
WM: (unintelligible)
P: there is something which at least with the database you must go a bit in the detail and look at it (.) SO where does this
WM: you should check for example=
P: =yes

Given WM's potentially face-threatening interruption of P in mid-utterance in excerpt (10), P produces an acknowledgement ("yes") such that the interruptions appears to be condoned by him.

Excerpt 11

        S: this thesis is for high concrete?
        P: (fast) for normal concrete or the thesis
        WM: (unintelligible)
        P: for high yeah yeah yes
        S: oh
        P: but what i mean is=
        WM: = behaviour doesn't change so much if it's high strength
        P: yeah yeah yeah
        WM: or low strength concrete or normal strength concrete
        P: so=

| WM: | =you can read this and and take the theory |
| P: | yes |

In excerpt (11), WM cuts P short when the latter is about to launch into an explanation designed to remove the student's misunderstanding of what his thesis is supposed to be all about. The professor again simply acknowledges this interruption and ostensibly agrees with him.

And the assistant WM also corrects or reformulates the professor's utterances.

Consider the relevant excerpts (12), (13) and (14)

Excerpt 12

P:	one one is just for one is only just for whatsoever (inhales) that we have some results TWO is usually the case you have this one with two meters distance
WM:	maybe it will be four
P:	and maybe if it's very long it's it's four (4) okay (…)

Excerpt 13

P:	without this application always it it it it it is easily you can design a a a a a a cantilever slab within one week (.) not more to do it=
WM:	=or a shorter time
P:	(fast) for a shorter everything is in our handout so it's it's not complicated (…)

Excerpt 14

| P: | basically something like help with wonderful words write something (.) because you write with very WONDERFUL words that you have a (.) very INTENSIVE theoretical part you have no time to do the design for bridge (.) and then we will see (.) because as i think you will have big problems after your results in (unintelligible) concretes and |

something I think it's too complicated for you it's too complicated

WM: too comprehensive

P: yeah yeah it's not so easy if you have no never done it it's not so easy and you should have some experience with it (…)

All these corrections and re-formulations in excerpts (12), (13) and (14) are passed by or repeated, and are thus implicitly or explicitly condoned.

Another potentially face-threatening act on the part of the student is his refusal to accept the professor's rejection of a request by renewing it. The student had asked the professor to write a letter of reference for him, which the professor refused to do point blank. But instead of accepting this refusal, the student repeats the request once more towards the end of the interaction. Consider excerpt (15) where the request is made for the first time and rejected and excerpt (16) where the request is renewed and again turned down:

Excerpt 15

P: then you should also er state this (.) er within your CV

S: but it's it's also in my CV though I mean I don't have any other records and er what about for example reference letters do they?=

P: =yes if you HAVE of course

S: er so can i ask YOU to write me a reference letter or?

P: mhhh no that no erm (.) I think the reference er would be tht I er support your erm application and we will do do it in in in in that way that you will give me your erm

S: CV

P: application

S: yah

P: your documents

S: yah

P: and we will er send it er to to the man who is er

supporting (soft) this

The professor's rejection of the student's request is very direct posing in fact a potential threat to the student's face. However, the student is clearly not at all intimidated by this rejection, as we can see in excerpt 16:

Excerpt 16

P:	but erm I think at the end (.) erm I just will okay I can give you this address just now
S:	yeah sure but I would erm also if this is not like er one of your colleagues I could ask you a er reference letter for this no it's like (..) is it okay? so because er for example in (town 3) or (town1)=
P:	= (soft) mhm=
S:	=you have some person that you know=
P:	=(soft) mhm
S:	and then you will send the documents so it's okay
P:	yah
S:	but I mean for (town5)or I don't know where else er it's probable that you will er well it's just like i will send the documents myself
P:	ja ja
S:	so it would be better if I had some erm feedback from some of the professors I was thinking but
P:	erm so you mean that it should be helpful to have a letter?
S:	yeah
P:	from me? (3sec) no it's not us usual to do so
S:	Okay so
P:	Those students are search searching by them by themselves

The fact that the student unashamedly renewed his request despite its previous explicit rejection may well be interpreted as challenging the professor's face given the hierarchical relationships holding in the institution "university". The student's insistence on procuring a letter of reference even though the professor's had explained that writing reference letters for individual students is highly unusual in this particular institution is clearly marked. The question now arises whether the professor perceived the student's behaviour as a threat to his face. The following interview with the professor (translated into English for easier comprehension) illuminates this question.

2.4   Perception of Potential Face-Threat in ELF Academic Advising Sessions

Asked by the interviewer (Int) about how he felt about the student's repeated request, the professor (P) did not see the student's behaviour as a challenge to his face.

Excerpt 17

Int: I found it odd that the student came twice with the same request, that is, he comes during the office hour to get a letter of recommendation. You say no, and here he comes again, I find it a little unusual er

P: Well, I would say it was important for him, and, while he is a student whom I see frequently, then it was also someone who must have been – who was – yes, quite experienced with English, er, he knew basically that he was a very good student but was not quite sure about his latest choice, and would see the professor as a mentor er who could help me and who is here to help me.

Int: hmm

P: And er well, he had it, like, when one wants it that way, is also so straightforward, ahm, take the decision for me er and support me in this, so, basically, he expected it that way, he believed it was the role of the professor, and he plainly could not understand ah how come I turn his request down.

In the following excerpt of another interview with a professor who advised an international student together with his assistant, the professor also does not ascribe any importance to the assistant's interruptions, corrections and reformulations discussed above, and does not regard them as a face-threat at all.

Excerpt 18

Int:	The question to you is whether you have (.) the no noticed and felt uneasy about it, whether your/you even thought further on that your authority uh
P:	no no no
Int:	for that
P:	ah
Int:	no? @
P:	to put it simply, these the uh
In1:	I would like to have the line-up/[…]
P:	I should say that it's the entire conversation/ […]
P:	here I would say that (name) he was a little brusque
In:	brusque
P:	I don't find it negative
Int:	no

The professor only concedes that the assistant (WM) was a bit "brusque", but he did not feel that this type of behaviour was intended as a challenge or threat to his face. In other words, the professor's face wants do not seem to have suffered from the various interruption, corrections and even reformulations of his utterances by his 'inferiors'. The professor remains in command during the interactions examined. What an analyst of the interaction from her etic standpoint would have interpreted as a face threat was thus, from his emic perspective, not felt to be one at all.

In sum, lower status ELF speakers' ostensibly face-challenging behaviour in university office hours did not seem to negatively affect a status-superior ELF speaker's face. Does this finding reflect a particular feature of ELF institutional office hours interactions, where speakers are, as it were, 'all in the same boat' using a language other than their mother tongue, such that different hierarchical perceptions obtain? Or does the speaker in authority feel so secure in his institutionally sanctioned role that he believes himself to be 'unchallengeable' regardless of the medium of the interaction (L1 or ELF)? These are open questions which this small case study cannot answer. Much more research will be necessary to filter out ELF specific features from general genre specific ones.

3 Conclusion

In the study described in this paper, interactions between academic advisors (professorial and support staff) and advisees (international students) in lingua franca English in a German university setting, the use of the following two strategies of identity construction was documented: code-switching and the *I*-plus-Verb constructions *I think* and *I mean.* Code-switching is used rather automatically and subconsciously, involving discourse markers or gambits such as uptakers, and it occurred at specific transitional points in the interaction.

The two expressions *I think* and *I mean* are not primarily used as semantically empty routines (as mostly happens in English L1 talk), but rather in their prototypical meanings of expressing a speaker's ideas and opinions, and signalling his or her identity.

The analysis also showed that the status-superior interactant, the professor, was interrupted and corrected, and sometimes his utterances were reformulated and finished for him. In one of the cases examined, a student did not accept the professor's rejection of his request for a letter of reference and proceeded to re-enact his request. Our assumption that such face-threatening behaviour would negatively affect the professors' face was disconfirmed in a post-hoc interview with him. Social factors may have played an important part in securing a stable role for the professor who seemed to be unassailable in his institutionally sanctioned position. It might only be through comparative institutional studies of L1 and ELF talk that the question of ELF specificity in identity- and face-related discourse behaviour can be resolved.

References

Baumgarten, N. and J. House (2007)   Speaker stances in native and
        non-native English conversation. In: Jan D. ten Thije and Ludger

Zeevaert   (eds.),   *Receptive   Multilingualism*,   195-216. Amsterdam: Benjamins.

Baumgarten, N. and J. House (2010) *I think* and *I don't know* in English as lingua franca and native English discourse.   *Journal of Pragmatics* 42:5. 1184-1200.

Cogo, A. and M. Dewey (2006)Efficiency in ELF communication: From pragmatic motives to Lexico-grammatical innovation. *Nordic Journal English Studies* 5(2): 59-94.

Dewey, M. (2009)English as a lingua franca: Heightened variability and theoretical implications. In: Anna Mauranen and Elina Ranta (eds.), *English as a Lingua Franca: Studies and Findings*, 60-83. Newcastle: Cambridge Scholars Press.

Eckert, P. and S. McConnell-Ginet (1992) Think practically and act locally: Language and gender community-based practice. *Annual Review of Anthropology* 21: 461-490.

Edmondson, Willis J.   (1981) *Spoken Discourse. A Model for Analysis.* London: Longman.

Edmondson, W. J. and J. House   (1981) *Let's Talk and Talk about it: A Pedagogic Iteractional Grammar of English.* München: Urban and Schwarzenberg.

Edmondson, W. J. and J. House   (2011) *Einführung   in   die Sprachlehrforschung* (eds.). 4th ed. Tübingen: Francke.

Firth, A.   (1990)   'Lingua Franca' negotiations: Towards an interactional approach. *World Englishes* 9(3): 69-80.

Firth, A.   (1996)   The discursive accomplishment of normality on 'lingua franca' English and conversation analysis. *Journal of Pragmatics* 26: 237-260.

Firth, A.   (2009)   The lingua franca factor. *Intercultural Pragmatics* 6(2): 147-170.

Grosjean, F.(2001)   The bilingual's language modes. In: J. L. Nicol (ed.), *Language Processing in the Bilingual*. Oxford: Blackwell

House, J. (2002) Communicating in English as a lingua franca. In: S. Foster-Cohen (ed.),   *EUROSLA Yearbook* 2: 243-261. Amsterdam: Benjamins.

House, J. (2003)English as a lingua franca: A threat to multilingualism? *Journal of Sociolinguistics* 7(4): 556-578.

House, J.(2008) (Im)politeness in English as a lingua franca discourse. In: M. Locher and J. Straessler (eds.), *Standards and Norms in the English Language*, 351-366. Berlin/NY: Mouton de Gruyter.

House, J. (2009) Subjectivity in English as lingua franca discourse: The case of *you know. Intercultural Pragmatics* 6:2. 171-194 (*Special Issue on English as Lingua Franca*, ed. Juliane House).

House, J. (2010) The pragmatics of English as a lingua franca. In Anna Trosborg ed. *Pragmatics Across Languages and Cultures. Handbook of Pragmatics, vol. 7.* Berlin/New York: de Gruyter Mouton, 363-390.

House, J. (2011) Global and Intercultural Communication. In: Gisle Anderson and Karin Aijmer eds. *Pragmatics of Society. Handbook of Pragmatics* vol 5. Berloin/Mouton: de Gruyter Mouton, 607-626.

House, J. and M. Lévy-Tödter (2009)Language, authority and face in academic English lingua franca advising sessions. In: Magdalène Lévy-Tödter and Dorothee Meer (eds.), *Hochschulkommunikation in der Diskussion,* 157-178. Frankfurt/Main: Lang.

House, J. and M. Lévy-Tödter (2010) Linguistic competence and professional identity in English medium institutional discourse. In: Birgit Apfelbaum and Bernd Meyer (eds.), *Multilingualism in the Workplace.* Amsterdam: Benjamins.

Hüllen, W.(1992)Identifikationssprachen und Kommunikationssprachen. *Zeitschrift für Germanistische Linguistik* 20: 298-317.

Martin, J.(1992) *English Text: System and Structure.* Amsterdam: Benjamins.

Pölzl, U.and B. Seidlhofer (2006)In and on their own terms: The 'habitat factor' in English as a lingua franca interaction. *International Journal of the Sociology of Language* 177: 151-176.

Seidlhofer, B. (2007) English as a lingua franca and communities of practice. In: *Anglistentag* 2006. Halle. Proceedings, 307-318. Trier: Wissenschaftlicher Verlag.

Wenger, E. (1989) *Communities of Practice.* Cambridge: Cambridge University Press.

Widdowson, H.(2003) *Defining Issues in English Language Teaching.* Oxford: Oxford University Press.

Notes

[1] I dedicate this chapter to my husband, Willis James Edmondson, who died on December 15th, 2009 after a long, courageously fought battle against a deadly illness – a battle he finally and tragically lost. Willis Edmondson was an admirably creative and innovative scholar, a genuinely free and independent person, and a wonderful human being. Over the many years of our life together, he has greatly inspired my work with the constructive comments and criticisms he so generously gave. I am eternally grateful to him.

Transcription Conventions

The transcription has been simplified for easier reading in this paper. The following conventions were used:

[ ] overlapping speech; translations from German

( ) description of non-verbal behavior

(1s)   length of pauses in seconds

(.)   very short pause

= latching

bold print : highlights points under discussion

(company 1): anonymized names of company

@   laughter

The voices of immigrant students in the classroom: discourse practices and language learning in a Catalan-Spanish bilingual environment

Josep Maria Cots (Universitat de Lleida)
Laura Espelt (Universitat de Lleida)

This paper aims at analysing the language learning context of a newly-arrived female teenage immigrant student during the first 10 weeks of the academic year in a bilingual secondary school. Inspired by Giddens' (1984) dynamic model of the relationship between structure and agency, the research reported focuses on (i) the discursive means and contexts that the educational institution offered the student to make the induction process as efficient and effective as possible and (ii) the student's use of these means in coping with three curricular languages different from her L1 (Catalan, Spanish and English) and in achieving a voice in the everyday social/learning practices of the classroom.

The analysis focuses on the connection between language learning practices and opportunities for self-expression, through which students can construct their identity, and which for Giroux (1988) constitute "the focal point" for a critical theory of education. We look at voice as an essential way of engaging in participation in a community of practice (Wenger, 1998) such as the school, whose definition of full membership tends to be based on their members' ability to perform discourse functions and to access specific linguistic/communicative resources.

The research presented follows a linguistic ethnographic approach in that (i) it adopts an intepretivist stance in identifying and describing patterns of language use as part of the social construction of reality, and (ii) it is mainly based on observational data, which is on certain occasions supplemented with information derived from semi-structured and informal interviews with students and teachers.

1 Introduction

This paper analyses the language learning context of a female teenage immigrant student during her first academic year in a bilingual secondary school. In doing this, we acknowledge the key contribution of the learner's social environment in the success or failure of the learning process, which we understand not only as the acquisition of a new communicative code but also as a process of becoming accepted as a member of a social group or institution. We look at context in terms of linguistic resources (Bourdieu, 1991) the access to which depends on social relations which are defined by individuals in a position of power. In this case, we look at a secondary school as a community of practice (Wenger, 1998), in which full membership is very much defined in terms of having adequate linguistic resources, mainly in Catalan. Therefore, it is important to explore the different discourse practices in which an immigrant student is expected to participate in order to begin to understand the strengths and weaknesses of the institution in helping the student to become a full member of the community.

Inspired by Giddens' (1984) dynamic model of the relationship between structure and agency, the research reported focuses on (i) the discursive means and contexts that the educational institution offers the students to make the induction process as efficient and effective as possible and (ii) the student's use of these means in coping with three curricular languages different from her L1 (Catalan, Spanish and English) and in achieving a voice in the everyday social/learning practices of the classroom. The analysis should allow us, in the first place, to explore the connection between language learning practices and opportunities for self-expression through which students can construct their identity, and which for Giroux (1988) constitute "the focal point" for a critical theory of education. In the second place, we look at the classroom as an essential setting for the newly-arrived student to engage and participate in a community of practice such as the school, whose definition of full membership tends to be based on their members' ability to perform discourse functions and to access specific linguistic/communicative resources.

The research presented follows a linguistic ethnographic approach in that (i) it adopts an interpretivist stance in identifying a situation of language use as part of the social construction of reality, and (ii) it is mainly based on observational data, which is on certain occasions supplemented with information derived from semi-structured and informal interviews with students and teachers. As mentioned above, the study focuses on the two main contexts of learning which a secondary school in a small town in Catalonia offers simultaneously to recently-arrived immigrant students: the 'reception classroom' and the 'mainstream classroom'. The main aim of the reception classroom (RC henceforth) is to facilitate the adaptation of the new students to the educational system in Catalonia by essentially teaching them the Catalan language. In this classroom the students generally spend about half of their ordinary school day during their first academic year. The rest of the time, they spend it in the 'mainstream classroom' (MC henceforth), which includes the group of local students corresponding to their age. The students in RC vary in age from 12 to 16 years old, an age range which corresponds to the four years of compulsory secondary education in Catalonia. Although Catalonia is a Catalan-Spanish bilingual autonomous community within Spain, the school system can be considered as Catalan, as this language is defined by the regional educational authority as the official language for the relationships with families, between teachers and between teachers and pupils. Spanish is taught as a subject language and some teachers in secondary schools can choose to teach their subjects in this language, if they are not competent enough in Catalan. The girl that we focus on for this study is Li Jiu (fictional name), who is 12 years old and of Chinese origin. The main source of data that we use for our analysis is a series of weekly day-long observations, with the corresponding field notes and video-recordings, of the first 10 weeks of the academic year 2008-09.

After a review of the sources that constitute the theoretical background of the study, through a brief 'vignette' into an ordinary day of Li Jiu we attempt to provide an ethnographic glimpse of the two main sites of learning for the immigrant students in the course of their daily routine: the reception classroom and the mainstream classroom. In section 4, we analyse the variation between each of these two contexts in terms of types of discourse practices afforded by the institution (structure) and how the immigrant student responds (agency) to the demands of the structure. The article closes with a section in which, we summarise our main findings and introduce a series of reflections in the line of increasing the effectiveness of the process of socialisation of the immigrant students into an educational community of practice.

2 Literature background

This study has been informed by two main research strands: language socialization (see, for instance, Ochs, 1993; Lave and Wenger, 1991; Watson-Gegeo, 2004; Zuengler and Miller, 2006) and critical applied linguistics (Kummaradivelu, 1999; Norton, 2000; Pennycook, 2001; Miller, 2003). From the perspective of language socialization, we look at language learning primarily as both a means for an individual to form part of a socio-cultural group and, at the same time, the result of the efforts made by the individual and the group to interact. We look at verbal communication not only as opportunities for input/output, but also for familiarisation with the social practices of the community. According to Ochs (1993), language acquisition is part of the process of becoming a competent member in a social group. For newcomers into a social group, language represents a powerful semiotic tool that will allow them to co-construct knowledge, beliefs and identities with the others. Watson-Gegeo (2004) points out that language learning, cultural knowledge and social behaviour are inseparable from the perspective of language socialization. Furthermore, all of the social practices in which second language learners participate take place in particular socio-cultural environments and they are linked to specific social, political and cultural meanings. Contexts influence the uses of linguistic forms but these forms also contribute to defining specific contexts.

Still from a language socialization perspective, Wenger (1998: 3) links cognition with social interaction and participation, and suggests the notion of 'community of practice' in order to place learning "in the context of our lived experience of participation in the world". For this author, newcomers in a community of practice start as peripheral participants in the social activities, and they may become full participants provided that they can access participation. From this point of view, peripheral participants do not acquire abstract knowledge which they will transfer to other contexts. Rather, they acquire a set of skills to act, to link themselves to others, and to get involved. Learning, therefore, is seen as a special type of social practice related to participation in context. The learners' ability to learn and act will not depend so much on their capacity for representing and storing abstract knowledge but on their level of engagement in the social practices in which they take part. Likewise, educational effectiveness is not based on the teachers' ability to model/manipulate the learners' conceptual representations, but on the ability to engage pupils in the learning activities.

From the point of view of critical applied linguistics, we can look at the educational institution and the socialization/learning achievements of newcomers as the interplay of 'structure' and 'agency' (Giddens, 1984). According to this author (1984: 17), structure can be considered both as a "patterning of social relations in time-space involving the reproduction of situated practices" and, at the same time, as "memory traces of these situated practices orienting the conduct of knowledgeable human agents". For Giddens (1984: 9), agency "refers not to the intentions people have in doing things but to their capability of doing those things in the first place", and it "concerns events of which an individual is the perpetrator, in the sense that the individual could, at any phase in a given sequence of conduct, have acted differently". The notions of structure and agency are considered by Norton and Toohey (2011: 426) as a shared premise in the study of identity and SLA, and they justify this with the following argument:

> Identity researchers must account for not only how structural conditions and social practices place individuals, but also how individuals struggle to situate themselves in the contexts in which they find themselves. (...) Methods for examining L2 learning and identity thus need to pay close attention to how individuals are placed by common societal practices, but also how they place themselves by engaging in societal practices in innovative ways.

These same authors, in their state-of-the-art article on identity, language learning and social change (Norton and Toohey, 2011: 414-415), provide us with a summary of the main contributions made by research to the study of language learning from the point of view of the language socialization and critical applied linguistics paradigms in the last 15 years. We take up the following four as premises for this article:

(i) A perspective of the individual language learner as situated in specific socio-cultural environments which are frequently inequitable.
(ii) The variety of forms of participation and identities that language learners can, or cannot, adopt in their social life in different communities of practice.
(iii) The impact of power in the language learner's access to social life and, consequently, to opportunities for developing their communicative skills in the target language.
(iv) The strong connection between access to practices and resources in specific settings and the language learner's process of identity construction.

The type of analysis we propose looks at the classroom as a social environment in which individuals enact particular roles and role-relationships that are in part institutionally determined (i.e. structure), but which are also constructed interactionally and *in situ* thanks to the autonomy and initiative of the individuals (i.e. agency). This perspective of the classroom has been supported by van Lier (1988: 50) for whom "the social world of the classroom (…) is a delicately balanced application of forces and sources of power, our task being to find out who and what provides the power, and who and what regulates it". Pennycook (2001: 121) is of the same opinion: "What we need (…) is an understanding of how schools operate within the larger field of social relations, how, as a key social institution they ultimately serve to maintain the social, economic, cultural and political status quo rather than upset it". In our analysis, we look at structure and agency as a series of 'affordances' (van Lier, 2004) or particular relationships between the immigrant student and the school environment, which promote or inhibit learning. For us, structure is instantiated mainly in the norms or routines that the institution, represented mainly by the teacher, enforces in the classroom. These norms or routines may also include the disposition of the physical environment and the use of particular learning resources. On the other hand, agency is identified in the classroom in the form of episodes in which the immigrant student takes the initiative and responds to the constraints of structure.

Within the critical applied linguistics perspective, the work of Norton (2000) and Miller (2003), focuses specifically on migrant language learners. In the first case, the author, working with adult immigrants in Canada shows the relevance of the language learning context for a comprehensive theory of identity and the impact of relations of power on social practices in which immigrant learners interact with target language speakers. Miller (2003) is a very direct antecedent of our study in that it aims "to understand the early linguistic adjustment of ESL students to high school" in Australia (p. 14) and to learn about "what conditions at school facilitate or constrain the acquisition of spoken English by recently arrived ESL students" (p. 15). The author concludes her work by situating audibility(i.e. being acknowledged as a competent language user) and legitimacy (i.e. having the right to speak and the contributions being accepted as valuable) as conditions for the learners' ongoing language development, and their capacity for self-representation, negotiation of identity and agency. Therefore, it is important to explore the extent to which social/educational practices in a school contribute to the audibility and legitimacy of the newly arrived immigrant students.

3   A vignette

Following the example of Wenger (1998), in this section we offer a vignette "to give some life" (p. 16) to our study and as an ethnographic approximation to the representation of an ordinary day at school for the newly-arrived immigrant student on whom we focus in this paper. In the analysis we carry out in section 4, based on the concepts of structure and agency, reference will be made again to some of the elements mentioned in this vignette.

Li Jiu arrives at school at 8:45. There are already many students waiting outside the school precinct, and all of them are busy chatting among themselves. When the gate opens, she goes to the reception classroom, where she finds her teacher. Today there are 10 students, all of whom are new in the school. None of them speaks Catalan, only a few speak some Spanish, except for an older girl who speaks Spanish very well. The students in this classroom are between12 and 16, and she is one of the youngest. They come from different countries: Dominican Republic, Romania, Morocco, Ghana and Mali. She is the only Chinese pupil in the classroom as well as in the school.

The students are seated around a square made up with the pupils' individual desks and they are very quiet at this time in the morning. Today, like other days, the teacher gives them a worksheet through which they learn Catalan words for animals, food, the family, numbers, colours, etc. The activities usually consist of finding the Catalan word corresponding to a picture and writing it next to it. The teacher lets them know that, if they do not know a word, they can make use of either a Catalan dictionary with pictures or one of the bilingual dictionaries they have in the small classroom library. They do not follow a specific course-book in the reception classroom, as they work with worksheets and other materials. Since the teacher allows them to help one another, she and Fátima, a 14-year old girl from Morocco, help each other by copying the words they do not know from the other. The two girls have become very good friends; they do not talk with anybody else in the reception classroom, and they always try to sit together.

After completing the worksheet, the teacher invites the class to play a vocabulary bingo. Each student has a card with pictures representing daily actions and they have to guess the name of the action in Catalan. Li Jiu is having a hard time playing because she does not know a lot of vocabulary in Catalan. Fátima sometimes tries to help her if she gets lost. During the game the teacher invites Li Jiu to say some numbers aloud, but she refuses by shaking her head. She recognises the number, but it is very difficult for her to pronounce it. The teacher insists, but she looks down to her desk until he says, always in Catalan, something like "Ok, Li Jiu you'll do it another day", and then she feels very much relieved. Her classmates seem to enjoy the game and sometimes they laugh at a classmate who makes a mistake. They love competing and want to win because the teacher jokingly said that the winner would win a motorbike. While announcing this, the teacher showed a picture of a motorbike and then everybody raised their hands and pointed at themselves, meaning "I want it for myself!".

When the bell rings to signal the end of the lesson and the beginning of recreation period, all the students leave the room very quickly. However, Li Jiu is not in such a rush and she waits for Fátima, because she does not want to be in the playground alone. Although they practically do not speak to each other, they eat their breakfast and walk around the playground holding hands; sometimes they point at something and they exchange smiles.

After recreation period, Li Jiu looks at her school schedule and notices that she has a Natural Sciences lesson with her 'mainstream group'. In the class she looks for Ester, her 'classmate-guide'. The teacher wants Li Jiu to sit next to Ester so that she can help her during the class. There are about 25 pupils in this classroom, everyone has their own individual desk and they sit separately. Each pupil has their own course-book and a notebook on the table. During the class they usually talk very little; they just listen to the teacher's explanations and look at the blackboard. The teacher tends to be in front of the class and explains the contents of the unit in the course book. She writes important concepts and schematic summaries with the main ideas, and asks the students to copy them in their notebooks. Li Jiu does not have a course-book and she has to look at her classmate-guide's course book. She does not follow the class, so she just copies what her classmate tells her to copy from her notebook.

Li Jiu's next lesson is also in her mainstream classroom, but only with some of the students because it is an optional subject. It is in English and it is called "Enjoy drama!". She does not like this class. The teacher often speaks in English and she always asks questions that the students have to answer. When she asks her, she refuses to answer by shaking her head and looking down onto her desk. Li Jiu cannot speak English, and she does not understand what the teacher is asking her. The students have a dossier with technical vocabulary about drama, and they combine the activities in the dossier with short performances in the class. Today they have to memorise a conversation at a restaurant and perform it. Li Jiu refuses to participate, and so she sits at the back of the room alone and just watches her classmates.

Li Jiu's last class is in the reception classroom again. Fátima is not there because she is in her mainstream classroom. Her classmates are already working at the computers. Each one has a computer and there is still one available for Li Jiu. She leaves her bag on her regular seat and looks at the teacher. He is already turning on the computer for her and asks her to go there. He tells her to go to a specific website for learning Catalan which is sponsored by the Department of Education in Catalonia (Generalitat de Catalunya, n.d.). She is already familiar with the site because they work with it every week. The pupils work individually. The interactive activities proposed on this site involve learning about and practising basic communicative routines and vocabulary associated with them. She seems to like this type of activities, probably because she understands the dynamics easily, she can work alone and she does not have to perform in public. The teacher is walking around the class checking how the students are carrying out the activity. She has worked at the computer for a whole class period when the bell rings indicating the end of the morning. She closes the site she was working at, turns off the computer, gets up, takes her bag and goes home without talking to anybody.

4 Structure and agency in the mainstream and the reception classrooms

In this section, we look at the school as a community of practice characterised by a series of socio-pedagogic activities in which the immigrant students need to take part in order to be considered as a full members. While some of these activities are shared between the RC and the MC, our analysis will also emphasise specific differences between the two settings which we have found during our observation.

4.1   Elements of structure

The first aspect that captures the attention of the observer in going from RC to MC is probably the physical distribution of the pupils and the learning materials employed (see Figure 1). In the first place, we find that in RC the students are sitting around a large table made up of individual desks and they all face each other. The teacher usually either stands near the blackboard or moves around this large table. In MC, the pupils sit in individual desks organised in rows with their gaze directed at the blackboard or the teacher, which are in front of them. These two particular arrangements may be symbolic of the relevance of social interaction among the pupils in RC, whereas in MC the emphasis seems to be placed on the transmission of information.

As for learning materials, perhaps the most important difference between the two settings is that in MC the course book for each subject is an essential tool, since most of the learning activities done in class follow it scrupulously. However, in RC there is no set course book and learning materials are prepared by the teacher from different sources. Since many immigrant pupils spend as much time, if not more, in RC as in MC, and they cannot always afford to buy a course book for each subject, they are deprived of a key resource for their full participation in the mainstream classroom. The absence of a set course book in RC is compensated by the teacher and the institution by making available to the students in the classroom alternative learning resources, such as computers, dossiers, dictionaries, readers, posters, games, etc. These different resources as well as the greater number of collaborative activities in which the pupils participate in RC allow for a degree of agency that is not found in MC.

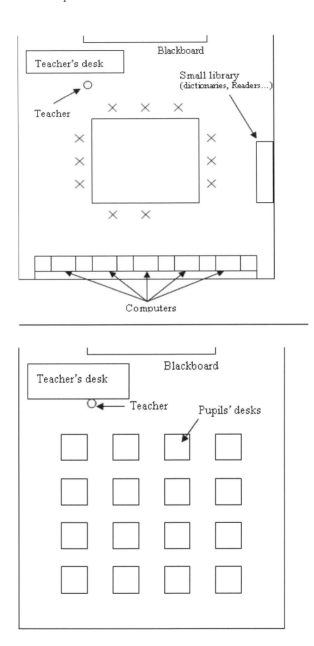

Figure 1: Physical arrangement of the reception (above) and the mainstream (below) classrooms.

The nature of the academic work in a secondary school classroom deserves attention as an affordance for the development of academic and communicative skills. In this case, we find that in both RC and MC, teachers show a tendency towards 'public performance' on the part of the pupils. That is to say, it is very often the case that their participation takes place in front of the rest of the class, adopting formats such as (i) a response to a question asked by the teacher, (ii) giving the answers for a written exercise which they have done as homework, (iii) an exercise (e.g. a dictation) to be done by one of the pupils at the blackboard, (iv) reading aloud a fragment from a text or (v) an oral presentation. In all of these situations, the pupils are expected to speak "loud and clear", as the RC teacher often reminds his pupils, so that the rest of the class can hear them. This type of public performance reflects a teacher-centred methodology which is still very dominant in secondary schools in Catalonia, and according to which the teacher is at all times in full control of the learning process and all the pupils follow the same pace in the learning activities. Nevertheless, from the point of view of language learning, forcing the students to use the language 'in public' may cause a great deal of anxiety in the learner and become an inhibiting factor in the participation and learning process.

Another aspect related to the nature of academic work in a secondary school is the definition of 'successful work', which generally refers to either getting the 'correct answers' for an exercise or reproducing as closely as possible to the original what the teacher or the course book says. In this sense, it is significant that copying information from the blackboard is an important activity in both RC and MC. Since a great deal of exercise correction is done 'in public', having the right answers is important for the pupil in order to be able to maintain their face in front of the rest of the class. This situation sometimes 'forces' the pupils to simply copy the answers from their partners without really understanding the question. In front of this implicit message about academic work which is conveyed to all the students, it might have been somewhat puzzling for Li Jiu to follow a direction such as the one the RC teacher gave her one day when Fátima was showing her the right answers to an exercise: "you can speak with your classmate but you cannot copy her answers". It is worth saying that this was a language activity requiring specific answers rather than discussion and, therefore, it was very likely the only way in which one pupil could help the other was to show her the right answer.

Another consequence of the teacher-centred methodology that abounds in secondary schools is that classroom interaction is very much dominated by the pattern Initiation-Response-Feedback (IRF). This interactional pattern leaves for the teacher virtually all the initiative for classroom interaction, thereby depriving the pupils from an opportunity to deploy their agency in initiating interaction. Furthermore, this triadic turn structure often involves the notion that there is only one right answer, which is the one the teacher knows. This connects very clearly with what has been said in the previous paragraph about the nature of 'successful' academic work, which is based on the idea that learning basically involves the acquisition/accumulation of knowledge essentially coming from two sources: the teacher and the course book. A third problem that this interactional pattern involves is that the teacher in their initiation turn does not usually allocate the response to a particular pupil and, therefore, the responses tend to be monopolised by the same pupils, those with either a more uninhibited personality or with a better knowledge of the subject matter.

One last element of structure which the immigrant student has to learn to deal with in a school located in an officially bilingual region is the use of languages. As has been mentioned before, in order to guarantee the transmission of Catalan among the population who have not acquired it in the family, and in order to balance the social use of the two languages, Catalan has been made the language of compulsory education in Catalonia, and Spanish and foreign languages are also present in the curriculum either as a subject or as a language of instruction. The educational policy establishes that at the end of compulsory education, all students should master both Catalan and Spanish and must have acquired some skills in (at least) one foreign language. Given this situation, the main function of RC is to provide the newly-arrived immigrant student with the necessary skills in Catalan to be able to integrate into the school. RC is a Catalan-immersion environment in which Spanish, the language which a majority of immigrant students use outside the school, is practically ignored. Interestingly enough, the RC teacher sometimes makes brief references to other languages with which the students may be familiar (e.g. Romanian, Arabic, French, etc.) in order to explain the meanings of certain words in Catalan. On the other hand, MC is not such a strict environment as RC from the point of view of language use, since the teachers may teach in Spanish if it is his/her L1 or, when Catalan is their L1, they sometimes code-switch momentarily into Spanish when addressing an immigrant student in order to facilitate their understanding. Likewise, the MC teacher accepts responses from the pupils in Spanish. In general, when comparing RC and MC from the point of view of languages, we could say that RC is a more monolingual environment than MC, since in the former only Catalan is accepted as medium of instruction, whereas in MC both Catalan and Spanish are present. However, in RC, due to the students' background more frequent references are made to linguistic and cultural diversity.

4.2   Elements of agency

In this section we want to focus on the acts of 'agency' that Li Jiu deploys in front of elements of structure such as those we have described above. One of the most noticeable acts that Li Jiu and her friend Fátima undertake in order to confront two of the elements of structure that we have discussed in the previous section has to do with the IRF interactional pattern and the 'public performance' of the students, which are common practices in both RC and MC. In this case, the students deployed a series of strategies aimed at avoiding being picked up by the teacher and exposed in front of the rest of the class. The first strategy involves not looking at the teacher and focusing their whole attention on the written exercise or whatever material they have on their desk. When, in spite of the 'activation' of the first strategy, they are selected by the teacher, they may simply refuse to go out, although not necessarily challenging the authority of the teacher;their attitude is one of showing a preference not to go out because they feel they will not be able to perform correctly. If neither of the two previous strategies works, and the pupil has no choice but to perform in public, they adopt a very low tone voice and they direct their gaze towards the floor. The low tone of voice is especially noticeable whenever the pupil is unsure about a specific lexical choice or the pronunciation of a word.

Collaborative work between the pupils can be considered as an element of structure, especially in RC, since the teacher often stresses the importance that the pupils work in pairs and "talk to each other". However, in MC collaborative work does not play such a relevant role. Indeed a great deal of the academic work that is done in the MC involves the pupils working individually in activities such as listening to the teacher, reading the text from the course book or doing exercises. It is probably because of the little relevance of collaborative work in MC that the school assigns a local classmate-guide to each immigrant pupil whom the school considers as in need of support in MC, as is the case of Li Jiu. The main task of this classmate during our observation was to help the immigrant pupil to follow the lesson. In the first term, we discover Li Jiu's agency in the Mathematics lesson when she shifts her gaze towards the student helper whenever she has finished her exercise, thereby requesting her to check whether it is right; after looking at the exercise, the responds with a nod and Li Jiuthanks her with a smile. During a later observation, although Li Jiu is still not very competent in Catalan or Spanish, we see that she deploys her agency by asking the classmate-guide to go with her to the library. Since she cannot do this verbally, she draws two girls on her notebook, with their respective names of

Ester and Li Jiu, walking towards a door where it says *biblioteca* (library). The resource to drawing and writing is quite common in the case of Li Jiu as a compensation strategy for her lack of communicative skills in Spanish or Catalan.

Collaboration between the pupils (mostly in pairs) is very much favoured by the RC teacher and in this context it can be considered as one more element of structure. However, as we have pointed out before, there are two circumstances that may explain the fact that the pupils, in general, show some degree of resistance to it. In the first place, they may not have a clear idea of what it means to 'collaborate' in a tradition of academic work in which what is mainly valued is the product, i.e. whether the pupil gets the answers right or not, rather than the process of discussion. This system does not rely so much on the capacity of the pupils to engage in reflective discussion as on the individual possession of specific knowledge. Therefore in MC there is very little collaborative work since, according to this view of education, it slows down the transmission and accumulation of knowledge. In the second place, although the RC teacher seems to promote collaborative work in the classroom, many of the activities that he asks the pupils to perform depend on whether they are in possession or not of a specific piece of knowledge (e.g. a word, a fact). If one of the two partners has it, the other simply needs to accept it or reject it,and there is not much to be discussed or elaborated in the answer. This paradox in collaborative work is further increased by the fact, which we have already pointed out, that the teacher expects the pupils to talk without copying from their partner if one of them knows the answer. In front of this situation, we have observed that the pupils sometimes do not follow the RC teacher's direction of doing the activity with a partner and they simply do it individually. This is something about which the teacher seems to be rather worried.

The most frequent kind of collaboration that we see between Li Jiu and her friend Fátima is of a more informal type and not necessarily promoted by either the teacher (asking them to work in pairs) or the school (i.e. assigning them a classmate-guide). Thus in RC, which is the only classroom in which they are together since, because of their age, they go to different MCs, we observe that they often choose to sit together. In this situation Fátima tends to adopt the role of expert, as she is older and more advanced in her linguistic and academic development. The help provided by Fatima may be requested by Li Jiu or simply given without previous request. This latter case occurs when Fátima, after doing her own exercise, takes a look at Li Jiu's exercise and realises that she is not doing it right. Furthermore, the two pupils take every opportunity to work together when the teacher allows them to do so, as in the case in which they are distributed in pairs when the whole class is working with the computers.

5 Conclusions

In this study we have applied the perspective of poststructuralist theories of language, identity and power to approach the experience of a newly-arrived immigrant student in a secondary school in Catalonia. Therefore, we have focused on (a) the individual language learner in a particular socio-cultural setting and (b) the learning process as the result of participation in different communities of practice, in which access to resources and relations of power play a key role.

With these premises in mind, in this paper we have begun to reflect on the extent to which the institutional environment of a secondary school offers to the newly-arrived immigrant student access to practices and resources to develop their communicative competence in the target language and to construct their identity. In the first place, we have focused on certain elements of 'structure' which, in our view, must be taken into consideration to explain the success or failure of the process of legitimate peripheral participation of the students. One of the main issues underlying some of the structural features we have pointed out in our analysis is related to the definition of the process of teaching and learning as (i) transmission of knowledge or as (ii) the learners' construction of knowledge through the interactional negotiation of meanings. In their movements between RC and MC, the immigrant students may be seen as travelling between the two definitions of teaching and learning, with the RC apparently leaning towards the latter and the MC tending to follow the former definition of teaching and learning. This can be seen in the different distribution of the pupils in the classroom (e.g. individual desks vs. sitting around a common table), in the presence or absence of particular teaching techniques (e.g. copying from the blackboard vs. playing games; individual work *vs.* pair-work), and in the learning resources employed (e.g. the course book as the only source of information vs. access to dictionaries and computer software). Another important impact of the transmission-of-knowledge perspective is the emphasis on the product rather than the process of learning. In this way, 'successful' academic work is that which contains the 'right' answers, rather than that which is the result of collaborative or individual analysis and reflection.

The 'transmission-of-knowledge' conception of teaching and learning tends to be associated with a teacher-centred, lockstep approach to teaching. This favours the appearance of two other structural elements in the classroom which may have an impact on the participation of the immigrant student. In the first place, we have seen that there is an emphasis on 'public performance' by the pupils in the classroom (e.g. reading part of a text aloud, reading the answers to an exercise, writing dictated words on the blackboard, etc.). This is probably the best way for the teacher to control that everybody follows the same pace in learning but also to make sure that the 'right' knowledge is conveyed. However, we have also seen that this may be an obstacle for the participation of immigrant students, who would probably feel more confident taking part in pair- or small-group communicative situations. The second element of structure which derives from a teacher-centred, lockstep approach is the dominance of the interactional pattern Initiation-Response Feedback (IRF), whose control depends entirely on the teachers and their capacity for managing the turns in an equitable manner.

Although our initial emphasis for this study was basically on the elements of structure that could have an impact on the participation of the immigrant students in the secondary school classroom, we have also considered possible elements of agency, through which the immigrant students resist the structure or adapt it to their capacities. We have tried to show how Li Jiu and Fátima avoid public performance (and possible failure) in the classroom by avoiding being selected, initially refusing to respond to the Initiation turn of the teacher and, if the teacher insists, making their performance as invisible as possible. As for collaborative work, while it is an institutionalised element of structure in MC, through the figure of the classmate-guide, in RC this collaborative work is more the result of the pupils' agency. We have seen that pupils adapt this collaboration to the demands from a transmission-of-knowledge view of teaching and learning, which emphasises 'right' answers rather than reflection, by using the opportunity to simply 'copy' or transfer specific information from one to the other rather than for analysis and reflection.

Underlying this study is the basic premise of socio-cultural theories of language learning (Vygotsky, 1978; Lantolf and Thorne, 2006) that all learning, and especially language learning, is a social process which takes place in specific socio-cultural and institutional environments and requires the engagement or participation of the individuals in those environments. In this sense, Lave and Wenger's (1991) notion of legitimate peripheral participation in a community of practice has been useful to us to explore the two main classroom settings in which newly-arrived immigrant pupils in a secondary school spend their first academic year: the reception and the mainstream classrooms. We are convinced, with Wenger (1998: 6), that in a school "communities of practice sprout everywhere" and that "in spite of curriculum, discipline and exhortation, the learning that is most personally transformative turns out to be the learning that involves membership in these communities of practice". The present study represents a contribution to shedding further light on the nature of the school's communities of practice and on their capacity for engaging immigrant students in their progress from peripheral to full participation.

References

Bourdieu, P. (1991) *Language and Symbolic Power*. Cambridge: Polity Press.

Generalitat de Catalunya (n.d.). *Vincles.*
    http://www.edu365.cat/eso/muds/catala/vincles/index.htm (accessed 10October 2011)

Giddens, A. (1984) *The Constitution of Society. Outline of the Theory of Structuration*. Cambridge: Polity.

Giroux, H. (1988) *Schooling and the Struggle for Public Life. Critical Pedagogy in the Modern Age*. Minneapolis: University of Minnesota Press.

Kummaradivelu, B. (1999). Critical classroom discourse analysis. *TESOL Quarterly* (33) 3: 453-484.

Lantolf, J. and L. Thorne (2006) *Sociocultural Theory and the Genesis of Second Language Development*. Oxford: Oxford University Press.

Lave, J. and E. Wenger (1991) *Situated Learning. Legitimate Peripheral Participation*. Cambridge: Cambridge University Press.

Miller, J. (2003). *Audible Differences. ESL and Social Identity in Schools*. Clevedon: Multilingual Matters.

Norton, B. (2000). *Identity in Language Learning: Gender, Ethnicity and Educational Change*. Harlow: Longman/Pearson Education.

Norton, B. and K. Toohey (2011) Changing perspectives on good language learners. *TESOL Quarterly*, 35 (2): 307-319

Pennycook, A. (2001) *Critical Applied Linguistics: A Critical Introduction*. Mahwah, NJ: Lawrence

Ochs, E. (1993). Constructing social identity: A language socialization perspective. *Research on Language and Social Interaction (26) 3: 287-306.*

van Lier, L. (1988) *The Classroom and the Language Learner*. London: Longman

Van Lier, L. (2004). *The Ecology and Semiotics of Language Learning: a Sociocultural Perspective*. Dordrecht: Kluwer Academic Publishers.

Vygotsky, L. (1978). *Mind in Society*. Cambridge: Cambridge University Press.

Watson-Gegeo (2004) *Mind, Language, and Epistemology: Toward a Language Socialization Paradigm for SLA*. *The Modern Language Journal*, v. 88, 331-350.

Wenger, E. (1998) *Communities of Practice: Learning, Meaning and Identity*. Cambridge: Cambridge University Press.

Zuengler, J. and Miller, E. (2006). Cognitive and socioculural perspectives. Two parallel SLA worlds? *TESOL Quarterly* (40) 1: 35-58.

Email openings and closings: pragmalinguistic and gender variation in learner-instructor cyber consultations

César Félix-Brasdefer (Indiana University)

This study, framed within the field of Computer-Mediated Discourse (Crystal 2006; Herring 2003), has two aims: first, it examines pragmalinguistic variation in the opening and closing moves in email messages (L2 Spanish and L1 English) sent from US undergraduate university-level students to their instructors of Spanish; second, it analyzes variation by gender to investigate the impact of this sociolinguistic variable on language use. The actional level and the macro-social factor of gender were used as the units of analysis for the present study (Barron & Schneider 2009). The data are analyzed with regard to the types of opening and closing moves and their frequency in 320 email messages sent by male and female students (200 written in L2 Spanish; 120 in L1 US English). Results are discussed with regard to pragmalinguistic variation in opening and closing moves, variation by gender, formal and informal features of email discourse, and politeness practices in learner-instructor cyber consultations in a foreign language context.

1 Introduction

Email communication in academic and non-academic contexts is ubiquitous. In academic settings email is by now the most preferred, pervasive, and efficient means of communication between students and instructors. Although openings (e.g. salutations, titles) and closings (e.g. farewells, signature) are optional elements of email messages, their presence helps maintain (or reinforce) the social relationships between the sender and the receiver. Similarly, their absence may hinder future communication or be perceived as impolite or inappropriate behavior by the recipient. One important feature of openings and closings in email discourse is the wide range of pragmalinguistic variation (Bou-Franch 2011; Crystal 2006; Kankaanranta 2005). The presence or absence of these elements in email discourse is constrained by various factors, such as the type of discourse (e.g. institutional vs. conversational), the relationship between the participants, based on factors such as power, distance, and degree of familiarity, frequency of interaction, gender, and the degree of politeness (Herring 2000). From a sociological view, Goffman (1971) refers to greetings and farewells as "access rituals", that is, greetings refer to "increased access" and farewells as "a state of decreased access" (p. 79). And, Brown and Yule (1983) proposed a functional dichotomy of language, namely, the transactional function (e.g. asking a professor for a letter of recommendation) and the interactional function (which includes some aspects of Malinowski's [1923] phatic function) (e.g. greetings and closings). In this chapter I will focus on the interactional aspect of email messages - openings and closings - sent by US undergraduate learners of Spanish to their instructors. Example (1) is an email message that includes a greeting and a closing, taken from the data that will be analyzed in this chapter (the wording of the email examples represents the original content of the sender's message).

(1)   L2 female learner: Email message sent to a female professor
       (in her late 40's)

       Hola Profesora [first name], 'Hi Professor […]'

       Sorry I missed class today. I am very sick with a sinus infection and complications due to my asthma. I have a doctor's note for you. I know our final portfolio's are due monday, and I received your oncourse message with today's class materials. Other than that,

       Is there anything else I need to review or do to be ready for Monday's class?

       Thanks,
       [Name & last name]

Email represents an asynchronous medium of electronic communication that prevails in student-faculty consultations. Due to its virtual nature, it has been observed that email discourse represents a hybrid means of communication that shares characteristics of both oral and written speech (Baron 2003: 87; Crystal 2006: 19; Herring 2003: 617; Yus 2001: 186). Some of the attributes that email discourse shares with face-to-face interaction include: an informal style, it is considered a linear medium in that information can be processed at the time it is received; it is characterized by relatively short, multiple turns; it generally has simple syntax; messages cannot be edited once they are sent; what is communicated most often requires some kind of response [i.e. illocutionary uptake); and information can be interpreted as humorous or sarcastic in specific contexts. However, at the same time, email is also different because written speech represents a non-linear medium since information is processed after it is read, the information is durable, texts vary greatly in length, emails can be edited before they are sent, some emotional information cannot be conveyed, and the addressee can respond at his/her convenience. And, unlike either spoken and written messages, email discourse, a hybrid medium of virtual communication, generally has the following attributes: it can be more informal than face-to-face speech, it can be edited and printed out, it may include a reply with the history present, it can be forwarded to others with or without the original sender's knowledge, introductions (e.g. "Dear Professor [last name]" or "Hi Professor") and closings can be omitted (e.g. "I look forward to your comments, thanks"). In addition, email discourse often utilizes compensatory strategies to replace social cues commonly used in face-to-face interaction, such as laughter, prosody (e.g. loudness [you are the BEST], duration [h:iiii], final rising intonation [are you still mad at me↑]), including emoticons (e.g., :-), :-(, etc.) to convey emotion. It should also be noted that the degree of formality or informality in email discourse can be related to the type of power distance culture (Hofstede 2001), namely, high (inequality) or low (equality) power distance, which can influence the openings and closings of email messages sent from a student to a professor, for example (Bjørge 2007).

The ability to write a polite or appropriate email in a second (L2) or foreign (FL) language depends on the learner's pragmatic competence, specifically on his/her pragmalinguistic and sociopragmatic knowledge (Leech 1983; Thomas 1983). Pragmalinguistic knowledge refers to the linguistic resources that are available in a particular language and that are necessary to express a specific communicative effect, as the linguistic and non-verbal resource used to write an email message to a professor (e.g. 'Dear professor, I was wondering if you would be able to write a letter of recommendation'). On the other hand, sociopragmatic knowledge refers to knowledge of social conventions at the perception level, such as an awareness of the differences in social distance or social power when writing an appropriate email to a professor vs. a fellow classmate. For example, when addressing a professor, the student has to select an appropriate opening ("Dear Professor [last name)]", "Professor [name]," "Hi John", "Hi', "Dear John,", or no greeting at all) and/or closing (e.g. "Thanks, Rob", "Bye, Rob", or 'Thanks and take care, Rob". It also refers to the appropriate use (or lack thereof) of polite behavior in email discourse (Watts 2003). The aim of this chapter is to examine the interactional aspect of email discourse in an FL context by analyzing the learners' pragmalinguistic and sociopragmatic ability to produce appropriate openings and closings in student-initiated email requests in cyber consultations sent to their instructors. It will also examine the role of variation by gender in producing opening and closing moves.

The present chapter is organized as follows. First, I review existing research on email discourse with attention to opening and closing moves. Then, I present the research questions for the current study, followed by the method of analysis. Finally, I provide the results, the discussion, and the conclusion.

2   Previous research on email openings and closings

The present study is framed within the field of Computer-Mediated Discourse (CMD) that has currently received significant attention in pragmatics research, specifically synchronous communication and the organization of social practices in email discourse (Biesenbach-Lucas 2006, 2007; Bloch 2002; Bou-Franch 2011; Bjørge 2007; Crystal 2006; Félix-Brasdefer 2012; Herring 2003; Waldvogel 2007; Yus 2001). Research on email discourse has shown that this medium is "an ideal tool for building and maintaining social relationships" (Baron 1998: 155). However, the maintenance and rapport-building of social relationships in an FL context may be hindered due to a lack of pragmalinguistic and sociopragmatic knowledge that prevents learners from appropriately developing a social relationship with a professor. Openings and closings in email conversations reflect a great deal of stylistic variation among members of university-based communities in Spain (Bou-Franch 2011) and in Norway, where English is used as a lingua Franca among international students whose native language is not Norweigian (Bjørge 2007). In the context of workplace interactions, greetings represent a means in which the writer "constructs his or her social and professional identity and relationship," while closings "help consolidate the relationship and establish a relational basis for future encounters" (Waldvogel 2007: 1). Similarly, the presence or absence of an opening or closing may be perceived as polite or impolite behavior in symmetric or asymmetric situations.

Crystal (2006) provides a detailed description and discussion of the structure and function of greetings and farewells in email discourse. According to the author, greetings and farewells are optional elements that show variation in form, and their presence is conditioned by the status and degree of social power and social distance between the writer and the recipient of the email. For instance, in a sample of 500 emails from people who knew the author (and with several kinds of social relationship and intimacy), "two-thirds [...] contained an introductory greeting" (p. 106) expressing various degrees of affect. The most frequent forms used in greetings sent to the author included "Dear David", "David", and "Hi David", as means of informal interaction. In contrast, farewells displayed a lower degree of variation in form, including both pre-closings (best wishes) and signature (e.g. thanks, David).

Waldvogel (2007) presents a comprehensive study of variation in the form of greetings and closings in email in two New Zealand workplaces, namely, an educational organization and a manufacturing plant. The author examined the impact of sociolinguistic variables such as status, social distance, and gender of the interlocutors in the production of greeting and closings. Results of the study showed variation not only in the use of these elements between the two organizations, but also variation in how these forms employed according to the aforementioned social factors. The greetings were analyzed in terms of elements that comprise them, such as no greeting, greeting word only (e.g. hi), first name only, greeting word + first name. Similarly, the closing data were examined according to the following elements: no closing, name only, farewell formula only, farewell formula + name, thanks only, and thanks + name. Results showed differences in the preference for opening moves between the two organizations, mainly, with respect to their presence or absence, and according to the status and degree of social distance between the sender and the recipient of the email. A great deal of variation was observed in the pattern of greetings and closings in both organizations. With regard to gender the author found that "women acknowledged their addressee more frequently than did men and made greater use of greetings and closings" (2007: 13). And in one of the organizations (Revelinu), men employed more forms expressing positive politeness. However, no difference was noted in the way men and women ended their messages. Overall, the author concluded that presence or absence of opening and closing moves in these emails was not necessarily attributed to polite or impolite behavior. Instead, it was noted that the selection and frequency of occurrence of opening and closing moves in these workplaces were considered the expected norm (or politic behavior [Watts 2003]).

Unlike the previous study that focused on workplace settings, Gains (1998) compared messages in academic (54 emails in different universities in the UK) and commercial contexts (62 emails at a UK insurance company). The commercial email messages in the insurance company were written in standard English in a semi-formal style, avoided features from conversational style, and the majority of the data (92%) did not contain a greeting. By contrast, in academic messages, writers used an informal (conversation) style including creative use such as humor and phatic exchanges. And, unlike commercial emails, the majority of the academic messages (63%) began with some form of opening such as the informal greeting "Hi," "Dear", or "Hellow," while 37% of the messages contained no greeting at all. In both academic and commercial messages, a closing was the predominant way of ending the message ("bye, "cheers," "thank you"). And, in a different institutional setting (university system in administrative departments), Lan (2000) found that non-native speakers of English in Hong Kong did not use a greeting form to open their messages (54%); while in the remaining 46% of the email data the opening was prefaced with *Dear*. However, it should be noted that the academic setting analyzed in the present study (student-faculty email consultations) differs from that of Lan (2000), which included emails sent to staff in administrative departments.

In general, it has been found that the type of community of practice in CMC (Murray 2000) influences the style, the form, the presence or absence, and frequency of openings and closings in email requests sent in academic and commercial settings. As in sociolinguistic research, where the concept of community of practice is used to analyze polite or impolite practices among men and women (Mills 2003), a community of practice in CMC determines the conventions or the norms that are appropriate and expected by the members of this community. In her dissertation on company-internal email communication in Lingua franca English, Kankaanranta (2005) examined 282 emails written by Finnish and Swedish employees. The author noted that greetings and closings in this business setting are relational and express involvement, and occurred in the majority of the messages.

Finally, openings and closings were examined exclusively in three academic settings. Based on Hofstede's (2001) notion of Power Distance (PD) cultures, Bjørge (2007) examined the openings (forms of address) and complimentary closings used by international students who used English as a lingua Franca in Norway. It was found that email messages written by those from high PD cultures included formal/conventional address forms and closings than low PD email messages whose preference was for informal or personal alternatives. In a different context, Economidou-Kogetsidis (2011) examined salutations in email requests written by Greek Cypriot university students of English to their professors. Overall, these learners showed a preference for formality (zero form of address) by using the lecturer's last name (or greeting only) rather than the first name. And Bou-Franch's (2011) innovative study focused on the variation observed in discourse practices, analyzing the opening and closing sequences in email exchanges with regard to the discursive practices used at a peninsular university. The email conversations were taken from two subsets within the same university community: 50 conversations between university lecturers (-Power, -Distance) and 50 email conversations between undergraduate students and their lecturers (+Power, + Distance). The data were analyzed using methodology from conversation analysis (Schegloff & Sacks 1973) and discourse analysis with respect to sequences and moves (Sinclair & Coulthard 1975; Stubbs 1983). In the study, the opening sequence included two moves, namely, greeting and self-identification. Closing sequences, on the other hand, consisted of three moves: expressions of gratitude, leave-taking, and signature. The focus of the study is on the stylistic variation observed in the various expressions employed to convey the illocutionary force of greetings and closings. The results of Bou-Franch's (2011) study showed sociopragmatic differences in email exchanges between equals (i.e. among lecturers) and unequals (i.e. students → lecturers). More importantly, the results of this study showed that opening and closing moves were influenced by both the relative institutional power and the conversational progression (two email exchanges vs. three email exchanges). While greetings predominated in both types of encounters (initial and response emails), "the closing sequence of non-initial emails sent down the institutional hierarchy [unequal encounters] displayed the least density" (2011: 1779). According to the author, this finding shows that the writers in this CMC speech community were careful in writing their messages, especially when corresponding with a person of higher status. Overall, the Peninsular email corpus showed a "highly sociable communicative style" (2011: 1783) that showed friendliness in order to maintain interpersonal relations in the aforementioned community of practice. The members of this university community share and use expected discourse practices to communicate with their fellow lecturers or with their instructors.

Taken together, the following observations ensue from these studies which investigated the relational dimension of email messages in different CMC speech communities. Unlike the text message, in which a request, for example, is an obligatory element, the presence or absence of greetings and closings in emails may be dictated by the type of the CMC speech community (e.g. academic vs. commercial setting), the degree of polite/impolite behavior or socially appropriate behavior conveyed in the message (Mills 2003; Watts 2003), the relationship between the writer and the receiver of the message, based on factors such as social power, social distance, and degree of familiarity (e.g. friends, workmates, student-professor) (Spencer-Oatey 1996), and the gender of the interlocutors (Antonopoulou 2011). With regard to gender in CMC studies, Herring (2000) provides an overview of studies in CMC where gender plays a significant role in the selection of social practices in synchronous and asynchronous discourse, and Mills (2003) provides a critical overview of impolite behavior among women. Further, the notion of a CMC speech community is important because it includes members that participate in a variety of social practices with other members of the community, as in students sending email messages to their professors during the academic semester in cyber consultations about their classes. And, although the studies above focused on the relational aspect of email discourse (opening and closing sequences), none focused on a CMC community among learners in an FL context. Most research on email discourse has focused on the request strategies used by learners of English and Spanish (Biensenbach-Lucas 2007; Félix-Brasdefer 2012; Hartford & Bardovi-Harlig 1996), but no attention was given to the preference for opening and closing moves.

The present study will investigate the following research questions:

1) In student-initiated email requests to instructors, what is the degree of pragmalinguistic variation observed in the opening and closing moves?
2) Does the gender of the sender influence the selection of the opening and closing moves?

3 Method

3.1 Data, participants, and procedures

The data for the current study is part of a natural email corpus of 320 email messages sent from US undergraduate learners of Spanish to their instructors. Of these, 200 were email requests sent in Spanish and 120 were sent in the students' native language, US English[1] . The email messages were sent to the students' instructors at a large Midwestern university during the course of the academic year. The data were collected during five semesters (2009-2011). All participants were learners of Spanish in third- and fourth-semester classes and all were taking courses in literature, composition, and/or linguistics in Spanish. The email messages were sent to 10 different instructors (four NSs of Spanish and six NNSs of Spanish) who agreed to participate in the study by sharing the email messages sent from their students during the course of a semester while they were teaching one of these classes. Seven were faculty members (in their 40's and 50's) and three were Associate Instructors (as they are called at this university) who are graduate students (in their late 20's and early 30's) with teaching responsibilities in upper-divission courses. Thus, the nature of the email requests sent to the graduate students may differ somewhat from those sent to faculty. Students sent email requests in English (their native language) or in L2 Spanish about class-related issues within the Department of Spanish and Portuguese at this US University (CMC speech community). All 320 email messages represent requests initiated by students to various instructors: 200 were written in Spanish (main corpus) and 120 in English.[2] Finally, due to the procedures used to collect the email data, it was not possible to collect information regarding the students' experience abroad.

3.2 Data analysis

Since all of the email requests in the present study represent requests initiated by students to instructors, the relationship between the students and the instructor was strictly academic, that is, distant (+D) and asymmetric with regard to social power (+P). It should be noted that these variables may be subject to change during the negotiation of the email exchange or during the course of the interaction or changes in the level of familiarity between the student and professor over the course of the semester (Fraser 1990; Spencer-Oatey 1996).

The data were analyzed according to previous classifications of opening and closing moves analyzed for Spanish (Bou-Franch 2011) and English (Kankaanranta 2005; Waldvogel 2007). For the current study, the classification in Table 1 was used to code and analyze the data:

Opening moves	Example	Closing moves	Example
		No Closing	
Greeting word only	"Hello"	Signature name only	"Jessica"
First name only	"John"	Signature name & last name	"Jessica Brown"
Greeting & name	"Hello" / "Hi John"	Leave-taking & name	"Sincerely (Regards), Jessica"
Greeting & title	"Hi/Hello Professor"	Leave-taking, name, & last name	"Sincerely, Jessica Brown"
Greeting, title, & name	"Hello Professor John"	Thanks, leave-taking, & name	"Thanks, Sincerely, Jessica"
Greeting, title, & last name	"Hello Professor Smith"	Thanks, leave-taking, name, & last name	"Thanks, Sincerely, Jessica Brown"
Title only	"Professor"	Thanks only	"Thanks" / 'Thanks a lot"
Title & name	Professor John	Thanks & name	"Thanks, Jessica"
Title & last name	Professor Smith	Thanks, name, & last name	"Thanks, Jessica Brown"
Title, name, & last name	Professor John Smith		

Table 1. Examples of opening and closing moves in student-initiated email requests sent to instructors.

In addition to the opening and closing moves, two additional elements were identified in the data, "self-identification" and "personal comment." (adopted from Bou-Franch 2011). "Self-identification" is the element prefacing the main message (e.g. 'This is Michael Allen from the 10:10 MWF class'). Personal comments were placed at the beginning or end of the text message. These are relational comments that express positive politeness (Brown & Levinson 1987) addressed to the instructor to open or end the message (e.g.

"I hope you're having a great summer!," "Have a good super bowl day," thank you and I hope you have a relaxing break," ¡Estoy nervioso! ("I'm nervous") ¡AH! But it'll be nice to be the first one done").

Following Barron and Schneider's framework on pragmatic variation (2009), the actional level was selected as the level of pragmatic analysis for examining pragmalinguistic variation in openings and closings (social practices), and the macro-social factor, gender, was selected in order to analyze its influence on language use in email discourse. The data were analyzed using both descriptive (frequencies and percentages) and inferential statistics (Chi-square tests).

Finally, the issue of inter-coder reliability during the coding of strategies should be addressed. The data were coded individually by the researcher and by a Mexican university-level female student (with advanced proficiency in English) who was trained to code the opening and closing sequences in the email data. In cases where a discrepancy occurred in the analysis, the researcher and the coder discussed the coding and arrived at an agreement. Overall, the coder and the researcher agreed on the coding of strategies for 95% of the data.

4   Results

This section presents the results for each research question with regard to pragmalinguistic variation observed in closing and opening moves (4.1) and the role of variation by gender (4.2) in student-initiated email requests sent to instructors of Spanish. Of the 320 email messages analyzed in this study, 62.5% (200 emails [128 initiated by females and 72 by males]), the main corpus, were written in Spanish and 37.5% (120 messages [71 initiated by females & 49 by males]) were written in English. The L1 English email data will be used for comparison purposes with the L2 Spanish emails.[3]

4.1   Pragmalinguistic variation of opening and closing moves

Opening moves (L2 Spanish emails)	% (frequency)	Opening moves (L1 English emails)	% (frequency)
No greeting	5.5% (11)	No greeting	9.2% (11)
Greeting word only	19% (38)	Greeting word only	32.5% (39)
First name only	4% (8)	First name only	3.3% (4)
Greeting & name	12% (24)	Greeting & name	4.2% (5)
Greeting & title	22% (44)	Greeting & title	11.7% (14)
Greeting, title, & name	3.5% (7)	Greeting, title, & name	7.5% (9)
Greeting, title, & last name	13% (26)	Greeting, title, & last name	10.8% (13)
Title only	7% (14)	Title only	5% (6)
Title & name	2.5% (5)	Title & name	1.7% (2)
Title & last name	11.5% (23)	Title & last name	13.3% (16)
Title, name, & last name	0% (0)	Title, name, & last name	.8% (1)
	100% (200)		100% (120)

Table 2. Opening moves in the L2 Spanish and L1 English data.

Overall, the majority of the L2 Spanish (94.5% or 189/200) and L1 English emails (90.8% or 109/120 emails) were introduced by an opening move, and the majority began with a greeting formula. Although the opening moves were used by the students in their first (11 of 11 types) and second languages (10 of 11 types) to initiate email messages, variation in these forms was more pronounced in the L2 Spanish data. Greeting and Title (22% or 44/200 emails) (e.g. *Hola Profesor*) and Greeting Word Only (19% 38/200 emails) (e.g. *Hola*) were the two most frequent greeting moves noted in the L2 Spanish emails, followed by three additional moves utilized with a range of 22 to 26 instances, namely, Title and Last Name (11.5% or 23/200 emails) (e.g. *Profesor* Smith), Greeting and Name (12% or 24/200 emails) (e.g. *Hola* John), and Greeting, Title, and Last Name (13% or 26/200 emails) (e.g. *Profesor* John Smith). The results of a Chi-square test that compared the frequencies (L2 Spanish) between Greeting and Title (most frequent) and

Greeting, Title, and Last Name (third most frequent) showed a significant difference (X^2 (1) = 4.630, $p \leq 0.031$). This shows that the students are not using these strategies with equal frequency. By contrast, in the L1 English group Greeting Word Only (32.5% or 39/120) (the second most frequent move in the L2 Spanish data) was the most frequent opening move. This was followed by three other less frequent moves with a range of 13 to 15, namely, Title & Last Name (13.3% or 16/120 emails), Greeting & Title (11.7% or 14/120 emails), and Greeting, Title & Last Name (10.8% or 13/120 emails). The result of a Chi-square test that compared the frequencies of the first (Greeting Word Only) and second (Title and Last Name) most frequent opening moves also showed significant differences (X^2 (1) = 9.61, $p \leq 0.002$). Again, when writing email messages in L1 English, the students are not using these opening moves with equal preference. The other variants noted in Table 2 were infrequently observed in the opening sequences of the L2 and L1 email data. And when the frequencies of the Greeting and Title opening move (most frequent in the L2 data) were compared between the L2 Spanish and the L1 English data, the results of a Chi-square yielded significant differences (X^2 (1) = 15.517, $p \leq 0.000$), thus, permitting us to reject the null hypothesis that this strategy is equally used in the L2 Spanish and the L1 English email data produced by the students in the present study.

The greeting move included a variety of informal (most frequent) and formal forms. The informal greeting *hola* 'hi' was the most pervasive formula used in the L2 Spanish data (65% or 130/200 emails). This informal greeting was used in various combinations: alone (*hola*), *hola* + title (*hola* professor), *hola* + professor's first name (*hola Carlos*), and *hola* + professor's last name (*Hola* Profesor Smith). Formal greeting variants (less frequent) noted in the L2 Spanish data included *señor* ('sir'), *señora* ('ma'am'), *profesor/a* ('professor') or the abbreviated form *Profe* (Prof) *estimado/a* ('dear'), or a salutation (infrequent) such as buenos días ('good morning') or *buenas tardes* ('good afternoon'). By contrast, in the L1 email data hola ('hello') (written in Spanish) was used 27% of the time (32/120 emails) in the L1 English data in similar combinations. Other greeting forms observed in the L1 English data included 'hi,' 'hello,' 'hey,' 'dear,' *hola, querido* ('dear'), *señor* ('sir'), *señora* ('madam').

Table 3 shows the overall distribution of closing moves indentified in the email data:

Closing moves	% (frequency) (L2 Spanish data)	Closing moves	% (frequency) (L1 English data)
No closing	1.5% (3)	No closing	1.7% (2)
Signature name only	7.5% (15)	Signature name only	4.2% (5)
Signature name & last name	3.5% (7)	Signature name & last name	5% (6)
Leave-taking & name	5% (10)	Leave-taking & name	1.7% (2)
Leave-taking, name, & last name	5% (10)	Leave-taking, name, & last name	5% (6)
Thanks, leave-taking, & name	3% (6)	Thanks, leave-taking, & name	.8% (1)
Thanks, leave-taking, name, & last name	3% (6)	Thanks, leave-taking, name, & last name	5.8% (7)
Thanks only	4% (8)	Thanks only	2.5% (3)
Thanks & name	26.5% (53)	Thanks & name	25% (30)
Thanks, name, & last name	41% (82)	Thanks, name, & last name	48.3% (58)
	100% (200)		100% (120)

Table 3. Closing moves in the L2 Spanish and L1 English data.

Unlike the variation observed in the opening sequences in both the L2 Spanish and L1 English data, the majority of the students chose one of two moves to close the message in both data sets, namely, Thanks, Name, & Last Name (L2 Spanish: 41% or 82/200 emails; L1 English: 48.3% or 58/120 emails) (see example 2a below) and Thanks & Name (L2 Spanish: 26.5% or 53/200 emails; L1 English: 25% or 30/120 emails) (see example 2b below) . The additional eight options were used infrequently by both groups.

The most frequent form employed to end an email message in L2 Spanish was 'thank you' or its variant *gracias* (58.5% or 117/200 emails) and intensified variants of this form (21.5% or 43/200 emails) such as *muchas gracias* ('thanks very much'), *gracias mucho* ('thanks much'), *mil gracias* ('a thousand thanks') or *muchisisisisisimas gracias* ('thank you sooooooo much'). In the L1 English data 'thanks' (e.g. 'thanks,' 'thanks again,' 'thanks for your time,' 'thanks in advance') predominated in the data (occurring in 50% of the corpus [(60/120 emails]), while the intensified forms 'thanks so much' or 'thanks a lot' were infrequently used (3% or 4/120 emails).

The following examples show email messages with opening and closing moves in the L2 Spanish (2) and L1 English data (3):

(2)   L2 Spanish opening and closing moves
    a. female student, #2.
        Hola, 'Hi'
        [Request]
        Muchos Gracias, 'Thanks so much'
            [Student's name+last name]

    b. Female student, #4.
        Hola Profesor,   'Hello Professor'
         [Request]
        Gracias! 'Thanks'
        [Student's name]

    c. female student, #57.
        Estimado Profesor, 'Dear Professor'
        [Request]
        Muchas Gracias! 'Thanks so much'
        Best,
        [Student's name only]

(3) L1 English opening and closing moves
    a. female student, #4.
        Hola, 'Hello'
        [Request]
        Thank you,
        [Student's name + last]

    b. male student, #9.
        Hi,
        [Request]
        Thanks a lot.
        [Student's name & last]

    c. male student, #9.
        Professor 'Last Name'
        [Request]
        Thanks!
        [Student's name only]

    d. female student, #14.
        Querida Profesora, 'Dear Professor' (female)

[Request]
Thank you,
and sorry for interrupting your break!
Sincerely,
[Student's name]

e. Female student, #19.

Hola Señor, 'Hello Sir'
[Request]
Muchas gracias. 'Thanks a lot'
[Student's name]

In addition to the opening and closing moves mentioned above, two additional moves were identified in the email data: self-identification (prefacing the email message) and personal comments at the beginning and end of the email message. These interpersonal moves were more frequent in the L2 Spanish data. The opening Self-Identification occurred in 11% (22/200 emails) of the L2 Spanish data and in only 5% (6/120 emails) of the L1 English data. Personal comments were also more frequent in the L2 Spanish data (20.5% or 41/200) than in the L1 English data (12.5% or 15/120 emails). In both data sets, personal comments were more frequently placed in the closing sequence. When writing an email in Spanish, students tended to include more personal comments both to open (14/200) and close the message (27/200) than when writing to their instructors in their native language (opening personal comment [2/120 emails] and closing personal comment [13/120 emails]). Examples of these interpersonal sequences are provided in (4, L2 Spanish) and (5, L1 English):

---

(4)   L2 Spanish: Personal comment (female student)

1   *Hola Dr.* [apellido]:   'Hello Dr. [last name]
2   →   *Primero, quería decirle que me gustó mucho su*
3   *presentación sobre los pedidos el sábado pasado.*
           'First, I wanted to say that I really liked your
           presentation about requests last Saturday'
4-11   [Request]
12   *Un saludo,*   'Regards'
13   [Student's name + last name]

(5)   L1 English: Self-identification (male student)
1   *Hola* [Professor's first name]
2 →   This is [name & last name] from the 10:10 MWF class.
3-7   [Request]
8   *Gracias*, 'Thanks'
9   [Student's first name]

In the L1 English data the opening greeting, as shown in Example 5 (line 1), and the closing move, as in Example 5 (line 8), were often written in Spanish, while the request was written exclusively in English. In these cases, the opening and closing moves are formulaic (ritualistic) expressions which are used to express solidarity with a professor at the beginning and end of the message. However, it is likely that due to insecurity in expressing ideas in the target language, the student selected his/her first language to issue the request to avoid any misunderstandings with the instructor.

4.2   The role of gender in email openings and closings

Variation by gender played an important role in the preference for opening and closing moves in the L2 Spanish and L1 English data. Table 4 shows the six most frequent opening moves identified in the email data by the gender of the sender of the email, namely, the student.[4]

	L2 Spanish Females (128/200)	L2 Spanish Males (72/200)	L1 English Females (71/120)	L1 English Males (49/120)
Greeting word only	23.4% (30)	11.1% (8)	31% (22)	34.7% (17)
Greeting & title	18.8% (24)	27.8% (20)	15.5% (11)	6.1% (3)
Greeting, title, & last name	14.8% (19)	9.7% (7)	5.6% (4)	18.4% (9)
Greeting & name	13.3% (17)	9.7% (7)	4.2% (3)	4.1% (2)
Title & last name	10.9% (14)	12.5% (9)	18.3% (13)	6.1% (3)
Title only	4.7% (6)	11.1% (8)	5.6% (4)	4.1% (2)

Table 4. Variation by gender in the six most frequent opening moves.

Opening an email message by means of a Greeting Word Only (e.g. *Hola* 'Hello/ Hi') was the most preferred strategy observed in the L2 Spanish female data (23.4% or 30/128 emails) and in the L1 English data (females [31% or 22/71 emails] and males [34.7% or 17/49 emails]) (e.g. 'Hello,'

'Hi'). This opening ranked third in the L2 Spanish male data (11.1% or 8/72 emails). The results of a Chi-square test that compared the frequencies of the Greeting Word Only in the male and female L2 Spanish data was significant $(X^2 (1) = 12.73, p \leq 0.000)$, showing that there are significant differences between males and females with respect to the openings of email messages in Spanish. The male writers in the L2 Spanish data selected Greeting & Title as the most frequent opening (27.8% or 20/72 emails), followed by Title & Last Name (12.5% or 9/72 emails) and other infrequent strategies shown in Table 4. Among the female writers in the L2 Spanish data, there was a preference for a Greeting Only move or in combination with a title or a name or last name (the first four openings in the L2 Spanish female data). In contrast, among the L1 English females, in addition to Greeting Word Only, they showed a preference for a more deferential style by opening the message with a title and the professor's last name (18.3% or 13/71) or a Greeting and Title move (15.5% or 11/71 emails). In the L1 English male data, writers also showed a preference for a deferential style by using a Greeting, Title, & Last Name (18.4% or 9/49 emails), thus, no significant differences were noted between the opening moves of males and females in L1 English.

Unlike the variation by gender observed in the opening moves, no major variation was noted in the closing moves, as seen in Table 5.

	L2 Spanish Females (128/200)	L2 Spanish Males (72/200)	L1 English Females (71/120)	L1 English Males (49/120)
Thanks, name, & last name	36.7% (47)	48.6% (35)	43.7% (31)	55.1% (27)
Thanks & name	29.7% (38)	20.8% (15)	28.2% (20)	20.4% (10)

Table 5. Variation by gender in the two most frequent closing moves.

When writing an email to an instructor, all students selected one of two main moves to close an email message, namely, Thanks, Name, & Last Name or Thanks & Name. Of these, the most formal moves, Thanks, Name, & Last Name, predominated in the email data. Overall, the frequencies of the other options for closing moves displayed in Table 3 were rather small.

5 Discussion

This study examined pragmalinguistic variation in the opening and closing practices as well as the role of gender in student-initiated email requests sent to their instructors of Spanish. Variation of opening and closing moves was analyzed according to the actional level (level of pragmatic analysis) and gender (Barron and Schneider 2009). Greetings and closings reflect the relational function of language (or phatic communication) that adds a social component to the email message (Brown & Yule 1983; Malinowski 1923). According to Bloch (2002) one of the functions of email in learner-instructor classroom interaction is "to establish a more personal relationship using this phatic form of language" (p. 125). In the L2 academic context examined in this study, openings and closings represent expected social practices in student-instructor cyber consultations and they contain characteristics of both formal and informal discourse, such as formal greetings (e.g. Dear Professor [last name]) and formal closings ("Thanks, Jessica Brown")

Research question #1 addressed the issue of pragmalinguistic variation in opening and closing moves. The eleven opening moves (Table 2) and the ten closing moves (Table 3) identified in the email data show a great deal of variation in both the L2 Spanish and the L1 English data sets, and this variation is influenced by the gender of the writer of the email. The majority of the emails examined in this study (over 90% in each data set) contained an opening move, and over 98% of the data analyzed ended the message with a closing move. And although these moves represent optional (structural) elements of an email message (Crystal 2006), their presence or absence may be influenced by the CMC community of practice, the setting in which emails are exchanged, the relative social power of and the degree of social distance between the writer and the recipient of the email message, among other factors. In workplace settings (asymmetric relationship) greetings and closings in email messages have been found to be much less frequent in educational organizations than in manufacturing plants (Waldvogel 2007). And in email messages sent to Crystal (2006) (with various kinds of social relationship and intimacy [p. 106]), opening moves were frequent in two-thirds of Crystal's messages sent to him from friends. In the present study, both greeting and closing moves predominated in the majority of the student-initiated email messages sent to their instructors (asymmetric relations) (90% or higher [Tables 2 & 3]). In the asymmetric relationship between a student and an instructor, the current study supports the findings of Gains (1998), in that the majority of the email messages (NSs of English) in an academic context began with an opening form. In particular, greeting moves reflected a more conversational style with the use of the informal greeting 'hi' or 'hello', a finding that approximates the behavior of the NSs of English in the current study. However, in the present study L2 email openings were more formal and deferencial (Table 2) than messages that students composed in their L1 (English). This finding is similar to the degree of formality observed among non-native speakers of English in Hong Kong in an academic setting (administrative departments) (Lan 2000) and among international students (of power distance cultures) who used English (in email messages) as a lingua Franca in Norway (Bjørge 2007).

In a different academic setting, namely among Spanish undergraduate students and their lecturers who exchanged emails, Bou-Franch (2011) found that opening moves such as greetings (93%) and self-identification (60%) predominated in unequal encounters (p. 1779). And in closing sequences, the following moves were used at least 60% of the time: thanking (63%), leave-taking (83%), and signature (63%). Thus, it seems that the preference for opening and closing moves is conditioned by the setting (e.g. insurance company vs. a university), the type of speech act accomplished (e.g. request, apology, or complaint), and the degree of social power and social distance between the writer and the recipient of the email message. The presence or absence of an opening or closing move may convey polite behavior or simply socially appropriate behavior that is neither polite nor impolite (Watts 2003). Whether an opening or closing move is perceived as polite or formal (e.g. 'Dear Professor [last name]'), depends on the interpretation on the part of the recipient of the email message. In the present academic context opening and closing moves are expected moves, and their absence as well as their form may be perceived negatively by the recipient of the message (Hartford & Bardovi-Harlig 1996). This observation, however, needs empirical support.

The finding that the majority of the emails began with a greeting move (e.g. Greeting Word only, Greeting & Title) shows that that students tended to use solidarity politeness with their instructor to express involvement (Scollon & Scollon 2011) or familiarity from the beginning of the email message. This finding is further substantiated by the fact that 65% of the L2 email messages (130/200 emails) were prefaced by the informal greeting *hola* (alone or in combination with other moves, such as Greeting & Name, Greeting, Title & Last Name). By contrast, the two moves mainly used to close an email message in the L2 Spanish and in L1 English data (i.e. Thanks, Name, & Last Name; Thanks & Name) reflect deference or hierarchical politeness (Scollon & Scollon 2001). Thus, when students in the academic context of this study open an email message, the tendency is to express solidarity politeness (or positive face) and the tendency in closing the message is to express deference politeness (or negative face) (Brown & Levinson 1987). Further, the finding that personal comments (embedded in opening and closing moves) were more frequent in the L2 Spanish email data than in the L1 English data, shows another example of solidarity politeness by means of making a positive comment to reinforce the instructor's positive face in an L2, before a request is made (Brown & Levinson 1987). As observed by one reviewer, it may be possible that these students are influenced by the politeness orientation of both their own culture (United States with an orientation to negative politeness) and that of the target language culture (a region of the

Spanish-speaking world, with an orientation toward positive politeness) (Félix-Brasdefer 2008; Márquez Reiter & Plancencia 2005).[5]

Given the pervasiveness of greetings and personal comments, and similar to the results of Bou-Franch (2011), the email data analyzed in the current study show a tendency toward "person first, business second" (p. 1784). Further, while CMC research has shown that email discourse is mainly characterized by an informal style, the results of the present study (and those in Bou-Franch 2011: 1783) suggest that academic email discourse is characterized by a formal style as well, as evidenced by the high frequency of formal opening (titles, last name) and, in particular, a preference for formal closing moves (Thanks, Name, & Last Name). Further, Bou-Franch's (2011) study provides strong evidence of "the pervasiveness and diversity of opening and closing mechanisms in certain situated email practices and therefore shows that the assumption that all email communication is the same, i.e. homogeneous, informal and generally lacking openings and closings is untenable." (p. 1783). The results of the present study support this observation.

Research question #2 examined the role of gender in opening and closing practices. In her critical review of CMC research, Herring (2000) reported gender differences in asynchronous CMC with regard to politeness. For example, women are more likely to be more polite (e.g., they thank and apologize more), while men seem to be less concerned with politeness practices. In the current study, there was evidence of variation by gender: in the female data, a wider variety of openings was used when writing an email to an instructor (L2 Spanish & L1 English). In contrast, among male students (L2 Spanish & L1 English) there was less variation and there was only one predominant opening move (Greeting Word Only, Table 4). Further, the female students (L2 Spanish or L1 English) and the male students writing in L1 English showed a preference for solidarity politeness by relying on conversational features such as the informal greeting ('Hello' or 'Hi'). On the contrary, the male students writing in L2 Spanish showed an inclination towards hierarchical or deference politeness (Scollon & Scollon 2001) by using more formal opening moves such as titles and the professor's last name. Previous research has also shown that women use more greetings than men when sending email messages in workplace settings, thus this study futher substantiates Waldvogel's (2007) findings and Holmes' (1995) observation that women are more likely than men to attend to the social and affective aspects of an interaction. For the present study, based on the frequency of greeting moves, females (L2 Spanish & L1 English) seem to show a greater preference for greetings than male students (in particular, in the L2 Spanish data). However, it should be noted that the opening move Greeting Word Only was also present in male email messages, although to a lesser degree. Finally, with regard to closing moves, the findings of this study support previous work (Waldvogel 2007) in that there is no difference in the way in which male and female students close their email messages sent to their instructors. A deferential style to close an email message was adopted in L2 Spanish, namely, Thanks, Name & Last Name and Thanks & Name, respectively. This finding further substantiates Crystal's (2006) observation that unlike greetings, which show variation (as in the various opening moves), closings show fewer possibilities of variation.

The results of the current study should be interpreted with caution, as only 320 email messages (200 in L2 Spanish and 120 in L1 English) were analyzed, and the email data were not evenly distributed by gender. As a result, these findings cannot be generalized to all learners of Spanish (males and females) writing email messages to their instructors in their native language or in an L2 or an FL context. Further, future studies should examine the influence of gender of both the writer and the recipient of the email message, especially since previous work in sociolinguistics shows that "it is the gender of the addressee rather than that of the speaker which emerges as a decisive factor." (Antonopoulou 2001: 252). In addition to examining a larger sample of email messages written in L2 Spanish and L1 English, data from native speakers from Spanish should be also analyzed for comparison purposes. In this respect, the results of the current study were discussed in light of the native speaker Spanish data presented in Bou-Franch (2011) which examined email exchanges between students and their lecturers at a university in Spain. An analysis of email conversations between learners and instructors, including the complete email exchange, will also complement our understanding of email discourse practices in student-instructor cyber consultations. Finally, studies on the perception of email discourse should focus on the perlocutionary effect of the message by examining issues of politeness or impoliteness on how the message was interpreted by the recipient(s) of the message. Although some of these issues have been investigated (e.g. Hartford & Bardovi-Harlig 1996; Haugh 2010; Hendriks 2010), we need to examine them at the discourse level and across email exchanges in FL learning contexts.

6 Conclusion

This study examined variation in the opening and closing sequences in email messages (L2 Spanish and L1 English) sent from undergraduate university-level students to their instructors of Spanish. Opening and closing sequences were analyzed in terms of moves. This study showed that there exists a great deal of variation in the ways to open and close an email message sent to an instructor. Opening moves are generally introduced by conversational features such as informal greetings ('Hi'), followed by other combinations that convey a formal style, whereas closing moves are characterized by a formal style. In this study the gender of the writer of the email message influenced the type and frequency of the opening moves. Finally, as it widely known, learning an L2 requires knowledge of the pragmatics of the L2 and sufficient exposure to the input of the target language. Specifically, when writing email messages in academic settings the learner needs to develop his/her ability with respect to both the pragmalinguistics (linguistic resources necessary) and the sociopragmatics (knowledge of appropriateness, social status, social power) when negotiating social practices in equal or unequal email encounters. To facilitate learners' knowledge of email discourse in an L2, pedagogical intervention should be implemented in the FL classroom (Félix-Brasdefer & Hasler 2012; Hasler Barker 2012; Ishihara & Cohen 2010; Tatsuki & Houck 2010) by providing the learners with explicit or implicit teaching as well as exposure to the pragmatics of email discourse of the target culture.

References

Antonopoulou, E. (2001) Brief service encounters: Gender and politeness. In A. Bayraktaroğlu & M. Sifianou (eds.), *Linguistics Politeness across Boundaries: The Case of Greek and Turkish* (pp. 241-269). Amsterdam/ Netherlands: Benjamins.

Baron, N. (1998) Letters by phone or speech by any other means: The linguistics of email, *Language and Communication* (18): 133-170.

Baron, N. (2003) Why email looks like speech: Proofreading, pedagogy and public face. In J. Aitchison and D. M. Lewis (eds.), *New Media Language* (pp. 85-94). London: Routledge.

Bjørge, A. K. (2007) Power distance in English lingua franca email communication. *International Journal of Applied linguistics* 17 (1):60-80.

Barron, A. and K. Schneider (2009) Variational pragmatics: Studying the impact of social factors on language use in interaction, *Intercultural Pragmatics* (6) 4: 425-442.

Biesenbach-Lucas, S. (2006) Making requests in E-mail: Do cyber-consultations entail directness? Toward conventions in a new medium. In K. Bardovi-Harlig, J. C. Félix-Brasdefer, and A. Omar (eds.), *Pragmatics & Language Learning*, vol 11 (pp. 81-107). [National Foreign Language Resource Center]. Honolulu, HI: University of Hawai'i Press.

Biesenbach-Lucas, S. (2007) Students writing emails to faculty: An examination of e-politeness among native and non-native speakers of English. *Language Learning & Technology* (11) 2: 59-81.

Bloch, J. (2002) Student/teacher interaction via email: the social context of internet discourse, Online *Journal of Second Language Writing* (11): 117-134.

Bou-Franch, P. (2011) Openings and closings in Spanish email conversations, *Journal of Pragmatics* (43): 1772-1785.

Brown, P. and S. Levinson (1987) *Politeness: Some Universals in Language Use*. Cambridge, UK: Cambridge University Press.

Brown, G. & G. Yule (1983) *Discourse Analysis*. Cambridge, UK: Cambridge University Press.

Condon, S. and C. G. Čech (1996) Functional comparison of face-to-face computer-mediated decision making interactions. In S. Herring (ed.), *Computer-Mediated Communication: Linguistic, Social, and Cross-Cultural Perspectives* (pp. 65-80), Philadelphia, PA: John Benjamins.

Crystal, D. (2006) *Language and the Internet* (2nd edition), Cambridge, UK: Cambridge University Press.

Economidou-Kogetsidis, M. (2011). "Please answer me as soon as possible": Pragmatic failure in non-native speakers' e-mail requests to faculty." *Journal of Pragmatics* 43: 3193-3215.

Félix-Brasdefer, J. C. (2008). *Politeness in Mexico and the United States: A Contrastive Study of the Realization and Perception of Refusals*. Amsterdam/Philadelphia: John Benjamins.

Félix-Brasdefer, J. C. (2012) E-mail requests to faculty: E-politeness and internal modification. In M. Economidou-Kogetsidis & H. Woodfield (eds.), *Interlanguage Request Modificationi (*pp. 87-118), Amsterdam: John Benjamins.

Fraser, B. (1990) Perspectives on politeness, *Journal of Pragmatics* 14: 219-36.

Félix-Brasdefer, J. C. & M. Hasler-Barker (2012) Compliments and compliment responses: From empirical evidence to pedagogical intervention. In L. Ruiz de Zarobe and Y. Ruiz de Zarobe (eds.), *Speech acts and Politeness across Languages and Cultures* (pp. 241-273). Bern: Peter Lang.

Gains, J. (1998). Electronic mail-A new style of communication or just a new medium? An investigation into the text features of email. *English for Specific Purposes* 18(1), 81-101.

Goffman, E. (1971). *Relations in Public: Micro studies of the Public Order*. New York: Basic Books.

Hartford, B. and K. Bardovi-Harlig (1996) "At your earliest convenience:" A study of written student requests to faculty. In L. Bouton (ed.), *Pragmatics and Language Learning Monograph Series*, vol. 7, (pp. 55-69), Urbana, IL: DEIL, University of Illinois.

Hasler Barker, M. (2012) *Effects of Pedagogical Intervention on the Production of the Compliment and Compliment Response Sequence by Second Language Learners of Spanish*, Unpublished doctoral dissertation, Indiana University, Bloomington.

Haugh, M. (2010) When is an e-mail really offensive: Argumentatativity and variability in evaluations of impoliteness. *Journal of Politeness Research* (6): 7-31.

Hendriks, B. (2010) An experimental study of native speaker perceptions of non-native request modification in e-mails in English, *Intercultural Pragmatics* (7) 2: 221-255.

Herring, S. (2000) Gender differences in CMC: Findings and implications, *CPSR Newsletter* 18(1). Retrieved on August 17, 2011 from http://cpsr.org/issues/womenintech/herring/

Herring, S. (2003) Computer-mediated discourse. In D. Schiffrin, D. Tannen, and H. E. Hamilton (eds.), *The Handbook of Discourse Analysis* (pp. 612-634), Malden, MA: Blackwell Publishing.

Hofstede, G. (2001) *Culture's Consequences*. 2nd edn. Thousand Oaks, CA: Sage.

Holmes, J. (1995) *Women, Men, and Politeness*, New York: Longman.

Ishihara, N. and A. D. Cohen (2010) *Teaching and Learning Pragmatics: Where Language and Culture Meet*, Harlow, England: Pearson.

Kankaanranta, A. (2005) Hei Seppo, Could You Pls Comment on This!" Internal Email Communication in Lingua Franca English in a Multinational Company. Ph.D. dissertation, Centre for Applied Language Studies, University of Jyväskylä. Retrieved August 17, 2011 from https://jyx.jyu.fi/dspace/handle/123456789/18895.

Lan, Li (2000) Email: A challenge to standard email? *English Today* 64 (vol. 16) (4): 23-29.

Leech, G. (1983) *Principles of Pragmatics*, New York: Longman.

Malinowski, B. (1923) The problem of meaning in primitive languages. In C. K. Ogden and I. A. Richards (eds.), *The Meaning of Meaning* (pp. 296-336), New York: Harcourt.

Márquez Reiter, R. and M. E. Placencia (2005) *Spanish Pragmatics*, Basingstoke: Palgrave/Macmillan.

Mills, S. (2003) *Gender and Politeness*, Cambridge, UK: Cambridge University Press.

Murray, D. E. (2000) Protean communication: The language of computer-mediated communication, TESOL *Quarterly* (34) 3: 397-421.

Schegloff, E. and H. Sacks (1973) Opening up closings, *Semiotica* (8): 289-327.

Scollon, R. and S. W. Scollon (2001) *Intercultural Communication*, Second edition, Malden, MA: Blackwell Publishing.

Sinclair, J., and M. Coulthard (1975) *Towards an Analysis of Discourse*, London, UK: Oxford University Press.

Spencer-Oatey, H. (1996) Reconsidering power and distance, *Journal of Pragmatics* (26) 1: 1-24.

Stubbs, M. (1983) *Discourse Analysis*, Oxford, UK: Basil Blackwell.

Tatsuki, D. H. and N. Houck (eds.) (2010) *Pragmatics: Teaching Speech Acts*, Alexandria, VA: TESOL.

Thomas, J. (1983) Cross-cultural pragmatic failure, *Applied Linguistics* (4) 2: 91-112.

Yus, F. (2001) *Ciberpragmática. El uso del lenguaje en internet* [Cyberpragmatics: Language Use in the Internet], Barcelona: Editorial Ariel.

Waldvogel. J. (2007) Greetings and closings in workplace email, *Computer-Mediated Communication* (12) 2: article 6. http://jcmc.indiana.edu/vol12/issue2/waldvogel.html.

Watts, R. (2003) *Politeness*, Cambridge, UK: Cambridge University Press.

Notes

---

1 Email requests from native speakers (NSs) of Spanish will not be examined here due to the low enrollment of NSs of Spanish in the Department of Spanish and Portuguese at this university.

2 The current project was approved by the Institutional Review Board at this Midwestern institution. All instructors provided their consent to participate in the study and agreed to send the researcher every request initiated by the student (and the instructor's follow up response to the student's initial request). All instructors were assured that all the information would be considered confidential and all identifying information from the students and instructor would be removed from each email.

3 The majority of email requests in both groups were requests for validation (e.g. asking the professor for clarification or confirmation), followed by requests for feedback (e.g. I don't understand what to do with section II of the homework), information (e.g. Will you be in your office after class?), action (e.g. Can you resend the syllabus please?) appointment (e.g., Can we meet tomorrow at 2pm to discuss the homework?), extension (e.g. Can I get two

more days to complete the final paper?) , and permission (e.g. Can I come to your morning section instead of our afternoon class on Friday?). (For details see Condon and Čech [1996: 73] & Félix-Brasdefer 2012).

[4] Although the gender of the interlocutor also influe nces the way the speaker opens the interaction, (Antonopolou 2001), in the present study I only focused on the gender of the sender of the email sender, namely, the student.

[5] As rightly noted by one reviewer, it is possible that the emai l data of some students were influenced by the length of residence abroad in a Spanish-speaking region which may favor a positive politeness orienta tion, as reflected in the personal comments observed in the op enings and closings in the L2Spanish email data. Although no data on study abroad were collected from the learners, this observation is worth e xploring in future studies that examine email discourse among students with and without exposure to the target culture.

Does gender influence task performance in EFL? Interactive tasks and language related episodes

Agurtzane Azkarai (Universidad del País Vasco)
María del Pilar García Mayo (Universidad del País Vasco)

There are differences in the way males and females use language (Aries, 1976; Ross-Feldman, 2005, 2007). However, the role that gender plays in second language acquisition (SLA) does not seem to have been studied in depth. This factor is fundamental for the Interaction Hypothesis (Long, 1996), as interaction opportunities have been claimed to depend on gender (Ross-Feldman, 2005, 2007).

This paper aims to investigate whether gender influences conversational interaction and whether different communicative tasks have an impact on the type of interaction matched (male-male and female-female) and mixed (male-female) gender dyads engage in. The results showed that type of dyad did not influence the incidence of language related episodes (LREs) when pairs work on specific tasks, that the different tasks influence the learner's production of LREs and that most LREs were resolved correctly.

1 Introduction

Several studies have shown that there are differences in the way males and females use language (Aries, 1976; Ross-Feldman, 2007; Tannen, 1990, among others). It seems that when men and women interact, men have more opportunities to participate and control conversational turns than women. However the role that gender plays in second language acquisition (SLA) does not seem to have been studied in depth. This individual variable is fundamental for the Interaction Hypothesis (Long, 1983; 1996), which states that conversational interaction facilitates second language (L2) learning. Input or modifications to the input received in the learning process might be different depending on social status, gender and culture of the participants. Thus, it is of special interest to consider these variables to contribute to a better understanding of such a complex phenomenon.

The main goal of this paper is to investigate whether gender influences conversational interaction and whether different communicative tasks have an impact on the type of interaction matched (male-male and female-female) and mixed (male-female) gender dyads engage in. Inspired by recent work carried out by Ross-Feldman (2007) with participants from El Salvador who were learning English as second language (ESL) in the USA, this paper examines the oral production of 12 (6 male, 6 female) Basque-Spanish bilinguals learning English as Foreign Language (EFL) in the Basque Country.

This paper is structured as follows: section 2 provides a brief overview of the Interaction Hypothesis (Long, 1996) and its main constructs: input, output and feedback. Special attention will be paid to Language Related Episodes (LREs) as they have been identified as the site where L2 learning may occur (Swain and Lapkin, 1998, 2001, 2002) and they are a key concept in this study. This background section will also provide information about the gender variable in first language (L1) and L2 acquisition and about tasks because they are the main data-gathering instrument in interaction research. Section 3 presents the study itself, its purpose and motivation, research questions entertained, participants and procedure. Section 4 comments the findings obtained from the experimental study and section 5 summarizes the main conclusions.

2   Background

2.1   The Interaction Hypothesis

Mackey (2007a) notes that since the early 1980s the relationship between conversational interaction and learning has been one of the core issues in L2 research, both in English as Second Language (ESL) (Mackey, 2007b) and in EFL (Alcón and García Mayo, 2008, 2009; García Mayo and Alcón, 2002, forthcoming). There is a wide range of empirical studies that deal with the relationship between interaction and learning pointing to the idea that interaction benefits learning. Back in 1978 Hatch argued that learners learn the structure of a language through interaction rather than learning grammar in order to interact. Krashen (1982, 1985), however, claimed that exposure to comprehensible input was a necessary and sufficient condition for L2 learning. Long's Interaction Hypothesis (1996) considered input as a foundational construct, the *sine qua non* of acquisition. However, *contra* Krashen, Long argues that comprehensible input alone is not enough to promote the process of L2 learning. There is enough evidence to date supporting Long's Hypothesis on the basis of all the detailed research carried out since the 1980s in Canadian immersion programs, where native speakers of English learned French, (Allen, Swain, Harley and Cummins, 1990; Genesee, 1987; Lambert and Tucker, 1972; Lyster, 2007; among many others). After several years and thousands of hours of exposure to real language, the learners communicated fluently but not accurately. They reached native-like levels in listening and reading but not in speaking and writing (Genesee, 1987), precisely the skills where the learners had to produce information.

Ellis (1992) had already observed that the need to communicate may raise learners' awareness of language with a resulting increase in attention to form and a heightened tendency to notice mismatches between input and output. Learners' attention to and noticing of mismatches between the input received and their output determines whether or not they progress (Schmidt and Frota, 1986). Attention and noticing, or conscious perception (for which attention is a prerequisite), are widely claimed to be both necessary and sufficient to focus items from linguistic input and store them in long-term memory, turning input into intake, at least for low-level grammatical items, such as plural or third person singular *s* (Schmidt, 1990, 1993, 1994).

Thus, although early researchers assumed that output did not play a significant role in the L2 acquisition process (Krashen, 1985) and that it only served as evidence that acquisition had occurred, Swain was convinced that learners' output had a number of benefits. Swain (1985 *et passim)* proposed the Output Hypothesis, which claims that the act of producing language (speaking or writing) constitutes part of the process of L2 learning. It is by producing language that (i) fluency (automatization) is promoted, (ii) attention to linguistic problems is drawn, (iii) syntactic processing rather than just meaning is encouraged and (iv) hypotheses about the target language are tested.

Besides input and output, feedback is another important construct in the Interaction Hypothesis. Feedback is the information that learners receive from their interlocutors about their language production and can come from teachers and/or other learners. The Interaction Hypothesis is primarily concerned with reactive feedback, which occurs as a reaction to some linguistic problem that any of the interlocutors has. Feedback can be provided explicitly by means of metalinguistic comments (for example when the teacher says "No, we don't say *x* in English; we say *y* because *x* is a noun"), or implicitly, which is the type of feedback interaction research is most interested in.

Another construct relevant in interactional work is that of language related episode (LRE). LREs are those occasions in which learners make use of interactional features to attend to linguistic elements in their conversation. They occur when learners focus on matters of language form and meaning and these include " […] *all* interaction in which learners draw attention to form, that is, those that focus on form in the context of meaningful communication as well as those that are set apart from such communication and simply revolve around question of form itself" (Williams, 1999: 595). Consider the following example:

(1) Male learner 1:   …that is-it is partly-partly inherited, no?
     Male learner 2:   How do you spell that?
     Male learner 1:   I-N-H-E-R-I-T-E-D? I think…I'm not sure but…

In this brief excerpt from data of the current study, male learner 2 does not know how to spell the word "inherited". He asks his partner who solves his doubt.

The use of LREs has been claimed to be directly related to language learning (Adams, 2007; Loewen, 2004). During an LRE a learner raises an issue about the target language and the other learner has the option to either join in the discussion or move on with the task at hand. The incidence of LREs varies depending on several factors such as learner's proficiency and learning activity (Ellis *et al.*, 2001a, 2001b; Loewen, 2003 2004; Swain and Lapkin, 1998, 2002; Williams, 1999, 2001).

2.2   The gender variable

Interaction may vary depending on several factors such as the participants' ethnic groups, social classes, culture or gender (Aries, 1996; Henley, 1995; Melzi and Fernández, 2004; Reid, Haritos, Kelly and Holland, 1995). Many studies in first language acquisition have shown that there are gender differences during conversational interaction among native speakers. For example, Tannen (1990) found that males and females acted differently from each other during the interaction with a same-gender friend. She also found that males generally discussed many topics briefly and that their discussions were more abstract and focused on less personal issues than females' discussions, while females talked more overall and discussed fewer topics than males.

There are also differences between males and females in mixed-gender settings that show that males discuss a wider range of topics in these settings, and that they seem to control conversational interactions. Females, on the other hand, restrict their topics during the conversation with males and allow the conversational control of men by making statements indicating solidarity and agreement with them (Aries, 1976; Bohn and Stutman, 1983).

West and Garcia (1988) found that men initiated the majority of topic changes curtailing women's topic development and failing to follow up on what women were discussing. Holmes (1994) found that females supported males' conversations more than males did with women's conversations:

"[…] while the men had the benefit of attentive, responsive and encouraging listeners, the women received relatively little support for their contributions, and were given less encouragement to continue when they did speak".

(Holmes, 1994: 161)

Itakura (2001) examined the conversations of female and male native speakers of Japanese who engaged in a ten-minute conversation in English and Japanese. What she found was that males were less dominant in their L2, English, than in their L1, Japanese. Itakura suggested that whether an individual has a self-oriented or other-oriented conversational style may play a role in whether conversational dominance translates from L1 to L2 as self-oriented speakers pursue topics that are of interest to them while other oriented speakers develop topics more collaboratively with their conversational partners. Depending on the context and the individuals involved, there may be differences in interactional style between males and females, and these differences cannot be assumed to automatically transfer from L1 to L2 (Ross-Feldman, 2007).

On the basis of the above-mentioned studies, it would seem that in male-female conversational interactions males have more opportunities to participate and control conversations than females. Moreover, depending on the gender of their conversational partner during interaction, speakers of both genders seem to alter their conversational moves. For example, Aries (1976) concluded that males spoke more than females, but that also both, males and females, directed more conversation to males than to females.

As for SLA, there have been some studies dealing with L2 interaction focusing on the role gender plays during L2 learning. Thus, in a study about the interactions of pairs composed of adult language learners, Gass and Varonis (1986) found that most negotiations occurred in male-female dyads, followed by male-male dyads. They suggested that males and females negotiated more in mixed-gender pairs than in matched-gender pairs and that men dominated the amount of talk and the performance of the task in mixed-gender pairs. Males also showed non-understanding with a greater frequency than females (Gass and Varonis, 1985; Kasanga, 1996).
Pica and her colleagues (Pica *et al.*, 1989; Pica *et al.,* 1991) found no significant differences for the incidence of negotiation in different types of dyads in conversation between learners and native speakers. However female native speakers negotiated more with male learners than with female learners and female learners negotiated more with female native speakers than with male native speakers. Pica *et al.* (1991) did not find any significant difference

for males, either learners or native speakers, but it seemed that female learners might be more sensitive to the influence of gender than males. Oliver (2002) studied the effect of gender on interactions between child language learners and she did not find any significant difference between male-male and female-female dyads.

Along the same lines but in an EFL setting, Alcón and Codina (1996) studied the impact of gender on negotiation and vocabulary learning in a situation of interaction. Results of the study indicated that learners' gender could not be considered a discriminating factor with regard to the amount of negotiation, although female involvement in negotiation was superior to males'.

More recently, Ross-Feldman (2007) analyzed the correlation between gender and conversational interaction. In her detailed study she investigated the influence of learner gender on L2 task-based interactions and the language learning opportunities that arose during such interactions. Specifically, she investigated the incidence and resolution of LREs in conversational interaction with the goal of shedding light on ultimate learning possibilities for males and females engaging in task-based interactions.

The participants in her study were 32 females and 32 males whose L1 was Spanish and who were learning English in an adult language-learning centre in the USA. Ross-Feldman's findings indicated that the gender of the learners participating in task-based interactions influenced the incidence and resolution of LREs. In mixed-gender dyads, the LREs initiated by males were resolved more often than those initiated by females. This might lead to a situation in which males have more opportunities to learn from the interaction than females. Moreover, LREs initiated by males were resolved in a more targetlike manner in mixed-gender dyads. On the other hand, LREs initiated by females were resolved more frequently in a targetlike manner on matched-gender dyads. So while males had more opportunities to learn a language in mixed-gender dyads, females have more opportunities in matched-gender dyads.

Males were advantaged in mixed-gender dyads because of their increased attention and they resolved questions about matters of language use. Females were advantaged in matched-gender dyads because their questions about language use were more likely to be resolved when they worked with other females. Similar to previous research findings on language and gender, topics raised by males in this study were resolved more often than those raised by females. The trend was for LREs initiated by learners of both genders to be resolved more often and in a more targetlike manner when interacting with females than with males. This would strengthen the possibility that the learning resulting from LREs could be influenced by the gender composition of the dyad, with males having more opportunities to learn in mixed-gender dyads and females having greater language-learning opportunities in matched-gender dyads.

Ross-Feldman concluded that, although both males and females seemed to be advantaged by working with female language learners, the learning that results from LREs may be affected by gender as well.

2.3   Tasks in conversational interaction

The goal of much interaction-based research involves manipulating the kinds of interaction that learners are involved in, the kind of feedback they receive and the kind of output they produce. In order to determine the relationships of the various components of interaction and L2 learning (Gass and Mackey, 2007), the most common way of gathering data is to involve learners in a variety of well-designed tasks.

Tasks are goal-oriented activities that facilitate the use of language in order to communicate meaning (Bygate *et al.*, 2001; Crookes, 1986; Long and Robinson, 1998; Nunan, 1991; Prabhu, 1987; Skehan, 1998; Willis, 1996). Tasks provide learners with opportunities to interact and receive and give information, and for this reason they are an ideal tool for both classroom use and for testing theoretical claims about L2 acquisition. They have become central to both L2 research and pedagogy and nowadays they provide a fruitful area of common ground between research and practice (García Mayo, 2007; Mackey, 2007a).

Pica, Kanagy and Falodun (1993) classified tasks depending on the type of information exchange they generate. For example, in one-way tasks only one interlocutor holds the information to be conveyed to the other participant. In a two-way task both participants have part of the information that needs to be shared. Tasks can also require an open outcome, that is when there is no predetermined answer or solution, or a closed outcome, when the task requires a specific solution. Research has shown that interaction is best promoted by tasks that have a two-way required exchange of information and a closed outcome (Pica et al., 1993).

In order for tasks to be successful, collaborative work is important. Interaction provides students with opportunities to engage in language learning processes that are going to facilitate their L2 learning. It is important then that students are encouraged to work in pairs collaboratively on language tasks, since they may reach grammatically correct decisions when working with their partners, or peers (Storch, 2001).

Some authors (Pica, 1991; Storch, 2001, 2007; among others) have demonstrated that working in pairs or in small groups (3 members) benefits the students with opportunities to give and receive feedback (Pica and Doughty, 1985; Varonis and Gass, 1985). These studies have shown that compared to teacher-fronted classes or Native Speakers (NS) - Non-Native Speakers (NNS) pairs, learners in groups or in NNS-NNS pairs engage in more modified interactions, or what Long (1983) calls 'negotiation of meaning'.

Storch (1999) investigated if students working in pairs and discussing their grammatical choices produced more accurate written texts than students working on similar exercises individually. Students tended to revise their text many times when working collaboratively whereas, when working individually, students completed their work quickly and did not revise their work before submitting it to the teacher. Collaboration and metatalk (talking about language) generated during interaction led to an improvement in the grammatical accuracy of the texts that were produced.

Storch (2001) analyzed if there was any connection between the way pairs interact and the quality of the final written output. Her results showed that there was evidence of speech co-construction, knowledge extension and scaffolding assistance in those pairs which adopted a collaborative orientation. Storch (2001) places importance on collaboration arguing that in her study pairs that collaborated produced more precise texts.

Kowal and Swain (1994) suggested that proficiency level between the members of the dyad may reduce collaboration in the learners' interaction. That is, students may be more demotivated when their partner is more competent or has a higher level in the language that he/she is learning. The results obtained by Storch (2001) demonstrated that this was not the case. In her study the more collaborative pair was the one in which the levels of both learners differed.

In more recent work Storch (2007) investigated the merits of pair work by comparing pair and individual work on a text editing task and the results she obtained showed that pairs took longer to complete the task. These results suggest that pairs paid more attention to items that needed amendment, and provide another explanation for the slightly larger number of corrections made by pairs compared to individuals. Interestingly, the study found no statistically significant differences in the accuracy of texts edited by pairs compared to those edited by students working individually. However, the pair talk data did show that a high proportion of LREs were resolved interactively, when the learners had an opportunity to use and reflect about language use. Seeking and receiving information, providing each other with explicit and implicit negative feedback gave most learners opportunities to learn. Providing an explanation is also beneficial for learners because it forces them to clarify and organize their own knowledge and enhance their own understanding. Repetitions or imitation may also facilitate the appropriation and internalization of new forms. It indicates that the learner has noticed his error and tries to correct it. Although Storch's (2007) study did not find statistically significant differences in the accuracy of texts edited by pairs compared to those edited by students working individually, the analysis of pair talk showed that learners benefited from working collaboratively in pairs on grammar-focused tasks.

3   The present study

3.1   Purpose and motivation

The present study aims to investigate whether gender influences conversational interaction and whether different communicative tasks have an impact on the type of interaction matched and mixed gender dyads engage in. It has been inspired by Ross-Feldman's (2007) recent work on the topic. As already mentioned participants in her study were learning English as a second language (ESL) and came mainly from El Salvador. These participants carried out different communicative tasks in mixed and matched-gender dyads. The findings obtained showed that women seemed to be ignored in most of the cases in which they initiated a LRE, while men obtained answers to all their doubts.

One of the reasons one might speculate this could have happened is the sociological context the participants came from. As mentioned above, Ross-Feldman's participants came mainly from El Salvador, a country where the role of women is very different from the one in most European countries. Specifically, Góchez (2006) reports that Salvadorian women are integrating gradually into the developmental process of the country but he provides data that indicate the disparities still existing between men and women. For example, just as an illustration, men have double *per capita* income than women. In the urban areas, there are 17.7% more poor women than men and women's salaries are 24.2% lower than those of men.

As the origin of the participants could have biased the findings of her study, the present paper reports the interaction between matched and mixed gender pairs of Basque-Spanish bilinguals learning English in an EFL context. The role of women in Europe is different from the one in Central America. Specifically, in the Basque Country women are present in politics, the university, private companies and most of them work outside the home, thus having economic independence from men, a point which sets them apart from the overwhelming majority of women in El Salvador.

From a methodological point of view, Ross-Feldman herself (2007: 76) calls for the use of more and different task types in order to fully explore how task and gender interrelate. In the study we have carried out, we have included not only the three tasks used by Ross-Feldman but also a fourth one, all of which will be described in section 3.4 below.

3.2   Research questions

On the basis of previous research carried out on the influence of gender in L2 interaction and the importance of LREs (cf. section 2), we entertain the following research questions for the current study:

   i. Does type of dyad (male-male (MM), female-female (FF), male-female (MF)) influence the incidence of language related episodes (LRE) when pairs are working on specific tasks?
   ii. How does the type of task used in conversational interaction influence the learner's production of LREs? Do information-gap tasks (picture placement and picture differences) generate more LREs than collaborative tasks (picture story and dictogloss)?
   iii. If LREs are generated, are they resolved or unresolved?

3.3   Participants

Twelve participants, six males and six females took part in this study. They were all born in the Basque Country and were Spanish-Basque bilinguals. Most of them (9) were students of English Philology and three of them were students of Basque Philology, all of them at the University of the Basque Country. Their English proficiency level was intermediate (lower or upper), as established by the standardized Quick Oxford Placement Test (Syndicate U.C.L.E., 2001). They were paired in dyads on the basis of their test results.

3.4   Procedure

Table 1 describes the tasks used in Ross-Feldman's study, which we have also used in ours in order to establish the appropriate comparisons. These tasks are similar to the one available in commercial ESL/EFL text books

	Picture Differences	Picture Placement	Picture Story
Description	Without showing each other their pictures, learners must work together to identify ten differences between the pictures	Without showing each other their pictures, learners must help each other place the missing objects in their pictures of a kitchen in order to make their kitchens identical	Learners work together to arrange eight pictures in the correct order to tell a story and then to write the story
Version A	People in a park	Each learner must place five items in his/her kitchen	Two travelers who accidentally switch luggage
Version B	People on a beach	Each learner must place five items in his/her kitchen	A girl with an unusual alarm clock who gets ready for school
Type	Information Gap	Information Gap	Collaborative
Flow of information	Two-way	One-way repeated	Two-way
Exchange of information	Required	Required	Optional
Outcome	Closed	Closed	Closed

Table 1: Tasks used in the present study

Ross-Feldman used two information gap tasks (picture differences and picture placement) and a collaborative task, but she did not include a type of task that has been reported to encourage learners to reflect in their own output, a focus-on-form task such as dictogloss (Wajnryb, 1990). She herself acknowledges that different task types should be used (Ross-Feldman, 2007:76) and that's why this study has included dictogloss as a fourth option. Dictogloss favors collaborative work (Wajnryb, 1990). It is an activity which has been claimed to encourage learners to reflect on their own output (Kowal and Swain, 1994; Swain, 1998; Swain and Lapkin, 1994, 2001). In dictogloss a short text is read (twice) at normal speed to the learners; the first time they just listen, and when the text is read the second time, students write down some key words they think will help to rewrite the original text. Both participants of the dyad work together to reconstruct the final version of the text and so, they refine their understanding of the language being used (García Mayo, 2002a, 2002b; Wajnryb, 1990). The dictogloss promotes the collaboration between both members of the pair and activates the cognitive processes necessary for the acquisition of second languages.

Dictogloss is designed to draw learners' attention to language form. During dictogloss, students come to notice their grammatical strengths and weaknesses and they try to overcome these weaknesses when attempting to co-produce the text (Nassaji, 2000: 247). Four texts were chosen from Wajnryb (1990). Two texts were taken from the pre-intermediate section: the first one was a 63-word passage entitled "A record on wheels" (page 34) and the second one was a 73-word passage entitled "Miracle plunge" (page 37). The other two texts were taken from the intermediate section of the same book. The first one was a 53-word passage entitled "Intelligence: nature or nurture?" (page 53) and the second one was an 87-word passage entitled "Tips for travelers: planning a trip". Texts of two different levels (pre-intermediate and intermediate) were chosen for the experiment since participants' results in the Oxford Placement Test were also two (lower or upper intermediate). The two pre-intermediate texts were presented in dyads in which participants' level was lower-intermediate (one text per dyad in order for participants not to repeat the same text) and the two intermediate texts were presented in dyads in which participants' level was upper-intermediate. Thus, participants had to complete a total of 4 different tasks (dictogloss, picture placement task, picture differences task and picture story task) with a partner of their same gender and with a partner of a different gender.

There were 6 mixed-gender dyads, that is, 6 MF dyads, and 6 matched-gender dyads, that is, 3 MM dyads and 3 FF dyads. Participants completed the task in a seminar room located at the Psycholinguistics Laboratory of the University of the Basque Country and all of the transcriptions where recorded and video-taped. Students granted permission for their data to be used for academic purposes.

Participants were free to complete the tasks in the order they wanted. The time they needed to complete each task lasted between 5 and 10 minutes. They were seated in front of each other so that they could not see their partner's pictures during the picture placement and the picture differences tasks.

Participants had to complete the experiment in two sessions. As they were students and they had different class schedules, in the first session they were paired either with someone of their same gender or someone of a different gender. In this first session, which lasted between 25-30', they were asked to complete the four tasks described above. The second took place a few days later (depending on the participants' agenda) and each participant had to complete the task with someone of their same or different gender, depending on the partner they had on the first session. In this last session, which also lasted between 25-30', participants had to complete the other version of the task. Finally, they were asked to complete an opinion questionnaire in order to express their opinions about the tasks, their partners and the experiment as a whole.

Ross-Feldman (2005) examines LREs to determine if gender differences exist in their frequency or type. She used the following coding-sequence of LREs:

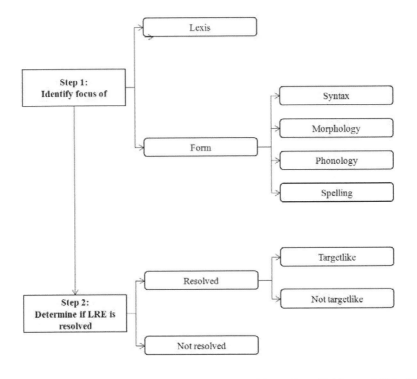

Figure 1: Coding-sequence of LREs.

As can be seen, the first step in coding her data was the identification of the focus (lexis or form) of the LRE. Secondly, Ross-Feldman determined whether the LRE was solved (resolved vs. not resolved) and, if so, how (targetlike vs. non-targetlike).

3.5   Data codification

Once the participants completed the tasks, all their conversational interactions, which amounted to 4 hours, 59 minutes and 59 seconds, had   to be transcribed. Then, the total incidence of LREs was analyzed as a proportion of LREs to the total turns taken by the learners to complete the different tasks. In this study the results were codified according to (i) the incidence of LREs, that is, the quantification of LREs in each dyad, (ii) the resolution (or not) of LREs and (iii) the resolution (correct or incorrect) of the LREs. Consider the following examples (from the current study):

(2) Example LRE: resolved: targetlike

1. Male learner:	And where is for example the blender?
2. Female learner:	What's that thing?
3. Male learner:	The thing you use to chock the fruit and make eh...
4. Female learner:	Ah! Yes, yes!

In example 2 above learners discuss the meaning of the word "blender" while doing the Picture Placement task.

(3) Example LRE: not resolved

1. Female learner:	Oh! Ah, no? Mine's, I don't know if it's a ball or a racquet...?
2. Male learner:	No.
3. Female learner:	Eh...Like to round and round and round all the time.
4. Male learner:	Yeah, no.
5. Female learner:	No? So, I've one machine of that here in the park.
6. Male learner:	Ok.
7. Female learner:	I don't know the name.

In the example above they discuss the word for "wheel". The female learner does not know the correct English word for it and asks her partner. However he does not solve her doubt and the LRE remains unresolved.

(4) Example LRE: resolved: non-targetlike

1. Female learner 1:	He's packing his luggage?
2. Female learner 2:	How do you write that?
3. Female learner 1:	Luggage? Like L-U-G-A-G-E.
4. Female learner 2:	A...A...
5. Female learner 1:	...G-A-G-E.
6. Female learner 2:	E?
7. Female learner 1:	L-U-G-A...
8. Female learner 2:	Lugaje [luɣaxe] [...]

In this case, the LRE is resolved. Female learner 2 asks for the correct spelling of "luggage", her partner resolves her doubt but in an incorrect way. This LRE is resolved in a non-targetlike manner.

4 Results and discussion

This section presents the findings of the data analysis we have conducted on the basis of the LREs produced by the different dyads. We will present the findings following the order of the three research questions posited above, which are repeated here for the reader's convenience:

  i. Does type of dyad (male-male (MM), female-female (FF), male-female (MF)) influence the incidence of language related episodes (LRE) when pairs are working on specific tasks?
  ii. How does the type of task used in conversational interaction influence the learner's production of LREs? Do information-gap tasks (picture placement and picture description) generate more LREs than collaborative tasks (picture story and dictogloss)?
  iii. If LREs are generated, are they resolved or unresolved?

The first research question focused on the potential differences in the incidence of LREs across the different dyads. The repeated-measures ANOVA shows that there is no significant group effect ($F = 0.25$, $p = 0.787$), that is, there is no significant difference between the LREs generated by matched (FF, MM) and mixed (MF) gender dyads. These results are in line with those reported by Ross-Feldman, who showed that the incidence of LREs across dyad type in each task was uniform, with the exception of the picture story task, in which MM dyads engaged in fewer LREs. Except for that case, type of dyad was not found to be significant.

The second research question focused on the influence of task type on the learners' production of LREs. The statistical analysis carried out shows that there is a significant task effect ($F = 4.90$, $p = 0.008$). This means that the differences in the production of LREs are task-dependent (García Mayo, 2002a, 2002b; Gass, Mackey and Ross-Feldman, 2005; Williams, 1999). There is also a significant Group x Task interaction effect ($F = 2.99$, $p = 0.023$), that is, different tasks are carried out differently depending on the dyads (FF, MM or MF). Figure 2 features the incidence of LREs in each task and each type of dyad:

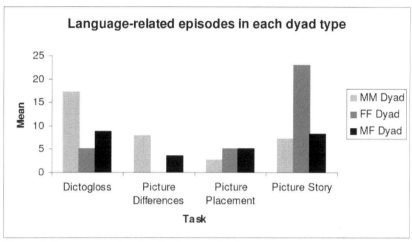

Figure 2: Language-related episodes per dyad

LREs were more common in the dictogloss (33.43%) and the picture story task (39.28%) as compared to the picture differences (12.54%) and the picture placement (14.76%) tasks. A plausible explanation for the difference between information-gap tasks (picture differences and picture placement) and collaborative tasks (dictogloss and picture story) could be based on the fact that both the dictogloss and the picture story task, involved not just conversational interaction with a specific goal (to complete the task) but also the production of a written text co-constructed by the two members of the dyad. In line with the findings in the study by Ross-Feldman (2007) and also in more recent work by Adams and Ross-Feldman (2008), the results of our study also point to the idea that tasks that include a writing component can push students to focus more on formal linguistic aspects during language production.

Ross-Feldman (2007) also reported that the tasks learners were engaged in seemed to have an effect on the incidence of LREs. Task was also a significant factor in her study, that is, there were significantly different proportions of LREs on different tasks: participants engaged in LREs most often on the picture story task, followed by the picture placement task and the picture differences task. The following figure represents the results reported on in Ross-Feldman (2007):

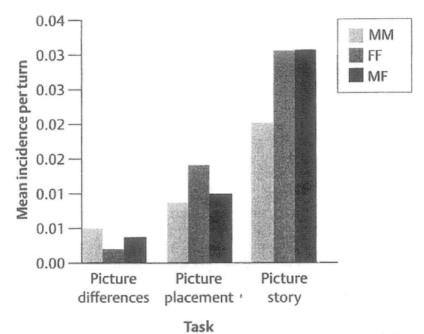

Figure 3: Language-related episodes in each dyad type in Ross-Feldman (2007)

The third research question focused on the resolution of LREs. We were interested in seeing whether those LREs produced were resolved or not and whether, if resolved, they were target-like. The overall finding is that most LREs were resolved in a target-like manner (77.72% targetlike, 7.52% non-targetlike and 14.76 not resolved). Figure 4 features the outcome of LREs resolution for each dyad and task type:

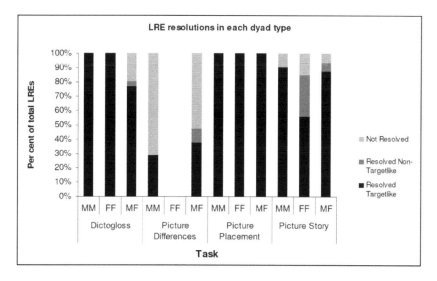

Figure 4: Language Related Episode resolutions in each dyad type

In what follows, we provide a description of the results obtained for each of the task types:
In the dictogloss all LREs were resolved correctly by matched-gender dyads (FF, MM dyads). In mixed-gender dyads (MF dyads), even if the majority of LREs were correct resolved (77.35%), a 18.87% of LREs was not resolved and a 3.78% was resolved but not in a targetlike manner.

In the picture placement task all LREs were resolved in a targetlike manner. In the picture differences task, there were no LREs in FF dyads. Moreover, most of the LREs were not resolved (70.84% in MM dyads and 52.38% in mixed-gender dyads) and very few were resolved in a targetlike manner (29.16% in MM dyads and 38.09% in mixed-gender dyads), a 9.53% was resolved in a non-targetlike way in MF dyads.

In the picture story task, in FF dyads 85.5% of the LREs were resolved (56.52% targetlike, 28,98% non-targetlike); 14.59% of the LREs were not resolved. In the case of MM dyads, almost all the LREs were resolved (90.95%), however 9.09% were not resolved. In mixed gender dyads (MF dyads), LREs were mostly resolved (88% in a targetlike manner and 6% in a non-targetlike manner), only 6% remained unresolved.

What these results suggest is that LREs that arose in the picture differences task seemed to be more difficult to resolve than in the other tasks. As can be seen, the majority of LREs was not resolved in this task in MM and MF dyads (LREs were not produced in FF dyads). We might speculate that it was the task-related vocabulary participants had to use in the park and beach scenes the one that caused problems, since participants were not familiar with some items they had to identify.

In MM dyads, except for the picture differences task, the majority of LREs was correctly resolved. In FF dyads, the majority of the LREs was resolved, however no LREs appeared in the picture differences tasks in this type of dyad, and in the picture story task, even if most of the LREs were resolved, a very high percentage of them was resolved in a non-targetlike manner.
In MF dyads, there is more heterogeneity in the resolution of LREs. In the dictogloss task, the picture story task and the picture placement task, LREs were mostly resolved in a targetlike manner. However, this type of dyad seems to have more difficulties with the LREs that arose during the picture differences task, since LREs were not resolved. These results are different from those obtained by Ross-Feldman (2007) as Figure 5 illustrates:

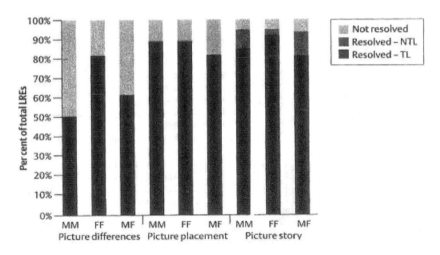

Figure 5: LRE resolution in each dyad type in Ross-Feldman (2007)

In order to provide a more complete picture of the findings obtained in Ross-Feldman's study and the present one, the following tables feature descriptive percentages of the results obtained in the three tasks that were used in both studies (picture description, picture placement and picture story). No statistical analysis could be carried out because we have had no access to the raw data in Ross-Feldman's study:

	THIS STUDY			ROSS-FELDMAN'S		
	MM dyads	FF dyads	MF dyads	MM dyads	FF dyads	MF dyads
Resolved Targetlike	29.16	0	38.09	50	81	60
Resolved Non-Targetlike	0	0	9.53	0	0	0
Unresolved	70.84	0	52.38	50	19	40

Table 2: Picture Differences task

It is interesting to see that the FF in our study did not produce LREs. The percentage of the LREs that remained unresolved in our study was very high (70.84% and 52.38% in MM dyads and MF dyads, respectively). In Ross-Feldman's study the percentages were lower (50%, 19% and 40% in MM, FF and MF dyads, respectively).

	THIS STUDY			ROSS-FELDMAN'S		
	MM dyads	FF dyads	MF dyads	MM dyads	FF dyads	MF dyads
Resolved Targetlike	100	100	100	89	89	82
Resolved Non-Targetlike	0	0	0	0	0	0
Unresolved	0	0	0	11	11	18

Table 3: Picture Placement task

In our study, all of the LREs were resolved in a targetlike manner in matched and mixed gender dyads. In the case of Ross-Feldman's study, even if the majority of LREs was resolved in a targetlike manner, a small percentage of them was not resolved (11%, 11% and 18% in MM, FF and MF dyads respectively).

	THIS STUDY			ROSS-FELDMAN'S		
	MM dyads	FF dyads	MF dyads	MM dyads	FF dyads	MF dyads
Resolved Targetlike	90,95	56,52	88	84	91	82
Resolved Non-Targetlike	0	28,98	6	11	4	14
Unresolved	9,05	14,5	6	5	5	4

Table 4: Picture Story task

The percentage of LREs resolved in a targetlike manner in MM and MF dyads was very similar, except for FF dyads (56.52% in our study and 91% in Ross-Feldman's study). FF dyads are different in both studies. In Ross-Feldman the three groups (MM, FF and MF) behave in a very similar way, whereas in our study FF dyads do not behave as MM and MF dyads do. Even if the percentage of LREs resolved is high (85.5%), it has to be taken into account that 28.98% of them was resolved in a non-targetlike manner.

On the basis of the resolution of LREs, both groups behave differently: the group in our study seems to be more heterogeneous, in the sense that in some tasks their resolution is complete and correct while in others there are no LREs or the resolution of LREs is incorrect or not carried out at all, as is the case in the picture differences or picture story tasks. In Ross Feldman's study these LREs were resolved in a targetlike manner most of the time, except for the Picture Differences task, in which the resolution of LREs was not as high as in the other tasks.

Even though there are some differences between this study and Ross-Feldman's, we can also find some similarities. In both cases it seems that there is no significant difference between LREs generated by matched and mixed-gender dyads, while the differences in the production of LREs are task-dependent. In Ross-Feldman's study the interaction between type of dyad and type of task was not significant, while in our case it is, meaning that tasks are carried out differently depending on whether dyads are matched or mixed.

The main finding in Ross-Feldman's study is that both males and females seem to be advantaged by working with female learners. In our study this is not the case, since participants seem to be more advantaged when they worked in matched-gender dyads than in mixed-gender dyads. One might speculate that the preference for matched-gender partners when carrying out tasks could be due to current methodological practice in most primary and secondary EFL classrooms, where teachers normally give the opportunity to choose partners and do not impose mixed dyads. Children prefer to work with someone of their same gender when they are asked to carry out a task in pairs.

It is also interesting to see our participants' opinion, since, as mentioned above; they completed a questionnaire after finishing the experiment. Even though in the present study we have not analyzed the qualitative data coming from their responses, they seem to point to the idea that half of the participants preferred to work with a female (6 participants); two of them (2) preferred to work with a male and the rest (4) had no problem working either with a female or a male. There seems to be some mismatch between the participants' responses, where they show preference for female partners, and the quantitative results, which reveal that they do better in matched-gender dyads.

5 Conclusion

This study set out to investigate whether gender could influence conversational interaction and whether different communicative tasks could have an impact on the type conversational interaction matched (male-male, female-female) and mixed (male-female) gender dyads engaged in. Gender is one of the least studied variables in SLA but it might be particularly relevant in studies conducted within the interactionist approach, which argues that conversational interaction can facilitate SLA by providing learners with opportunities to receive input, produce output and be offered appropriate feedback.

Inspired by recent work by Ross-Feldman (2007) with learners from a very different sociological background – learners from El Salvador learning English in an ESL context-, we conducted a study with 12 Basque-Spanish intermediate learners of English in an EFL context. The different dyads carried out four tasks, two information-gap tasks (picture description and picture placement) and two collaborative tasks (dictogloss and picture story). Task performance was operationalized in terms of language-related episodes (LREs) as they had been shown to be a site where L2 development might occur (Swain and Lapkin, 1998, 2001). On the basis of previous research on issues related to gender and task types, we entertained three research questions. In the first one we asked about whether the type of dyad could influence the incidence of LREs and we found that, in line with Ross-Feldman, there was no significant difference between the LREs generated by matched (female-female, male-male) and mixed (male-female) gender dyads.

In our second research question we asked about how task type could influence the learners' production of LREs and we found that, also in line with Ross-Feldman, the differences in the production of LREs were task-dependent and that different tasks were carried out differently depending on the dyads (female-female, male-male or female-male).

In our third research question we focused on the resolution of LREs and we found that most LREs were resolved in a target-like manner, also along the lines of the results obtained by Ross-Feldman.

We should not conclude this study without making reference to the shortcomings that it does have. On the one hand, this could be considered a pilot study on the general issue of gender and interaction because of the small number of participants that took part in it. Further studies need to be carried out with a more robust sample in order for the general findings in this study to be supported. Data obtained in interaction-based work needs to be transcribed and codified and, even though we only had 6 dyads, their interaction amounted to almost 5 hours, which could be analyzed with other research questions in mind.

Thus, we need to collect data controlling some important individual variables and future work needs to consider learner's motivation (Dörnyei, 2009). For example, work by Dörnyei and Kormos (2000) has suggested that learners were more willing to communicate if they had a positive attitude towards the task they are engaged in and the same researchers have also claimed that the motivation of the interlocutor might also play a role in learning. Recent reviews on the interaction approach (García Mayo and Alcón, forthcoming) indicate that interaction research is currently considering individual variables (attention, working memory capacity, motivation) but there is clearly room for much more detailed research in this area. Tragant (2006) has produced a questionnaire that classifies learners on the basis of motivational factors. We intend to use it in future work as it is clear that motivation is a variable that needs to be controlled for when carrying out task-based interaction.

In conclusion, this study has shown that (i) type of dyad (male-male (MM), female-female (FF), male-female (MF)) does not influence the incidence of LREs when pairs are working on specific tasks, (ii) different tasks used in conversational interaction influence the learner's production of LREs (with those containing a written requirement generating a higher number of LREs), and (iii) most LREs were resolved in a target-like manner. All these findings will have to be further researched with a more robust number of participants, whose motivation will have to be measured with appropriate tools in order to establish appropriate motivation-matched dyads.

References

Adams, R. (2007) Do second language learners benefit from interacting with each other? In Mackey, A. (ed), *Conversational Interaction in Second Language Acquisition,* Oxford: Oxford University Press.

Adams, R. and L. Ross-Feldman (2008) Does writing influence learner attention to form? In D. Belcher and A. Hirvela (eds*)* *The Oral-Literate Connection,* Michigan: The University of Michigan.

Alcón, E. and V. Codina (1996) The impact of gender on negotiation and vocabulary learning in a situation of interaction, *International Journal of Psycholinguistics* (12): 21-35.

Alcón, E. and M.P. García Mayo (2008) Incidental focus on form and learning outcomes with young foreign language classroom learners. In: Philp, J., R. Oliver and A. Mackey (eds) *Second Language Acquisition and the Younger Learner: Child's Play?* Amsterdam: John Benjamins.

Alcón, E. and M. P. García Mayo (Guest eds) (2009) Interaction and language learning in foreign language contexts, *International Review of Applied Linguistics* (47) 3 (special issue).

Allen, P., M. Swain, B. Harley, and J. Cummins (1990) Aspects of classroom treatment: Toward a more comprehensive view of second language education. In Harley, B. et al., (eds) *The Development of Second Language Proficiency*, Cambridge: Cambridge University Press.

Aries, E.J. (1976) Interaction patterns and themes of male, female, and mixed groups, *Small Group Behaviour* (7) 1: 7-18.

Aries, E.J. (1996) *Men and Women in Interaction: Reconsidering the Differences,* New York: Oxford University Press.

Bohn, E. and R. Stutman (1983) Sex-role differences in the relational control dimension of dyadic interaction, *Women's Studies in Communication* (6): 96-104.

Bygate, M., P. Skehan, and M. Swain (2001) Introduction. In Bygate. M., P. Skehan and M. Swain (eds) *Task-based Learning: Language Teaching, Learning and Assessment*, London: Longman.

Crookes, G. (1986) *Task Classification: A Cross-disciplinary Review*, Center for Second Language Classroom Research Social Science Research Institute: University of Hawai'i at Manoa.

Dörnyei, Z. (2009) Motivation and the vision of knowing a second language. In: Beaven, B. (ed) *IATEFL*, 2008: Exeter conference selections. Canterbury: IATEFL: 16-22.

Dörnyei, Z. and J. Kormos (2000) The role of individual and social variables in oral task performance, *Language Teaching Research* (4): 275-300.

Ellis, R. (1992) *Second Language Acquisition and Language Pedagogy*, Clevedon: Multilingual Matters.

Ellis, R., H. Basturkmen and S. Loewen (2001a) Learner uptake in communicative ESL lessons, *Language Learning* (51): 281-318.

Ellis, R., H. Basturkmen and S. Loewen (2001b) Preemptive focus on form in the ESL classroom, *TESOL Quarterly* (35): 407-432.

García Mayo, M. P. (2002a) The effectiveness of two form-focused tasks in advanced EFL pedagogy, *International Journal of Applied Linguistics* (12) 2: 156-175.

García Mayo, M. P. (2002b) Interaction in advanced EFL pedagogy: A comparison of form-focused activities, *International Journal of Educational Research* (37): 323-341.

García Mayo, M.P. (ed) (2007) *Investigating Tasks in Formal Language Learning*, Clevedon: Multilingual Matters.

García Mayo, M.P. and E. Alcón (Guest eds) (2002) The role of interaction in instructed language learning, *International Journal of Educational Research* (37) Special issue: 3-4.

García Mayo, M.P. and E, Alcón (forthcoming) Negotiated input and output. Interaction. In Herschensohn, J. and M, Young-Scholten (eds) *The Handbook of Second Language Acquisition*, Cambridge: Cambridge University Press.

Gass, S. and A. Mackey (2007) Input, interaction, and output in second language acquisition. In VanPatten, B. and J. Williams (eds) *Theories in Second Language Acquisition: An Introduction*, Mahwah, NJ: Lawrence Erlbaum Associates.

Gass, S. and E. Varonis (1985) Task variation and nonnative/nonnative negotiation of meaning. In Gass, S. M. and C. Madden (eds), *Input in Second Language Acquisition,* Rowley, MA: Newbury House.

Gass, S. and E. Varonis (1986) Sex differences in non-native speaker/non-native speaker interactions. In Day, R. R. (ed), *"Talking to Learn": Conversation in Second Language Acquisition*, Cambridge, MA: Newbury House.

Gass, S., A. Mackey and L. Ross-Feldman (2005) Task-Based Interactions in Classroom and Laboratory Settings, *Language Learning* (55) 4: 575-611.

Genesee, F. (1987) *Learning through Two Languages: Studies of Immersion and Bilingual Education*, Cambridge, MA: Newbury House.

Góchez, R. E. (2006) http://www.gestiopolis.com/canales5/adepro/participacion-de-lamujer-en-el-salvador.htm Retrieved in June 2008.

Hatch, E. (1978) *Discourse Analysis and Second Language Acquisition.* In Hatch, E. (ed) *Second Language Acquisition,* Rowley, MA: Newbury House: 402-435.

Henley, N. M. (1995) Ethnicity and gender issues in language. In Landrine, H. (ed), *Bringing Cultural Diversity to Feminist Psychology: Theory, Research, and Practice.*

Holmes, J. (1994) Improving the lot of female language learners'. In Sunderland, J. (ed), *Exploring Gender: Questions and Implications of English Language Education,* London: Prentice Hall.

Itakura, H. (2001) *Conversational Dominance and Gender: A Study of Japanese Speakers in First and Second Language Contexts.* Philadelphia: John Benjamins.

Kasanga, L.A. (1996) Effect of gender on the rate of interaction: some implications for second language acquisition and classroom practice. *I.T.L., Review of Applied Linguistics* (111) 2: 155-192.

Kowal, M. and M. Swain (1994) Using collaborative language production tasks to promote students' language awareness, *Language Awareness* (3) 2: 73-93.

Krashen, S. (1982) *Principles and Practice in Second Language Acquisition,* New York: Pergamon Institute of English.

Krashen, S. (1985) *The Input Hypothesis: Issues and Implications,* Oxford: Pergamon.

Lambert, W.E. and G. R. Tucker (1972) *Bilingual Education of Children. The St. Lambert experiment,* Rowley, MA: Newbury House.

Loewen, S. (2003) Variation in the frequency and characteristics of incidental focus on form, *Language Teaching Research* (7) 3: 315-345.

Loewen, S. (2004) Uptake in incidental focus on form and second language learning, *Language Learning* (54) 1: 153-188.

Long, M. H. (1983) Native speaker/non-native speaker conversation and the negotiation of comprehensible input, *Applied Linguistics* (4) 2: 126-141.

Long, M.H. (1996) The role of the linguistic environment in second language acquisition. In Ritchie, W. C. and Bhatia, T. K. (eds), *Handbook of Second Language Acquisition,* New York: Academic Press.

Long, M. H. and P. Robinson (1998) Focus on form: Theory, research and practice. In Doughty, C. and Williams, J. (eds), *Focus on Form in Classroom Second Language Acquisition.* Cambridge: Cambridge University Press: 15-41.

Lyster, R. (2007) *Learning and Teaching Languages through Content: A Counterbalanced Approach,* Amsterdam/Philadelphia: John Benjamins.

Mackey, A. (2007a) Interaction as practice. In DeKeyser, R. (ed), *Practice in a Second Language: Perspectives from Applied Linguistics and Cognitive Psychology,* Cambridge: Cambridge University Press.

Mackey, A. (2007b) Introduction. The role of conversational interaction in second language acquisition. In A. Mackey (ed), *Conversational Interaction in Second Language Acquisition: A Collection of Empirical Studies,* Oxford: Oxford University Press.

Melzi, G. and C. Fernández (2004) Talking about past emotions: Conversations between Peruvian mothers and their preschool children, *Sex Roles* (50): 641-657.

Nassaji, H. (2000) Towards integrating form-focused instruction and communicative interaction in the second language classroom: some pedagogical possibilities, *The Modern Language Journal* (84) 2: 241-250.

Nunan, D. (1991) Communicative tasks and the language curriculum, *TESOL Quarterly* (25): 279-295.

Oliver, R. (2002) The patterns of negotiation for meaning in child interactions, *Modern Language Journal* (86): 97-111.

Pica, T. (1991) Classroom interaction, negotiation, and comprehension: redefining relationships, *System* (19): 437-452.

Pica, T. and C. Doughty (1985) Input and interaction in the communicative language classroom: A comparison of teacher-fronted and group activities. In Gass, S. M. and C. Madden (eds), *Input in Second Language Acquisition*, Rowley, MA: Newbury House.

Pica, T., R. Kanagy and J. Falodun (1993) Choosing and using communication tasks for second language instruction and research. In Crookes, G. and Gass, S. M. (eds), *Tasks and Language Learning*, Clevedon: Multilingual Matters.

Pica, T., L. Holliday, N. E. Lewis and L. Morgenthaler (1989) Comprehensible output as an outcome of linguistics demands on the learner, *Studies in Second Language Acquisition* (11): 63-90.

Pica, T., L. Holliday, N. E. Lewis, D. Berducci, and J. Newman (1991) Language learning through interaction: What role does gender play? *Studies in Second Language Acquisition* (13): 343-376.

Prabhu, N.S. (1987) *Second Language Pedagogy*, Oxford: Oxford University Press.

Reid, P. T., C. Haritos, E. Kelly, and N. E. Holland (1995) Socialization of girls: Issues of ethnicity and gender development. In H. Landrine (ed), *Bringing Cultural Diversity to Feminist Psychology: Theory, Research, and Practice*, Washington, DC: American Psychological Association: 93–112.

Ross-Feldman, L. (2005) *Task-based interactions between second language learners: Exploring the role of gender*, Georgetown University: Washington D.C. Doctoral Dissertation.

Ross-Feldman, L. (2007) Interaction in the L2 classroom: does gender influence learning opportunities? In Mackey, A. (ed), *Conversational Interaction in Second Language Acquisition: A Collection of Empirical Studies*, Oxford: Oxford University Press.

Schmidt, R. (1990) The role of consciousness in second language learning, *Applied Linguistics* (11): 129-158.

Schmidt, R. (1993) Awareness and second language acquisition, *Annual Review of Applied Linguistics* (13): 206-226.

Schmidt, R. (1994) Implicit learning and the cognitive unconscious: Of artificial grammars and SLA. In N. Ellis (ed), *Implicit and Explicit Learning of Languages.* London: Academic Press.

Schmidt, R., and S. Frota (1986) Developing basic conversational ability in a second language. A case study of an adult learner of Portuguese. In Day, R. (ed), *Talking to Learn: Conversation in Second Language Acquisition,* Rowley, MA: Newbury House.

Skehan, P. (1998) *A Cognitive Approach to Language Learning*, Oxford: Oxford University Press.

Storch, N. (1999) Are two heads better than one? Pair work and grammatical accuracy, *System* (27): 363-374

Storch, N. (2001) How collaborative is pair work? ESL tertiary students composing in pairs, *Language Teaching Research* (5) 1: 29-53.

Storch, N. (2007) Investigating the merits of pair work on a text editing task in ESL classes, *Language Teaching Research* (11) 2: 143-159.

Swain, M. (1985) Communicative competence: Some roles of comprehensible input and comprehensible output in its development. In S.M. Gass and C. G. Madden (eds) *Input in Second Language Acquisition*, Rowley, MA: Newbury House: 235-256.

Swain, M. (1998) Focus on form through conscious reflection. In C. Doughty and J. Williams (eds), *Focus on Form in Classroom Second Language Acquisition,* Cambridge: Cambridge University Press.

Swain, M., and S. Lapkin (1994) *Problems in output and the cognitive processes they generate: A step in second language learning*, Report of Year 1 of SSHRC grant. Toronto: OISE, Modern Language Centre.

Swain, M. and S. Lapkin (1998) Interaction and second language learning: Two adolescent French immersion students working together, *Modern Language Journal* (82): 320-337.

Swain, M. and S. Lapkin (2001) Focus on form through collaborative dialogue: Exploring task effects. In M. Bygate, P. Skehan and M. Swain (eds), *Researching pedagogic tasks: Second Language*

Learning, Teaching and Assessment, London, UK: Pearson Education.

Swain, M. and S. Lapkin (2002) Talking it through: Two French immersion learners' response to reformulation, *International Journal of Educational Research* (37): 285-304.

Syndicate, U.C.L.E. (2001) *Quick Placement Test,* Oxford: Oxford University Press.

Tannen, D. (1990) Gender differences in topical coherence: creating involvement in best friends' talk, *Discourse Processes* (13) 1: 73-90.

Tragant, E. (2006) Language learning motivation and age. In: Muñoz, C. (ed) *Age and the Rate of Foreign Language Learning,* Clevedon: Multilingual Matters.

Varonis, E. and S. M. Gass (1985) Non-native/non-native conversations: A model for negotiation of meaning, *Applied Linguistics* (6): 71-90.

Wajnryb, R. (1990) *Grammar Dictation,* Oxford: Oxford University Press.

West, C. and A. Garcia (1988) Conversational shift work: a study of topical transitions between women and men, *Social Problems* (35) 5: 551-575.

Williams, J. (1999) Learner-generated attention to form, *Language Learning* (49) 4: 583-625.

Williams, J. (2001) The effectiveness of spontaneous attention to form, *System,* (29): 325-340.

Willis, J. (1996) *A Framework for Task-based Learning,* Oxford: Collins.

Acknowledgments

The authors want to thank the participants of the study because without their time this project would not have been possible. The first author wants to thank the Basque Government for a pre-doctoral scholarship (Reference Number: BFI 08.281) and acknowledge funding from UFI11/06 (University of the Basque Country). The second author wishes to acknowledge funding from the following research grants: FFI2009-10264 and CSD2007-00012 (Spanish Ministry of Education), IT-311-10 (Basque Government) and UFI11/06 (University of the Basque Country)

Exploring learners' noticing of corrective feedback through stimulated recall

Patricia Salazar (Universitat Jaume I)

Corrective feedback has been the focus of a growing body of empirical research over the past two decades. Indeed, from Truscott's (1996) claims that it is ineffective and should be rejected, corrective feedback has received much interest and a vast number of studies have investigated various issues such as effectiveness, types of feedback, uptake and learners' noticing of CF. It is this last topic that we will centre on in this paper, as it has been claimed (Schmidt, 2001) that CF may enhance learners' noticing of the linguistic forms. One possible way to examine learners' noticing is by means of stimulated recall interviews, which allow for learners' verbalization of their thoughts at the time of performing a task.

In order to ascertain how the feedback provided was noticed, the participants in the study received two different types of CF (a more implicit and more explicit version) when discussing their mistakes on a written task. This conversation was tape-recorded and on the following day they carried out a stimulated recall interview in which they were asked to report what they were thinking at the moment of obtaining feedback.

The information recalled from the participants reveals that regardless of obtaining a more implicit or more explicit type of CF, it was most of the times noticed as such, and the participants provided an array of reports in their recalls which show that they were able to notice that their errors were not targetlike and tried to look for a more grammatical reformulation. Therefore, despite the sometimes conflicting findings (e.g. Sheen, 2007; Bitchener, 2008) about the effectiveness of CF, we believe that it plays an important role in helping students notice their mistake, as the stimulated recall methodology we have used has shown.

1 Introduction

After many years of intense debate on the value of corrective feedback (CF) on learning, it is now widely assumed that it is beneficial (Russell and Spada, 2006; Mackey, 2007; Sheen, 2010). Nonetheless, due to the vast number of issues related to the provision of CF, such as amount of feedback, source of feedback or learners' proficiency level, it is difficult to provide a full and accurate picture of the best method to offer CF. One of the most hotly debated topics when dealing with CF is the type of feedback (i.e., explicit or implicit). A broad definition of CF would refer to "any feedback provided to a learner, from any source, that contains evidence of learner error of language form" (Russell and Spada, 2006: 134). This information about what is not acceptable in the target language is termed *negative evidence* (Gass, 2007) and it provides the language learner with information about the incorrectness of a foreign language (FL) form or structure via CF in response to his/her ungrammatical production.

In addition to the positive impact of CF on L2/FL learning, many studies have reported that students want and expect CF on the part of their teachers, both on their oral output (Panova and Lyster, 2002; Russell, 2009) or on their written production (Fathman and Whalley, 1990; Ferris and Roberts, 2001; Chandler, 2003).

This small-scale study aims at exploring how FL learners noticed two distinct types of CF on their written production via a stimulated recall interview. In spite of the some alleged inherent problems of this methodology, it has been extensively employed in the field of language learning. This chapter will first deal with the impact of explicit and implicit CF on learning and the concept of noticing as an essential condition to learn will also be briefly examined (section 2). An analysis of the stimulated recall procedure will be presented in section 3. The study carried out will be discussed at length in section 4 and, finally, the main conclusions stemming from the study will be commented in section 5.

2   Effectiveness and noticing of CF

It is claimed that through CF, learners may notice the mismatch between their errors and the corrections they receive, either by the teacher or by their more proficient peers. According to Schmidt's (1993) *Noticing Hypothesis*, noticing is essential to learn anything that is new. For this reason, the degree of explicitness of CF that is needed to promote noticing is a crucial issue in current research on CF. In Carroll and Swain's (1993: 361) words, explicit feedback is "any feedback that overtly states that a learner's output was not part of the language-to-be-learned". On the other hand, these authors include confirmation checks and clarifications requests as implicit feedback as learners must deduce why their utterance is nontargetlike. Thus, different types of CF may be graded along a continuum between implicit and explicit feedback and much research has sought to examine what type of feedback is more conducive to learning. Although the boundary between explicit and implicit feedback is sometimes not easily drawn, traditionally, implicit feedback has embraced recasts, repetition and any kind of feedback that is not intended to overtly draw the learners' attention to their ill-formed production (Carroll and Swain, 1993). In contrast, if feedback clearly indicates that the learners' output is not acceptable, it is deemed to be explicit. The dichotomy implicit/explicit feedback is necessary as some research has claimed that explicit feedback is more effective than implicit feedback in language learning.

In a recent meta-analysis of CF, Li (2010) shows the superiority of explicit feedback over implicit feedback in the short term. Li's analysis thus corroborates previous findings (e.g. Ellis *et al.*, 2006; Sheen, 2007) that groups receiving explicit CF outperform both the control group and the implicit feedback group. Moreover, the positive role of explicit CF in Sheen's (2007) study is maintained in the delayed posttest. This finding clearly contradicts Li's (2010) research in that implicit feedback is slightly more effective than explicit feedback on long-delayed posttests. A possible explanation for this outcome is that implicit feedback may be more beneficial "to the development of implicit knowledge (L2 competence)" (Li, 2010: 344). As mentioned earlier, Schmidt (2001) claimed that noticing was an essential requirement for the conversion of input to intake. The concepts of noticing, awareness and attention in language learning grew in importance in the mid-90s with studies examining second language acquisition under a cognitive approach (e.g. Schmidt, 1993; Alanen, 1995). The main assumption underlying this framework is that some level of attention to form is needed for acquisition to take place, as second language acquisition is claimed to be a conscious process, unlike first language acquisition. Support for Schmidt's position comes from Alanen (1995), who showed that learners that were able to verbalize the rules of specific targeted features performed much better than those who could not.

In sum, it is clear that CF is a complex issue due to the many factors at stake (i.e., timing of outcome measures, length of treatment, learners' age, etc.). In an attempt to shed some light on the topic, the present study aimed at investigating whether and how participants noticed CF via verbalization of their thoughts.

3 Stimulated recall

The analysis of reflections on mental processes originated in the fields of philosophy and psychology but soon were applied systematically in numerous language studies, including test-taking, reading, vocabulary choice, strategy use or pragmatics (Gass and Mackey, 2000; Gass, 2001; Salazar, in press). By means of verbal reporting, insightful data may be elicited, both simultaneously (e.g., think-aloud) and retrospectively, as in the case of stimulated recall (SR henceforth). In 1954, Bloom put forward that through the use of SR, "a subject may be enabled to relive an original situation with great vividness and accuracy if he is presented with a large number of the cues or stimuli which occurred during the original situation" (Bloom, 1954: 25). In order to check the reliability of recall, this author recorded classroom events and asked participants to recall a particular event. It was found that if recalls took place a short period of time after the event (48 hours), recall was 95% accurate and accuracy diminished as more time elapsed between the event and the recall. Over time, research has incorporated SR in language learning. For example, Mackey's (2000) study employed SR to explore whether second language students noticed and benefited from teacher feedback. Sixteen intermediate level students belonging to two different classes were asked to report what they noticed during class and whether that information was new to them. Learners' reports about what they noticed were shown to have a positive impact on their second language developmental processes.

The case study reported by Nabei and Swain (2002) examined language learning of a Japanese learner through teacher's recasts. Stimulated recall was used to elicit the learner's awareness of feedback. The findings revealed that more attention was paid to language form than to meaning; in addition, receiving feedback helped this student learn English. More recently, Yoshida (2008) carried out a study which analyzed teachers' choice and learners' preference of CF types. The SR interviews indicated that teachers overused recasts as a form of feedback due to time restrictions in the classes. On the other hand, learners' reports showed that they preferred clarifications or elicitations to be able to find the correct answers themselves, rather than being provided with the correct form immediately after their nontargetlike utterance.

As can be observed, the main aim of the above research studies which have employed SR is to gather learners' accounts of their thought processes. Frequently, SR methodology is used in conjunction with other data collection methods as a means of data triangulation.

4   The study

4.1   Rationale and research questions

This chapter reports on a small-scale study aimed at investigating whether CF was noticed by 8 students when discussing their mistakes on a written task in the FL context. The study attempted to add to some claims (Hyland, 2003) pointing to the need of more research focusing on a small number of learners to better understand how feedback is incorporated in their language learning process. In addition, we also wished to contribute to the increasing research on the use of SR in order to elicit students' verbalizations.

Bearing in mind previous research on the topic, we formulated the following research questions:

1)   Will learners report noticing of corrective feedback? If so, will explicit corrective feedback be more noticed than the implicit version?
2)   If learners notice CF, will it have an impact in the long term?

4.2   Participants

Eight Spanish university students majoring in English Philology volunteered to take part in the present study. Their level of proficiency in English was upper-intermediate or B2 according to the descriptors in the Common European Framework of Reference. This level was determined by means of a *Quick Placement Test* (Oxford University Press) the subjects completed prior to the study. Out of the eight participants, seven were females and one male, and their mean age was 22 years old. The participants were randomly assigned to the two different versions of feedback (4 to the implicit type and 4 to the explicit one).

4.3   Data collection procedure

The participants were required to write an assignment or *Project Work* on one of the four skills (listening, speaking, writing and reading) as part of their mark in one of their subjects of their degree. A draft of the Project Work was turned in to their teacher who corrected content, organization and grammatical mistakes and gave it back to each student in an interview in which feedback on their mistakes was provided[1]. Two types of feedback were offered: Feedback 1 (F1 henceforth) consisted of mere repetition with rising intonation of the learner's error. In order to keep it as implicit as possible, no further comment was provided. Example 1 illustrates this type of feedback:

Example 1: Feedback 1 (Italics indicate the teacher's reading of the erroneous segment)
Teacher: *The students have to look up in the dictionary all the words that they do not know and write it down.* Write it down?
Student 1: and note it, and note it
Teacher: *all the words that they do not know and write it down?*
Student 1: ah! and write them down

In Feedback 2 (F2 henceforth), the teacher repeated the learner's error and made it more explicit by adding the question *Is this correct?*, pointing out an overt comment on the grammaticality or accuracy of the wrong expression, as can be seen in the following example:

Example 2: Feedback 2

Teacher: *I have chosen the speaking skill as I think is the most...*Is this correct?

Student 2: no, as I think it is

The interviews in which errors were commented on were tape-recorded and transcribed. The day after each of these interviews took place, the subjects were asked to have a second interview in order to carry out a stimulated recall session to make students verbalize their thoughts at the moment of receiving feedback. In order to stimulate recall, the tape with the conversations of the first interview was played back to the subjects and stopped to ask them a series of questions (see Appendix 1) designed to make them verbalize their thoughts about the first interview.

In the present study, "noticing" was operationalized as those students' reports in which they recognized and/or commented on teacher's CF in the recall interview, in line with previous research (i.e., Mackey *et al.*, 2000; Egi, 2004) which also used oral verbal reports to measure learners' noticing.

We adhered to Gass and Mackey's (2000) proposals for increasing validity and reliability of recall. As for validity, in this study the time delay between task performance and recall was minimized (SR sessions took place the day after CF sessions). According to these authors, key to the reliability issue is the need to i) reduce anxiety, ii) stimulate to remember rather than present a new perspective, and iii) allow the student to produce a relatively unstructured answer. In the present study the participants felt comfortable as they knew the interviewer (she was one of their lecturers), they were asked questions conforming Gass and Mackey's (2000) SR protocol and they were also allowed to code switch into their mother tongue (Spanish or Catalan) to verbalize their thoughts more precisely.

Depending on participants' availability, between 5 and 6 weeks after the SR session, they were provided with a tailor-made posttest which included all the mistakes each of them had made and had been tackled in their individual interview.

The results of presenting the subjects with two versions of CF are beyond the scope of the present chapter and are reported elsewhere (Salazar and Martí, 2010).

4.4   Results and discussion

Our first research question asked, on the one hand, about whether participants would report that they noticed CF, and on the other, about what type of CF (explicit or implicit) would be more noticed.

It was apparent from students' verbalizations that they were accessing their recollections of the first interview, and that they were trying to report their thoughts at that time, as Examples 3 and 4 show[2]:

Example 3: Feedback 1
Student 1: when you said me "early stages" I remember that I was looking for another preposition. I was saying "an, on, at" or… but I remember that it was a preposition… just a preposition I was looking for

Example 4: Feedback 2
Teacher: I'd like you to try to remember what you thought at the moment we were having our conversation, not now but then, right?
Student 6: well, I thought that at first sight I thought that it was correct but then I realize that "you have to" is a structure of obligation so it's better to put "should"
Teacher: OK

These examples show that students noticed the CF provided by the teacher. Figure 1 illustrates the complete sequence of the students' verbalizations: when asked to elicit their recalls of the CF interview, students could report that they noticed the CF they had been provided with or not. In the first case, delayed repair or no repair could take place in the tailor-made posttest. On some occasions, participants did not report noticing of CF, but delayed repair did nevertheless occur in the tailor-made posttest. This could be due to students' under-reporting of thoughts, since they may have noticed CF but did not report them during the SR interview, as Egi (2007) also put forward.

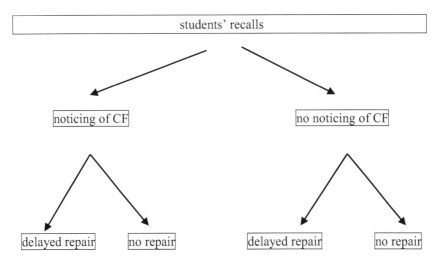

Figure 1. Sequence of students' recall verbalizations.

The total number of errors was 41, out of which 33 (or 80.4%) were reported in the SR interviews. This may imply that participants perceived CF as such; however, this finding partially answers our first research question. In an attempt to provide the full answer, we need to examine the extent to which implicit and explicit CF were noticed.

Tables 1 and 2 show the number of mistakes analyzed in the present study and which were noticed after teacher's CF in the SR interview. From a quantitative perspective, 17 or 73.9% of errors were perceived in the implicit version of feedback, whereas 16 or 88.8% of errors were noticed under the explicit version. These results point to the fact that explicit CF was more salient and therefore noticeable, in line with previous research (Ellis *et al.*, 2006; Sheen, 2007).

In light of these results, we may claim that not only did the participants in the study notice the CF provided, but also both versions of CF reached a high level of noticing by students. However, it seems that under the explicit condition, students were more aware of the feedback received, approaching 90% of their total amount of mistakes. This outcome supports Lasagabaster and Sierra's (2005) research that teachers should offer more explicit correction, especially correction that learners can understand and notice.

	F1 (implicit feedback)	
	number of mistakes	mistakes noticed after feedback
S1	8	6
S2	5	3
S3	6	4
S4	4	4
Total	23	17

Table 1. Noticing of mistakes under implicit feedback.

	F2 (explicit feedback)	
	number of mistakes	mistakes noticed after feedback
S5	5	5
S6	5	5
S7	3	2
S8	5	4
Total	18	16

Table 2. Noticing of mistakes under explicit feedback.

In most cases, the combination of CF and SR seems to be effective in determining, first, that the learners recognized that they were being corrected, and second, that they understood the nature of the problem and looked for a targetlike alternative.

The second research question we posed referred to whether noticing of CF would have an effect in the long term. The results reported in Table 3 suggest that a vast majority (82.9%) of the mistakes which had been noticed in the SR session were corrected in each student's tailor-made posttest. The delayed effect of CF may be proved by the fact that in the implicit version of CF, two mistakes had not been noticed in the SR interview but were, nevertheless, repaired in the tailor-made posttest. Not surprisingly, over 12% of the errors which had not been noticed and reported were not corrected in this posttest (3 mistakes belonged to implicit CF and 2 to explicit CF).

		number of mistakes	mistakes noticed in SR and corrected in tailor-made posttest	mistakes not noticed in SR and corrected in tailor-made posttest	mistakes not noticed in SR and not

					corrected in tailor-made posttest
	S1	8	6	1	1
	S2	5	4	1	0
F1	S3	6	4	0	2
	S4	4	4	0	0
	S5	5	5	0	0
F2	S6	5	5	0	0
	S7	3	2	0	1
	S8	5	4	0	1
Total		41	34 (82.9%)	2 (4.8%)	5 (12.1%)

Table 3. Noticing of mistakes and their correction in the delayed posttest.

These findings seem to suggest that noticing of CF, as attested in the SR sessions, had an impact on the long-term production of the corrected grammatical items in the tailor-made posttests. This is an important result which adds to some claims (Gass, 1997; Bitchener *et al.*, 2005) that noticing the mismatch between learners' errors and the corrections they receive may be conducive to long-term learning. Moreover, Mackey (2000) found a relationship between reporting what her learners had noticed and their second language development, as greater development was shown for the structures the learners reported most frequently.

5 Conclusion

This study aimed at gaining further insights into learners' noticing of CF via stimulated recall methodology. The first research question we formulated asked about what type of CF (explicit or implicit) the participants would notice best. According to our findings, both versions of feedback were noticed and reported, although a higher percentage was achieved in the explicit feedback condition.

As far as our second research question is concerned, it centered on the impact of CF in the long term. By means of tailor-made posttests, we were able to show that over 80% of the total number of mistakes that had been reported was corrected in this posttest. It is also worth mentioning that two mistakes which had not been noticed and/or reported were nevertheless corrected in the tailor-made posttest.

Despite the encouraging finding referring to learners' noticing of implicit and explicit feedback and their results in the delayed posttest, a word of caution is needed, in the sense that the SR procedure may be considered a research tool and a learning tool (Mackey, 2005). This implies that SR may grant learners an opportunity to learn from their mistakes and this could be the reason why the results in the tailor-made posttest are so positive. In this line, we should also mention some other problems inherent in SR: we concur with Yinger's (1986: 271) claims that "the subjects report what they are currently thinking and take the opportunity to elaborate the reasons for their interpretation of the videotape", instead of reporting their thoughts at the moment of the task. In the same vein, Tjeerdsma (1997) points out the possibility that the learners are reacting to what is watched on the videotape (in this study, they may have reacted to what they listened to), rather than recalling their performance. This may imply that, despite the immediacy of the recall, the students might have included, consciously or not, a degree of reflection to their accounts, thus reporting mental events that did not occur (Russo *et al.*, 1989).

The study is subject to a number of limitations: first, the small sample and the level of participants make our results tentative, as our findings might be different if a larger number of participants with different levels of proficiency had taken part in the study.

For pedagogical purposes, the fact that learners reported that they did notice CF is an important finding as far as the use of CF in the classroom context is concerned. Thus, the present study supports research (e.g., Russell and Spada, 2006) pointing to the effectiveness of CF for grammar learning. In this vein, the finding that implicit CF was noticed is an interesting one as some previous research (Mackey *et al.*, 2000) showed that recasts, that is, implicit feedback, failed to be identified as feedback.

Further research should examine learners' noticing of feedback on other linguistic areas such as phonology and lexis (Mackey *et al.*, 2000) as well as more implicit an explicit versions of CF. Moreover, longitudinal research employing SR as complementary data for understanding thought processes may also shed further light on noticing of CF and FL learning.

References

Alanen, R. (1995) Input enhancement and rule presentation in second language acquisition. In Schmidt, R. (ed.) *Attention and awareness in foreign language teaching.* Honolulu: University of Hawai'i Press.

Bitchener, J. (2008) Evidence in support of written corrective feedback, *Journal of Second Language Writing* (17) 2: 102-118.

Bitchener, J., S. Young and D. Cameron (2005) The effect of different types of corrective feedback on ESL student writing, *Journal of Second Language Writing* (14) 3: 191-205.

Bloom, B. (1954) The thought processes of students in discussion. In French, S. J. (ed.) *Accent on teaching: Experiments in general education*, New York: Harper.

Carroll, S. and M. Swain (1993) Explicit and implicit negative feedback: an empirical study of the learning of linguistic generalizations, *Studies in Second Language Acquisition* (15) 3: 357-386.

Chandler, J. (2003) The efficacy of various kinds of error feedback for improvement in the accuracy and fluency of L2 student writing, *Journal of Second Language Writing* (12) 3: 267-296.

Egi, T. (2004) Verbal reports, noticing and SLA research, *Language Awareness*, (13) 4: 243-264.

Egi, T. (2007) Recasts, learners' interpretations, and L2 development. In Fathman, A. and E. Whalley (1990) Teacher response to student writing: focus on form versus content. In Kroll, B. (ed.) *Second language writing: Research insights for the classroom*. Cambridge: Cambridge University Press.

Ferris, D. and B. Roberts (2001) Error feedback in L2 writing classes. How explicit does it need to be? *Journal of Second Language Writing* (10) 3: 161-184.

Gass, S. (1997) *Input, interaction, and the second language learner*, Mahwah, N.J.: Lawrence Erlbaum Associates.

Gass, S. (2001)

Gass, S. (2007 en Li no)

Gass, S. and A. Mackey (2000) *Stimulated recall methodology in second language research*, Mahwah, N. J.: Lawrence Erlbaum Associates.

Hyland, F. (2003) Focusing on form: student engagement with teacher feedback, *System* (31) 2: 217-230.

Lasagabaster, D. and J. M. Sierra (2005) Error correction: Students' versus teachers' perceptions, *Language Awareness* (14) 2-3: 112-127.

Li, S. (2010) The effectiveness of corrective feedback in SLA: a meta-analysis, *Language Learning* (60) 2: 309-365.

Mackey, A. (2000) *Interactional feedback on L2 morpho-syntax: Learners' perceptions and developmental outcomes*, paper presented at the American Association of Applied Linguistics Conference, Vancouver, Canada.

Mackey, A. (2005)

Mackey, A. (2007) (ed.) *Conversational interaction in SLA*. Oxford: Oxford University Press.

Mackey, A., S. Gass and K. McDonough (2000) How do learners perceive interactional feedback?, *Studies in Second Language Acquisition* (22) 4: 471-497.

Nabei, T. and M. Swain (2002) Learner awareness of recasts in classroom interaction: A case study of an adult EFL student's second language learning, *Language Awareness* (11) 1: 43-63.

Panova, I. and R. Lyster (2002) Patterns of corrective feedback and uptake in an adult ESL classroom, *TESOL Quarterly* (36) 4: 573-595.

Russell, J. and N. Spada (2006) The effectiveness of corrective feedback for second language acquisition: a meta-analysis of the research. In Norris, J. and L. Ortega (eds.) *Synthesizing research on language learning and teaching*. Amsterdam: Benjamins.

Russell, V. (2009) Corrective feedback, over a decade of research since Lyster and Ranta (1997): Where do we stand today?, *Electronic Journal of Foreign Language Teaching* (6) 1: 21-31.

Russo, J. E., E. J. Johnson and D. L. Stephens (1989) The validity of verbal protocols, *Memory & Cognition* (17) 6: 759-769.

Salazar, P. (in press) Production of refusals: insights from stimulated recall. In Martí, O. (ed.) *Refusals in instructional contexts and beyond*. Amsterdam: Rodopi.

Salazar, P. and O. Martí (2010) Corrective feedback and repair: the case of treatable and untreatable errors. In Caballero, R. and M. J. Pinar (eds.) *Ways and modes of human communication*. Universidad de Castilla-La Mancha: Servicio de Publicaciones.

Schmidt, R. (1993) Awareness and second language acquisition, *Annual Review of Applied Linguistics* (13): 206-226.

Schmidt, R. (2001) Attention. In Robinson, P. (ed.) *Cognition and second language instruction.* Cambridge: Cambridge University Press.

Sheen, Y. (2007) The effects of corrective feedback, language aptitude, and learner attitudes on the acquisition of English articles. In Mackey, A. (ed.) *Conversational interaction in second language acquisition*, New York: Oxford University Press.

Sheen, Y. (2010) Introduction. The role of oral and written corrective feedback in SLA, *Studies in Second Language Acquisition* (32) 2: 169-179.

Tjeerdsma, B. L. (1997) A comparison of teacher and student perspectives of tasks and feedback, *Journal of Teaching in Physical Education* (16) 4: 388-400.

Truscott, J. (1996) The case against grammar correction in L2 writing classes, *Language Learning* (46) 2: 327-369.

Yinger, R. J. (1986) Examining thought in action: a theoretical and methodological critique of research on interactive teaching, *Teaching and Teacher Education* (2) 3: 263-282.

Yoshida, R. (2008) Teachers' choice and learners' preference of corrective feedback types, *Language Awareness* (17) 1: 78-93.

Notes

1. For the purposes of the present study, only grammar mistakes have been taken into account.
2. Students' verbalizations have not been corrected for grammatical accuracy.

Appendix 1

INSTRUCTIONS FOR STIMULATED RECALL (adapted from Gass and Mackey, 2000)

Lecturer's instructions:
"What we're going to do now is watch the video of our first interview yesterday. I am interested in what you were thinking at that time. I can hear what you were saying by looking at and listening to the video, but I don't know what you were thinking. So, what I'd like you to do is tell me what you were thinking, what was in your mind at that time.

Questions:
What were you thinking here/then?
I see you're laughing, what were you thinking here?
What was in your mind at that time?

Backchannels:
Uhm
OK
Right

Code switching in classroom discourse: A multilingual approach

Laura Portolés Falomir (Universitat Jaume I)
Sofía Martín Laguna (Universitat Jaume I)

Cross-linguistic influence and the fluent alternation of several languages have been the focus of interest of recent research (García, 2009; Muñoz, 2007; Safont, 2001). The present study analyzes cross-linguistic influence and language switches in the oral production of English by 25 Catalan-Spanish bilingual children in a Spanish primary school. With that aim, we first identify the most common types of code-switch and their function in an EFL classroom by using Williams and Hammarberg's (1998) categorization of code-switches. Second, we test the applicability of such model by examining to what extent and in what manner the background languages (L1 and L2) are used during English production (L3) in the context of the Valencian Community, where Catalan and Spanish coexist. The data obtained show that both learners and teachers code-switch into Spanish rather than Catalan during interaction in English, thus assigning Spanish an instrumental role. In line with previous research, we suggest that these results may have been motivated by contextual factors (Muñoz, 2007).

1 Introduction

Research on cross-linguistic influence (henceforth CLI) in foreign language acquisition has exclusively focused on the role of the native language in an additional language. However, the spread of English as a lingua franca and the growth of minority languages have promoted the study of multilingualism (Alcón and Safont, in press). In the last decade, wide research has been conducted on the influence of a non-native language on an additional language (De Angelis and Dewaele, 2009).

The present study examines cross-linguistic influence and language switches in the oral production of English by Catalan-Spanish bilingual learners. It has two main purposes. First, it aims at examining what type of code-switch and function are the most common in the EFL classroom. To this aim, Williams and Hammarberg's (1998) categorization of code-switches will be used. Second, this study seeks to analyze to what extent and in what manner the background languages (L1 and L2) are used in English production (L3). With this purpose, we will test the applicability of the role model proposed by Williams and Hammarberg (1998) based on the findings of the oral production of a learner of L3 Swedish.

2   Literature Review

2.1   Classroom Discourse in multilingual contexts

Instructional settings constitute a kind of 'ecosystem' where learning originates as a result from the convergence of pedagogical and social aspects through interaction (van Lier, 2004). Over the last decades, researchers have contributed to broaden our knowledge about classroom discourse and its effects from a variety of perspectives. On the one hand, from a pedagogical point of view, early studies on classroom discourse focused on teachers' questions and their influence on students' contribution to the discourse (Barnes, 1969), and also investigated who controls the discourse topic (Flanders, 1970). The identification of patterns in classroom discourse has also received a great deal of attention (see Sinclair & Coulthard, 1975 for the teacher initiation-student response-teacher feedback (IRF) sequence; see Bellack *et. al* (1966), who introduced the concept of 'move' and described several types of pedagogical moves in classroom interaction (structuring, soliciting, responding, reacting); and the difference between 'instructional register' and 'regulative register' suggested by Christie (2000: 186-190).

On the other hand, in the language classroom, discourse is the medium through which teachers and learners interact that also allows most teaching to take place. Therefore, language is at the same time the means and the goal of the lesson. In this regard, one might say that linguistic choices in the classroom matter when language learning is the goal and understanding how code choice works is essential for a multilingual approach. In addition to the aspects mentioned above, interaction in the classroom makes it a social event that entails the fluent alternation of several languages, especially in multilingual contexts, an issue that has been the focus of interest of recent research (García, 2009). The access to "different linguistic features or various modes of what are described as autonomous languages, in order to maximize communicative potential" is known as 'translanguaging' (García, 2009:140). As pointed out by García (2009), translanguaging is a broad term that includes aspects such as code-switching.

Levine (2011) provides a comprehensible theoretical framework together with empirical evidence from English-German bilingual classrooms. Her research findings show that code choice is a significant factor, and that it may differ depending on the roles and discursive goals adopted by the speakers engaged in interaction. Given that, to our knowledge, code-switch has received scant attention in instructed contexts where two languages coexist in the community and English is a third language for the students, our aim in this study is to contribute to this research area, taking into account cross-linguistic interaction among the coexisting languages (L1 Spanish, L2 Catalan, L3 English).

2.2 Multilingualism and TLA

In the last decades, the spread of English as a lingua franca and the revitalization of minority languages have raised interest on the study of multilingualism. Multilingualism is the norm rather than the exception. In fact, most of the citizens in different European countries know two languages at least, due to the sociolinguistic context they are in (Cenoz *et al.*, 2001). In addition, the introduction of at least one foreign language in the school curriculum is a common practice in multilingual societies in Europe, as it is the case of the Valencian Community (Safont, 2007), where three languages coexist. As a result, many schools offer a multilingual school system in which the students study a majority language (Spanish), an official minority language (Catalan) and an international foreign language (English).

In line with this recent phenomenon, there is wide research on third language acquisition (henceforth TLA) in order to exploit the benefits of multilingual education. TLA is a complex and dynamic phenomenon with specific characteristics that differ from Second Language Acquisition (henceforth SLA). Jessner (2006) argues that learning a third language is very different from learning a second language. Following this line of research, Cenoz (2003:72) states that "TLA processes should form the basis for studying bilingual and monolingual learning and not vice versa". In this vein, multilingualism refers to any type of language acquisition, but as Jessner (2008) reports, qualitative changes are found in language learning as languages are involved. The multilingual system is "not the product of adding two or more languages but a complex system with its own parameters exclusive to the multilingual speaker" (Jessner, 2003:48). As Safont (2005) indicates, the third language learner has a unique linguistic system which is influenced by the relationships established among the languages involved.

Cook (1991) and Grosjean (1985) propose a holistic view to approach multilingualism suggesting that the parts of a whole are dynamically interrelated and should not be studied in isolation. This perspective contrasts with the monolingual view in which the multilingual speaker is seen as several monolingual speakers in one person. In this regard, Herdina and

Jessner (2002:7) stated "as long as bilinguals are measured according to monolingual criteria, they appear to be greatly disadvantaged both in linguistic and cognitive terms". Taking this idea into account, Herdina and Jessner (2002) proposed the so-called Dynamic Model of Multilingualism (henceforth DMM) in order to account for the complexity that multilingual acquisition presents. In this model, languages are seen as dynamic systems which are in constant interaction, and transfer phenomena are recognized as significant features in multilingual systems (Jessner, 2003:48).

2.3   Cross-linguistic interaction: code- switching

The transfer phenomena between languages, known as cross-linguistic influence (henceforth CLI), is the area which has received most attention in SLA and TLA studies (Clyne, 1997; Cenoz *et. al.* 2001). In TLA, there are more possibilities to investigate than in SLA, that is, the influence of L1 on L2, L1 on L3, L2 on L1, L2 on L3 and L3 on L1. Therefore, though CLI should form the basis of transfer phenomena studies, the term Cross-linguistic interaction (henceforth CLIN) is preferred in TLA because more than two languages are involved (Jessner, 2003). This widespread phenomenon is seen as an evidence of multilingual competence and a proof that a multilingual is not the sum of several monolinguals. In this sense, it is clear that CLIN is not a sign of a problem or language deficit as traditional research has assumed. CLIN is seen as an umbrella term for all the existing transfer phenomena which comprise interference, code-switching and borrowing. Although there is terminological confusion among researchers about the nature and type of transfer phenomena, what is clear is that multilingualism should be the standpoint (Jessner, 2003). In this study, we are going to refer to code-switching as "the changes from one language to another in the course of conversation" among bilingual or multilingual speakers (Li Wei, 2007:14).

Code-switching is a common practice in multilingual classrooms (Cenoz, 2003, Muñoz, 2007; Tremblay, 2006; Unamuno, 2008), though studies have shown that individuals tend to code-switch more frequently in natural and spontaneous settings rather than in instructional settings. Thus, Dewaele (2001) compared the amount of code-switches among trilinguals in an informal and a formal situation and the results showed that code-switches were less frequent in the formal situation.

In recent research, the influence of the L1 and L2 on L3 production in the EFL classroom has been widely investigated (Cenoz, 2003, Muñoz, 2007; Lindqvist, 2009; Safont, 2001; Tremblay, 2006; Williams and Hammarberg, 1998). Williams and Hammarberg (1998) proposed a model based on the findings of a case study on the oral production of a learner of L3 Swedish. They found that the influence of English (L1) and German (L2) on L3 had different functions, even having a high level of competence in both languages. Findings showed that English played an *instrumental role* (i.e. it was used for eliciting words from the interlocutor and metalinguistic functions) whereas German played a *default supplier role* (i.e. "to furnish linguistic material for the speech production in L3" (Hammarberg, 2009: 102), in the sense that it seemed to be used more automatically, unconsciously and without any communicative aim. Williams and Hammarberg proposed a set of factors that determine the choice of instrumental language and another set of factors which determine the choice of the default supplier language. The factors that seem to be responsible for the activation of the instrumental language are the following ones: (1) *Personal identification* with the language in question; (2) The *status of the language*; and (3) *Language for communication* between the interlocutors: learners' language choice for code-switching may be determined by the interlocutor's use of languages (Grosjean 1998). We consider appropriate to add an additional dimension to this set of factors, i.e. the sociolinguistic learning context, which may be relevant in the choice of the instrumental language (Muñoz, 2007; Cenoz, 2003; Tremblay, 2006).

In contrast, for the activation of the default supplier language, Williams and Hammarberg (1998) consider the following factors as key to understand the relationships between languages:

1) *Typological and cultural similarity*: The typological and cultural distance of the languages plays an important role in language learning. According to Singleton (1987), the general tendency for the speakers is to borrow items from languages that are typologically closer. Ringbom (2001) finds that the transfer of form is more common across related languages whereas the transfer of semantic patterns and word combinations is nearly always based on the L1. In his studies about the type of transfer that Finnish students produce in their L3 (English), he showed that Finnish students transferred more lexicon from the L2 (Swedish in this case) rather than from the L1. In other words, Finnish native students perceive the similarity between English and Swedish.

2) *Level of Proficiency*: There is also research regarding the proficiency on the languages involved. In fact, learners with a low level of proficiency in the L2 tend to use the L1 as the main source for transferring (Möhle, 1989; Ringbom, 1987; Tremblay, 2006). In this sense, unless the level of the L2 is high, the influence L2 has on L3 is marginal. Similarly, L1 influence decreases with the increase in the L3 proficiency; trilingual learners

transfer more when they are less proficient in their foreign languages (Cenoz, 2001).

3)   *Recency of use*: The recency of use refers to the tendency to transfer more from the foreign language actively used by the speaker. As Cenoz (2005) remarks, TLA is not a mechanical process and the exposure to the languages could vary throughout the learning process. In Hammarberg's (2001) study, her informant transferred more from the foreign language she most recently used.

Apart from that, a number of different taxonomies have been used to classify instances of code-switching. In some cross-linguistic studies, code-switching has been classified depending on the functions and intentionality (Williams and Hammarberg, 1998; Hammarberg, 2001; Hammarberg, 2009). According to Hammarberg (2001:25), language switches are "expressions in languages other than L3 that are not phonologically or morphologically adapted to the L3". This author identifies four major types of categories: EDIT, META, INSERT and WIPP. These categories are divided depending on the function and intentionality the switch has in the conversational context. In this sense, the first three aforementioned categories appear to have a pragmatic or intentional purpose (for instance introduce a self-repair, make a comment or ask a question) whereas WIPP switches, which stand for *Without Identified Pragmatic Competence,* occur as part of the utterance formulation in the L3 without any pragmatic function.

EDIT switches are used to introduce self-repairs interactive feedback signals or beginning of turntakes. The META group comprises two subcategories. META COMMENT involves instances of switches about comments on the communicative situation or the text itself and META FRAME involves questions about L3. The INSERT group contains those switches which intend to elicit the L3 word from the interlocutor to overcome lexical problems. Finally, WIPP switches seem to correspond to lapses which are immediately followed by the correct target form without changing intonation and hesitation. Williams and Hammarberg (1998) suggested that WIPP switches were mainly produced by the default supplier language whereas the rest of the categories were produced on the basis of the instrumental language. The WIPP category has also been referred to as *non-intentional language switches* (Poulisse and Bongaerts, 1994). These authors suggest that *non-intentional language switches* "are not preceded by any signs of hesitation and did not stand out from the rest of the utterance by a marked intonation" (Poulisse and Bongaerts, 1994: 43).

Lindqvist (2009) applied Williams and Hammarberg's (1998) model in order to investigate the factors influencing the roles of the L1 and the L2 in French L3 oral production in six case studies of learners from diverse linguistic backgrounds. The data were collected from several interviews and retellings of a cartoon, a video film and a picture with a French native speaker. The results showed that the L1, mainly when it was English, was activated as an instrumental language. The activation of a supplier role was less clear, and was interpreted to have been determined by formal similarities between French and the L1 and the L2.

In addition to the pragmatically functional language switches suggested by Williams and Hammarberg (1998), further studies on CLI have analyzed the influence of contextual factors on CLI, both in primary and secondary school contexts (Cenoz, 2003; Muñoz, 2007).

Cenoz's (2003) study on CLI focused on children's development of the multilingual mental lexicon in two different times, fourth and sixth year of primary education. The participants were 20 bilingual learners (Spanish and Basque) who had received instruction in English from the age of four in a Basque medium-school. Students were asked to tell the wordless "Frog story" and all the instances of cross-linguistic influence were analyzed. The findings indicated that the three languages were activated in the classroom discourse, though only two languages were expected to be activated (as this study focused on the English classroom in a Basque-based school). Although Basque is used as a vehicular language in this school, Spanish is the majority and dominant language in this sociolinguistic context. Students preferred the use of Spanish for non-intentional switches when their level of awareness was lower and they did not have enough time to ask for help, which can be accounted for in relation to language distance. In contrast, the Basque language was used when the level of awareness was higher and the students tried to get information from the interlocutor.

These findings were discussed in relation to the results obtained by Muñoz (2007) in Catalonia. Muñoz (2007) examined the use of previously learned languages in 29 secondary school learners' productions by means of a story-telling task. The subjects were Catalan-Spanish bilinguals who had learned French as the first foreign language at school and were learning English as a fourth language. The analysis distinguished lexical transfer (including borrowings and foreignisings) from code-switching. Similar to the present study, code-switches were sub-categorized into explicit appeals for help (Hammarberg, 2001), clarification requests, and meta-comments (Hammarberg, 2001). Muñoz (2007) concluded that transfer from French was very low and, in most cases, the L1 played a significant role. Regarding lexical items, Catalan-dominant learners only used Catalan as a supplier language, whereas Spanish-dominant learners borrowed mostly from Spanish and family bilinguals from both. At the clause level, the findings were similar, with a slight preference for Catalan. This author argued that contextual factors, i.e. Catalan being the language of the school and the preferred one outside the classroom, determine the language choice. Comparing these results to Cenoz's (2003) study on Spanish-Basque bilingual learners, where there was a preferential use of Spanish in contrast to Basque in code-switches, Muñoz (2007: 89) argued that the fact that both Catalan and Spanish belong to the same language family may account for the differences in the patterns observed in both studies.

From our perspective, the status of Basque in the Basque Country is not the same as Catalan in Catalonia. Although the vehicular languages of the schools in the studies mentioned above are held by the minority language (Basque and Catalan respectively), the dominant presence of these minority languages in the sociolinguistic context outside the school differs widely. For this reason, participants in Cenoz's (2003) study tended to code-switch more in the majority language (Spanish) rather than in the minority language (Basque), even if the main language of instruction was Basque.

Although the same minority language (Catalan) is shared in the context of our study, namely that of the Valencian Community, with the one in the aforementioned study by Muñoz (2007) in Catalonia, the status and vitality of the minority language is very different in each community. The presence of Catalan in the context of our study is not as frequent as in Catalonia. As Safont (2001:373) indicated in her study carried out in the Valencian Community, "we have lived (and still are living) a process of *castilianisation,* where a constant code-switching from Castilian to Catalan takes place in Catalan oral production". This factor may be decisive in the participants' activation of languages when speaking.

Safont-Jordà (2001) analyzed the role of the L1 (Catalan) and L2 (Spanish) in the oral production of L3 (English) as far as intentional and non-intentional language switches were concerned. The participants were 20 undergraduate bilingual learners in their first to third year at a university in the Valencian Community. Subjects were distributed three different tasks: a picture description (describe objects in English), story retell (listen to short stories in the mother tongue (Catalan) and retell them in English) and a discussion. Results indicated that students with lower level of English were the ones who transferred more from one language to the other to overcome lexical problems. The outcomes also demonstrated that the code-switching was more often employed in the story retell. As Safont (2001) suggested, the fact that students listened to the story in their mother tongue may be a decisive factor for code-switching into Catalan when trying to retell the story in English. In this vein, Catalan was mainly employed for commenting aspects of the L3 production, that is, metalinguistic comments. The role of the Catalan language was clearly instrumental; however no specific role may be attributed to Spanish as it was used arbitrary by the participants without any clear purpose. As happened in Lindqvist's (2009) and Muñoz's (2007) study, the activation of the supplier role was less clear.

With reference to the activation of languages, Muñoz (2007), Lindqvist (2009) and Safont (2001) argue that L1 rather than L2 is the most important source of influence on L3, in contrast to other studies (Hammarberg, 2001; Cenoz, 2003). In this regard, De Bot (2004) hypothesizes that the L1 is a more solid system than the L2 because it is more frequently used. In this sense, we may state that there are more instances of instrumental code-switches rather than supplier switches.

As reviewed above, Williams and Hammarberg's (1998) model has been considered a useful tool in determining the roles of the instrumental language and supplier language in L3 production, though it has not been much used in research studies on code-switching (Lindqvist, 2009). In line with the DMM, further research is needed to ascertain whether such model can be applied to learners with different linguistic profiles, taking into account both their background languages and the target language.

3   Method

3.1   Research questions and hypotheses

Following this line of research, this study examines Williams and Hammarberg's (1998) model on primary school students in a bilingual community where English as a foreign language is introduced at an early age. Finally and considering CLI as a key factor for learners' L3 acquisition (Cenoz, 2003; Muñoz, 2007; Lindqvist, 2009), the present study addresses the following questions:

a)   Do the instances of code-switching have a pragmatic purpose or not? What type of non-adapted language switches is the more predominant in EFL classroom?

b)   Which is the main source of influence the L1 or L2?

c)   Do the L1 and L2 have different functions in L3 oral production? (Lindqvist, 2009)

Considering the above research questions and the empirical evidence on the effect of the L1 and L2 on students L3 in several studies (Williams and Hammarberg, 1998; Hammarberg, 2001; Lindqvist, 2009) we formulate the following hypotheses:

H1. The most common language switches during English classes have a pragmatic purpose.

H2. The non-adapted language switches which are more predominant in language classroom are the META-COMMENT (comments on the communicative situation or the text itself).

H3. Both the teacher and students code-switch into Spanish due to several reasons: (1) the teacher and most of the students have Spanish as L1; (2) Spanish is the majority language in the community; (3) the language for communication among teacher and students is Spanish and (4) the school context and learning setting is mainly Spanish-based.

H4.   Due to the reasons mentioned above, Spanish will be the instrumental language.

3.2   Context of the study

The present research was undertaken in the Valencian Community, a Spanish bilingual community where two official languages are recognized, Spanish and Catalan, in accordance with the Autonomous Statute of 1982. In Spain, we find Catalan speakers in Catalonia; the Valencian community; the Balearic Islands; a stretch of land between Catalonia and Aragon, known as La Franja; and in a small region of Murcia known as Carxe. According to the latest sociolinguistic survey (Pons and Sorolla, 2009:31), 78'2% of the population understands Catalan, while 57'6% can speak it, 54'9 can read it and 32'5 can write it. In general terms, the Valencian Community presents the lowest rates of bilingualism within the population among the regions where Catalan is considered as a co-official language (see Table 1). In Catalonia and the Balearic Islands, Catalan is no longer a minority language, in fact, it is the predominant language of education, culture and mass-media. Taking into consideration these data, language-in-education policies in the

Valencian Community are not strong enough to foster the development of linguistic competence in the minority language.

	Understand	Speak	Read	Write
Catalonia	**97.4**	**84.7**	**90.5**	**62.3**
Valencian Community	**78.2**	**57.6**	**54.9**	**32.5**
Balearic Islands	**93.1**	**74.6**	**79.6**	**46.9**

Table 1. Linguistic Competence in Catalan-speaking communities. Source: Pons and Sorolla (2009)

Nevertheless, current language policies are much more pluralistic than those used some decades ago. Regarding bilingual programs, there are three different educational programs which aim at fostering bilingualism in different ways (*Consell de la Generalitat Valenciana*, 1984).

1. The PIP *(Programa d'Incorporació Progressiva)* model is education in Spanish with the progressive introduction of Catalan. In the early stages of education, Spanish is the language of instruction in all subjects, except for the Catalan subject. In the following years, the subjects taught in Catalan increase progressively. This program is recommended for Spanish-speaking children.

2. The PIL *(Programa d'Immersió Lingüística)* model is also thought for Spanish speakers but the difference is that the Catalan language is used as a means of instruction since early ages. In contrast, Spanish is introduced progressively from the third year of primary school as a means of instruction. This program adopts an immersion methodology to guarantee the integration of children in the target community.

3. And finally, the PEV *(Programa d'Educació en Valencià)* model is Catalan-based. It is addressed for Catalan speakers and only ten per cent of the instruction is in Spanish

3.3   Participants

The participants in this study were a group of 25 children in the third year of primary education at a school in the Valencian Community, Spain, and the teacher of English as a foreign language. The students' group was constituted by 15 females and 10 males between the ages of 8 and 9. The teacher, who held a bachelor in English Philology, was 28 years old.

The school follows the PIP *(Programa d'Incorporació Progressiva)* model, which consists in education in Spanish with the progressive introduction of Catalan as previously mentioned. Regarding the introduction of English as a foreign language, the participants had been learning English since they were 5 years old approximately. Their proficiency in English was low as compared to the official languages (Catalan and Spanish) in this region. These participants can be considered receptive or passive bilinguals, i.e. "speakers who are capable of comprehension, but produce little or no speech" (Sherkina-Lieber, Perez-Leroux & Johns 2011: 301), because they can understand Catalan but they do not tend to produce it.

3.4   Analysis

The oral data that were used in this study were collected at a normal EFL classroom at the end of April. The teacher was required to follow her daily English lessons, though focusing on oral tasks in order to get more data on code-switching phenomenon in oral productions. One of the researchers was present in the class with the aim of voice-recording the 50-minute class. Then, the recording was transcribed following the conventions established in Appendix 1. The transcript of the English lesson was analyzed following Williams and Hammarberg's (1998) categorization of code-switches presented in the table below (see Table 2).

NON-ADAPTED LANGUAGE SWITCHES	FUNCTION	LANGUAGE ROLE
EDIT (self-repairs, interactive feedback signals or beginning of turntakes)	**pragmatic or intentional purpose**	**Instrumental**
META COMMENT (comments on the communicative situation or the text itself)		
META FRAME (Questions and comment about the L3 performance)		
INSERT (Switches to overcome lexical problems)		
WIPP (Without identified pragmatic purpose)	**non- intentional function**	**Supplier**

Table 2. Williams and Hammarberg's classification of language switches.

4 Results and discussion

The data obtained from the recording and transcript showed that multilingual classrooms offer a wide variety of patterns and that language systems may be simultaneously interacting. However, in this study, only two languages were activated, English as the language of instruction in the EFL classroom, and Spanish as the dominant language of the school and the family context.

With the aim of testing Hypothesis 1 and 2, we made a comparison between the instances of code-switching with pragmatic functions (eliciting words or commenting on the text itself) and those instances without pragmatic function. In this sense, EDIT, INSERT and META categories belong to the non-adapted language switches which have pragmatic function and WIPP switches belong to the switches without pragmatic or intentional function. The table below (see Table 2) offers a summary of the results obtained.

CATEGORY	N	FUNCTION
EDIT	10	pragmatic or intentional purpose
META COMMENT	13	
META FRAME	6	
INSERT	11	
WIPP	0	non- intentional function

Table 3. Results of the categories found.

As expected taking into account the results from previous studies (Hammarberg, 2001; Lindqvist, 2009; Safont, 2001), in our analysis most of the non-adapted language switches occurring in the classroom have a pragmatic function. The main reasons for code-switching are: (a) for ease of expression and economy of speech, (b) owing to learners' limited competence and insecurity and (c) for translation. Interestingly enough, no instances of non-intentional switching have been found. All the language switches have a pragmatic function in the conversational context. As Table 3 shows, the most common category is the meta-comment. Both learners and teachers tend to use their dominant language for ease of expression in order to manage the communicative situation.

In what follows, instances of pragmatically code-switches from our corpus are provided. The category EDIT is widely used among participants for restructuring the conversation (e.g. *ehm, ehh, vale*). In example 1, the student code-switches into Spanish as a self-repair tool for saving time to think about what she is going to say.

(1) Sn: it's fish (3:0) erm <it's yellow and ***bueno*** yellow (.) red and pur purple> (3.0)

Our results show that the META group is the most frequent category used in the classroom. Students need to resort to their dominant language in order to resolve problems arising in a communicative situation or when doing a task. The main reason may be that their available verbal resources in the foreign language are very limited.

Regarding META COMMENTS, in example 2, the teacher asks a student about what he is drawing. He immediately answers "a car". Then, the teacher asks "is it your car?" but the student does not understand the question due to her limited English proficiency and introduces an interactive signal (edit category) in order to suggest the teacher to repeat the utterance. The teacher repeats the sentence and the student code-switches into Spanish "*No te entiendo.*" The teacher tries to make herself understood again by exaggerating the intonation and finally, the students say "yes" aloud. The student comments on the task in his mother tongue in order to understand what is going on.

(2)   T: what are you drawing? (4.0) a house an animal?
      S22: errrm a car
  T: is it your car?
        S22: *ehhh*?
        T: is that your car?
        S22: *no te entiendo*
        T: is it your car?
        S22: YEEEEES

META FRAME involves questions about L3. In the present study, the teacher is the one who uses more expressions in order to elicit words from the learners. As can be observed in example 3, the teacher asks the students about the meaning of certain words, such as the Spanish word "*bañera*". She wants to check if the students already know the word.

(3)   T: ok do you remember how do you say LISTEN how do you
           say *bañera* in English?
  SS: BATH:

In only one occasion, one student directly asks for the meaning of a word in English as the example 4 shows.

(4)   Sn: *ᵒcómo se dice colmillos?ᵒ*
  T: I think it's: tusk

The INSERT group contains non-L3 items to overcome lexical problems in L3. The teacher code-switches into Spanish six times immediately after certain words in order to offer the direct translation. She may probably consider that these words are unknown for the students, as it is the case in examples 5 and 6.

(5)   T: ok. she is going to::: record
          well she is going to re<u>cord</u> with this she is
          going to (2.0) °record is ***grabar***° [the class

(6)   ohh congratulations ***enhorabuena*** I like this (2.0) your first
          communion

The students also tend to translate English words into Spanish in order to check if their translations are correct. In the example below (7), the teacher introduces the title of the new unit "In the park". Immediately after, one of the students tries to translate this expression with a doubtful intonation. The teacher confirms the student's translation but giving the correct form.

(7)   T: in the park
          Sn: ***dentro del parque?***
          T: yes ***EN el parque*** ok in the park

In example 8, the teacher asks where the ice-cream is. One of the students answers in Spanish because he does not know the word in English. Then, one of his classmates offers the correct word in English. As example 9 illustrates, one of the students is describing an animal and she code-switches into Spanish to say "*escondite*" because she does not know the English word.

(8)   T: yes where is his ice cream?
          Sn: [***al suelo***
          Sn: [floor

(9)   S6: her name is Laden. her color is white. her like carrots
          and vegetables. the favourite game is ***escondite***
          ((laughter))it can jump but it can't fly.

All the code-switches mentioned above have intentional meaning and pragmatic function. In this sense, we may say that code-switching is a useful strategy in EFL classroom interaction for reducing the overall comprehension burden. In contrast, we have not found any instance of non-intentional switch (*i.e.* WIPP switches seem to correspond to lapses which are immediately followed by the correct target form without changing intonation and hesitation). These findings suggest that WIPP switches may not happen in beginner learners, though these findings contradict previous results which advocate that beginner learners' oral language contain more unintentional switches than more advanced learners' speech (Poulisse and Bongaerts, 1994; Muñoz, 2007).

In summary, our results offer evidence that confirm hypothesis 1 and hypothesis 2 since the code-switches in our data have a pragmatic function and the most general category is the METACOMMENT. With the aim of testing Hypothesis 3 and 4, we made a comparison between the instances of code-switching with communicative aims (elicit words or comment on the text itself) and those instances without communicative aims. With these data, we separated the language that played an instrumental role from the language that played a supplier role. We further analyzed the reasons for these findings.

In our study, three languages were available in the participants' repertoire, though only two of them (Spanish and English) were activated. In contrast, in Safont's (2001) study, the three languages were activated because Catalan was the participants' mother tongue and Spanish the predominant language of the immediate context. In a similar study conducted by Cenoz (2003) on trilingual speakers in a predominant Basque school, three languages were activated (Basque, Spanish and English). The reason may be that Basque was the language of the school and Spanish was the majority language of the sociolinguistic context of the community. For instance, in Unamuno's study (2008) on code-switching in a primary school in Barcelona where Catalan is the official language of the institution, results showed a preference for the use of Catalan in the English language classroom in issues related to the management and completion of assigned activities, even though most of the participants were immigrants.

In the present study, we have seen that Spanish plays an instrumental role in the English classroom. It is used with a clear communicative aim in order to elicit words from the interlocutor, in clarification requests, in metalinguistic functions and in reorganizing the conversational pattern. These results support De Bot's (2004), Safont's (2001) and Lindqvist's (2009) findings that the L1 is the main source of influence in L3 production. Moreover, the fact that all the learners used Spanish as an instrumental language is due to the interlocutor's use of language and the instructional sociolinguistic setting. In fact, Lindqvist (2009) suggests that no matter whether Spanish represents the L1 or the L2, it plays an instrumental role in both cases because it is the language shared between the participants. As a result, even those participants whose mother tongue is Catalan show a preference for the activation of Spanish due to these factors. In this vein, we may say that the main reason for code-switching into Spanish may be motivated by contextual factors (Muñoz, 2007), such as the sociolinguistic context of the school and the interlocutor. This school follows a PIP linguistic model which means that classes are conducted in Spanish. In addition, the linguistic landscape and the language of communication among teachers and children is mainly Spanish. In this sense, the language used by the interlocutor (the teacher) during the English class for code-switching is always Spanish. This factor strongly determines students' activation of languages (Unamuno, 2008).

Regarding the supplier role, it has been far more difficult to identify it because there were not WIPP switches in the conversation and the only language used was Spanish. We can assume that there is no evidence of the role of the supplier language in this conversation. Both contact languages (Spanish and Catalan) are from the same linguistic family (i.e Romance family), while the English language belongs to the Germanic family. In this sense, language distance does not seem to play a role in this study since neither of the two languages is typologically close to English. In contrast, Cenoz's study (2003) of Spanish (L1), Basque (L2) learners of English showed a preference for the Spanish in WIPP lapses because Spanish is more typologically closer to English than Basque. The recency of use and the proficiency level do no seem to play a role in the present study, though more data on those aspects will be necessary to determine language choice. Learners with a poor command on oral English tend to switch more frequently into their dominant languages.

Summarizing hypotheses 3 and 4, both of them are confirmed. It could be said that students' preferred language for code-switching was Spanish because (1) the teacher and most of the students have Spanish as L1; (2) Spanish is the majority language in the community; (3) the language for communication between teacher and students is Spanish, and (4) the school context and learning setting is mainly Spanish-based. Due to these reasons, Spanish plays an instrumental role in this EFL classroom.

In line with Levine (2011), the findings in this study provide further evidence to debunk the myth that the English as a foreign language classroom is monolingual, since the English language interacts with other languages, which are constantly activated and deactivated. In this respect, Levine explains that "in the educational setting, the choices we make to use the L1 or the L2 interact with and influence how communication takes place, and how learning might happen" (Levine 2011: 102). In the case of this study, where

Catalan and Spanish are the languages of the community, code-switching into Spanish rather than Catalan takes place. This can be accounted for by contextual factors (Muñoz, 2007), such as the students following a PIP (Spanish-based) model at school.

5 Conclusion

Multilingual classrooms where three languages coexist are excellent laboratories for analyzing the interaction among languages and the students' cross-linguistic awareness. A central assumption in this study is that language systems in a multilingual classroom interact and influence each other. Students may use their linguistic repertoire for different functions and intentions. At first sight, we may consider that code-switching is a common phenomenon in EFL classroom, although, as Dewaele (2001) suggests, code-switching in academic situations is not as frequent as in spontaneous situations because students tend to avoid it. This paper supports the evidence that code-switching is not a blockage or deficiency in language learning, but may be a strategy in classroom interaction. Instances of code-switching are intentional, in the sense that they are used for conveying pragmatic functions in the context of the situation. Translation is a widely used strategy in the EFL classroom. This practice is positive for helping students to convey the meaning, though overuse of code-switching for translation may have a negative influence. It has been found that the most common code-switching category is the METACOMMENT. These results may imply that students need to resort to their dominant language in order to overcome comprehension problems and to make comments on the learning task or the situation.

This study suggests that the L2 does not influence students' L3 oral production. Two main reasons come into the ground. The first one is that teachers' language practices in the management of the English class may be determinant for students' language choice (Unamuno 2008). The teacher's preference for addressing her students in Spanish is a major influence for the learners' language choice. And the second main factor is that instances of code-switching are strongly determined by the sociolinguistic context and learning setting. In this sense, we may assume that school language policies have a strong impact on classroom language use. In this line, further research should be carried out in schools from the Valencian Community in order to make a comparative analysis between PEV linguistic models (mainly Catalan-based) and PIP models (Spanish-based). Research on children's cross-linguistic influence in Catalan-based models may to provide us with more comprehensive results about the interaction of languages and the role of each language in the acquisition of a third language.

Multilingualism is a core aspect of today's society and further research should be conducted in order to analyze language processes in multilingual contexts. This study lays ground about the importance of protecting the minority languages and promoting language policies for implementing multilingual education.

References

Alcón, E. and P. Safont (in press) English and multilingualism. In Chappelle, C. (ed) Encyclopedia of Applied Linguistics, New York: Wiley & Sons.

Barnes, D. (1969) Language in the secondary classroom. In Barnes, D., J. Britton and H. Rosen (eds) Language, the learner and the school, Harmondsworth: Penguin.

Bellack, A.A., H.M. Kliebard, R.T. Hyman and F.L. Smith (1966) The Language of the Classroom, New York NY: Teachers' College Press.

Cenoz, J. (2001) The effect of linguistic distance, L2 status, and age on cross-linguistic influence in third language acquisition. In Cenoz, J., B. Hufeisen and U. Jessner (eds) Cross-linguistic influence in third language acquisition: Psycholinguistic perspective, Clevedon: Multilingual Matters.

Cenoz, J. (2003) Cross-linguistic influence in third language acquisition: Implications for the organization of the multilingual mental lexicon, Bulletin Suisse de linguistique appliquée (78): 1-11.

Cenoz, J. (2005) Learning a third language. Cross-linguistic influence and its relationship to typology and age. In Hufeisen, B. and R. Fouser (eds) Introductory Readings to L3, Tübingen: Stauffenburg.

Cenoz, J., B. Hufeisen and U. Jessner (2001) Cross-linguistic influence in third language acquisition: Psycholinguistic perspectives, Clevedon: Multilingual Matters.

Christie, F. (2000) The language of classroom interaction and learning. In Unsworth, L. (ed) Researching Language in Schools and Communities. Functional Lingusitics Perspectives, London: Cassell.

Clyne, M. (1997) Some of the things trilingual do, International Journal of Bilingualism (1): 95-116.

Consell de la Generalitat Valenciana (1984) Decret 79/1984 de 30 de juliol. Diari Oficial de la Generalitat Valenciana 186.

Cook, V. (1991) The poverty of the stimulus argument and multicompetence, Second Language Research (7): 103-117.

De Angelis, G. and J.M. Dewaele (2009) The development of psycholinguistic research on crosslinguistic influence. In Aronin, L. and B. Hufeisen (eds) The exploration of Multilingualism, Amsterdam: John Benjamins.

De Bot, K. (2004) The multilingual lexicon: Modeling selection and control, International Journal of Multilingualism (1) 1: 17-32.

Dewaele, J.M. (2001) Activation or inhibition? The interaction of L1, L2 and L3 on the language mode continuum. In Cenoz, J., B. Hufeisen and U. Jessner (eds) Cross-linguistic influence in third language acquisition: Psycholinguistic perspective, Clevedon: Multilingual Matters.

Flanders, N.A. (1970) Analysing teacher behavior, Reading MA: Addison-Wesley.

García, O. (2009) Education, multilingualism and translanguaging in the 21st century. In Mohanty, A., M. Panda, R. Phillipson and T. Skutnabb-Kangas (eds) Multilingual Education for Social Justice: Globalising the local, New Delhi: Orient Blackswan (former Orient Longman).

Grosjean, F. (1985) The bilingual as a competent but specific speaker-hearer, Journal of Multilingual and Multicultural Development (6): 467-477.

Grosjean, F. (1988) Exploring the recognition of guest words in bilingual speech, Language and Cognitive Processes (3) 3: 233-274.

Hammarberg, B. (2001) Roles of L1 and L2 in L3 production and acquisition. In Cenoz, J., Hufeisen, B. and Jessner, U. (eds) Cross-linguistic influence in third language acquisition: Psycholinguistic perspectives, Clevedon: Multilingual Matters.

Hammarberg, B. (2009) Activation of L1 and L2 during production in L3: a comparison of two case studies. Processes in third language acquisition, Edinburgh: Edinburgh University Press.

Herdina, P. and U. Jessner (2002) A Dynamic model of Multilingualism: Perspectives of change in psycholinguistics, Clevedon: Multilingual Matters.

Jessner, U. (2003) The nature of cross-linguistic interaction in the multilingual system. In Cenoz, J., B. Hufeisen and U. Jessner (eds) The multilingual lexicon, Netherlands: Kluwer Academic Publishers.

Jessner, U. (2006) Linguistic Awareness in Multilinguals: English as a Third Language, Edinburgh: Edinburgh University Press.

Jessner, U. (2008) A DST model of multilingualism and the role of metalinguistic awareness. Second language development as a dynamic process, Special issue Of Modern Language Journal (92) 2: 210-283.

Levine, G.S. (2011) Code Choice in the Language Classroom, Bristol: Multilingual Matters.

Lindqvist, C. (2009) The use of the L1 and the L2 in French L3: examining cross-linguistic lexemes in multilingual learners' oral production, International Journal of Multilingualism (6) 3: 281-297.

Li Wei (2007) Dimensions of bilingualism. In Li Wei (ed) The Bilingualism Reader, London: Routledge.

Möhle, D. (1989) Multilingual Interaction in Foreign Language Production. In Dechert, H.W. and M. Raupach (eds) Interlingual Processes, Tübingen: Gunter Narr.

Muñoz, C. (2007) Cross-lingusitic influence and language switches in L4 oral production, Vigo International Journal of Applied Linguistics (4): 73-94.

Pons, E. and N. Sorolla (2009) Informe de la llengua catalana (2005-2007), Barcelona: Observatori de la Llengua Catalana – CRUSCAT. Dossier 13.

Poulisse, N. and T. Bongaerts (1994) First language use in second language production, Applied Linguistics (15): 36-57.

Ringbom, H. (1987) The Role of the First Language in Foreign Language Learning, Clevedon: Multilingual Matters.

Ringbom, H. (2001) Lexical transfer in L3 production. In Cenoz, J., B. Hufeisen, and U. Jessner (eds) Cross-linguistic influence in third language acquisition, Clevedon: Multilingual Matters.

Safont, M.P. (2001) Unintentional and Intentional Codeswitching in Third Language Oral Production. In Björklund, S. (ed) Language as a Tool. Immersion Research and Practices. Proceedings of the University of Vaasa, Vaasa: University of Vaasa.

Safont, M.P. (2005) Third Language Learners: Pragmatic production and Awareness, Clevedon, UK : Multilingual Matters.

Sherkina-Lieber, M., A.T. Perez-Leroux and A. Johns (2011) Grammar without speech production: The case of Labrador Inuttitut heritage receptive bilinguals, Bilingualism: Language and Cognition (14): 301-317.

Sinclair, J. M. and M. Coulthard (1975) Towards an analysis of discourse: The English used by teachers and pupils, London: Oxford University Press.

Singleton, D. (1987) Mother and other tongue influence on learner French, Studies in Second Language Acquisition (9): 327-46.

Tremblay, M.C. (2006) Cross-linguistic influence in third language acquisition: the role of L2 proficiency and L2 exposure, Ottawa Papers in Linguistics (34): 109-119.

Unamuno, V. (2008) Multilingual switch in peer classroom interaction, Linguistics and Education (19): 1-19.

Van Lier, L. (2004) The Ecology and Semiotics of Language Learning: A Sociocultural Perspective, Boston, MA: Kluwer.

Williams, S. and B. Hammarberg (1998) Language Switches in L3 production: Implications for a polyglot speaking mode, Applied Linguistics (19) 3: 295-333.

Acknowledgements

As members of the LAELA (Lingüística Aplicada a l'Ensenyament de la Llengua Anglesa) research group at Universitat Jaume I (Castellón, Spain), we would like to acknowledge that this study is part of a research project funded by (a) the Spanish Ministerio de Ciencia e Innovación (FFI2008-05241/FILO), (b) Fundació Universitat Jaume I and Caixa Castelló-Bancaixa (P1.1B2011-15), (c) FPU program of the Spanish Ministry of Education and (d) VALi+d program of Conselleria d'Educació de la Generalitat Valenciana.

Appendix 1

Transcription Conventions

.	Falling intonation.
?	Rising intonation.
!	Exclamation talk.
,	Comma indicates a level, continuing intonation; suggesting non-finality.
[ ]	Brackets indicate overlapping utterances.
(.)	Period within parentheses indicates micropause.
(2.0)	Number within parentheses indicates pause of length in approximate seconds.
ye:s	Colon indicates stretching of sound it follows.
<u>yes</u>	Underlining indicates emphasis.
YES	Capital letters indicate increased volume.
°yes°	Degree marks indicate decreased volume of materials.
(yes)	Between parentheses indicate transcriber doubt about hearing of passage.
(xxx)	Unintelligible speech.

>yes<	Speeded-up talk
<yes>	Slow-down talk.
((laugh))	Aspects of the utterance, such as whispers, coughing, and laughter, are indicated with double parentheses.
Bold	Code-switching.
SS	Students.
Sn	Unknown Student.
S1	Student 1.
T	Teacher.
R	Recorder.